THE
EVERYTHING®
Healthy
Green Drinks Book

Dear Reader,

I'd like to start this book off with a "congratulations to you!" The fact that you are taking a proactive role in improving your health and the quality of your life through sound nutrition is something you should be very proud of. So many people are becoming increasingly aware of the profound effect nutrition has on their overall health. Their interest in quality nutrition, how to consume it, and how to optimize their daily diet at every snack and meal has increased as well.

Personally, as a wife and mother of three young children, I strive to make nutrition a top priority in order to maintain and optimize the health of everyone I love. I know the challenges of making nutritious ingredients appealing enough to little ones and grown-ups alike, and I've used that experience to create the recipes I've included here . . . so consider them "tried and true."

Professionally, as a writer of six health-focused books with recipes that include clean, whole foods, I've been ecstatic to hear all the positive feed-back from readers who are embarking on new, nutritious ways of living, and are using smoothies and juices to include more fruits and vegetables in their daily diet. The sole purpose of this book is to help everyone who is trying to eat and drink healthier, and would like new and delicious ideas for how to do it.

I wish you the absolute best in your healthful endeavors, and hope you enjoy every recipe in this book as much as I do. Cheers to great health!

Sincerely,

Britt Brandon

Welcome to the EVERYTHING® Series!

These handy, accessible books give you all you need to tackle a difficult project, gain a new hobby, comprehend a fascinating topic, prepare for an exam, or even brush up on something you learned back in school but have since forgotten.

You can choose to read an Everything® book from cover to cover or just pick out the information you want from our four useful boxes: e-questions, e-facts, e-alerts, and e-ssentials.

We give you everything you need to know on the subject, but throw in a lot of fun stuff along the way, too.

We now have more than 400 Everything® books in print, spanning such wide-ranging categories as weddings, pregnancy, cooking, music instruction, foreign language, crafts, pets, New Age, and so much more. When you're done reading them all, you can finally say you know Everything®!

QUESTION

Answers to
common questions

FACT

Important snippets
of information

ALERT

Urgent
warnings

ESSENTIAL

Quick
handy tips

PUBLISHER Karen Cooper

MANAGING EDITOR, EVERYTHING® SERIES Lisa Laing

COPY CHIEF Casey Ebert

ASSISTANT PRODUCTION EDITOR Alex Guarco

ACQUISITIONS EDITOR Eileen Mullan

ASSOCIATE DEVELOPMENT EDITOR Eileen Mullan

EVERYTHING® SERIES COVER DESIGNER Erin Alexander

Visit the entire Everything® series at *www.everything.com*

THE
EVERYTHING®
Healthy
Green Drinks
Book

Britt Brandon

Aadamsmedia
Avon, Massachusetts

For the loves of my life: my amazing husband, Jimmy, our beautiful daughters Lilly and Lonni, and our awesome son JD, who inspire me to live life to the fullest every day, and make me that much more passionate about living as healthy as I can and as long as I can so I can spend many more wonderful days with them.

An Everything® Series Book.
Everything® and everything.com® are registered trademarks of F+W Media, Inc.

Published by
Adams Media, a division of F+W Media, Inc.
57 Littlefield Street, Avon, MA 02322. U.S.A.
www.adamsmedia.com

Contains material adapted and abridged from *The Everything® Giant Book of Juicing* by Teresa Kennedy, copyright © 2013 by F+W Media, Inc., ISBN 10: 1-4405-5785-3, ISBN 13: 978-1-4405-5785-9; *The Everything® Green Smoothies Book* by Britt Brandon with Lorena Novak Bull, RD, copyright © 2011 by F+W Media, Inc., ISBN 10: 1-4405-2564-1, ISBN 13: 978-1-4405-2564-3; *The Everything® Juicing Book* by Carole Jacobs, former nutrition editor, *Shape* magazine and Chef Patrice Johnson with Nicole Cormier, RD, copyright © 2010 by F+W Media, Inc., ISBN 10: 1-4405-0326-5, ISBN 13: 978-1-4405-0326-9.

ISBN 10: 1-4405-7694-7
ISBN 13: 978-1-4405-7694-2
eISBN 10: 1-4405-7695-5
eISBN 13: 978-1-4405-7695-9

Printed in the United States of America.

10 9 8 7 6 5 4 3 2

Library of Congress Cataloging-in-Publication Data

Brandon, Britt.
 The everything healthy green drinks book / Britt Brandon.
    pages cm
    Includes index.
    ISBN-13: 978-1-4405-7694-2 (pb)
    ISBN-10: 1-4405-7694-7 (pb)
    ISBN-13: 978-1-4405-7695-9 (ebook)
    ISBN-10: 1-4405-7695-5 (ebook)
    1.   Blenders (Cooking) 2.   Smoothies (Beverages) I. Title. II. Title: Healthy green drinks book.
    TX840.B5B46 2014
    613.2--dc23

                           2014008245

Many of the designations used by manufacturers and sellers to distinguish their product are claimed as trademarks. Where those designations appear in this book and F+W Media, Inc. was aware of a trademark claim, the designations have been printed with initial capital letters.

Always follow safety and commonsense cooking protocol while using kitchen utensils, operating ovens and stoves, and handling uncooked food. If children are assisting in the preparation of any recipe, they should always be supervised by an adult.

Cover images © melpomen/natika/Tetiana Vitsenko/123RF; © StockFood/Eising Studio - Food Photo & Video.

This book is available at quantity discounts for bulk purchases. For information, please call 1-800-289-0963.

Contents

Acknowledgments

I would like to thank my managing editor at Adams Media, Lisa Laing, for giving me the opportunity to write books just like this—books that are intended to share information that is necessary for people intending to live healthier, happier lives. Without Lisa, I would have never had my dreams of writing and sharing information about achieving better health with others come to fruition.

I would also like to thank my editor, Eileen Mullan, who has been one of the most wonderful editors I've worked with, and has made creating this book an absolute delight!

Last, but most importantly, I would like to thank my husband, Jimmy. My life, my career, and my happiness (all of which I am beyond thankful for everyday) I owe to the amazing support, friendship, and love I have found in my best friend, the love of my life, my husband.

Introduction

While many people make concerted efforts to exercise daily, eat clean, and live healthy lifestyles, it can become difficult to maintain those healthy ideals when your daily menu gets stale or redundant. With everything that the average day includes, from work to household chores to daily errands, creating quick and easy green drinks that contain essential vitamins, nutrients, phytochemicals, and powerful antioxidants can be a true lifesaver.

The hundreds of creative recipes in this book are intended to save you from the repetitious, everyday smoothies, juices, and drinks you've become bored with and give you new and exciting ideas for fruits, vegetables, and other additions that can make your delicious, nutritious green drinks something you look forward to again!

The realization that the Standard American Diet, summed up fittingly with the acronym "SAD," lacks a number of macronutrients, micronutrients, and vitamins has led a growing number of people to improve their diet and, therefore, their health. Any kind of deficiency in the essential dietary elements our bodies need to function and thrive is considered malnutrition, and a startling percentage of people are living with illnesses and diseases because they are malnourished. It is clear that consuming quality, clean, whole foods that provide the dietary essentials your body and brain need for optimal performance can change your life and improve your health.

While delving into a delicious apple, crunching on a cup of cabbage, and noshing on a handful of nuts may be easy ways to eat your favorite foods, you can consume a wider variety of fruits, vegetables, healthy liquids, etc. by choosing a delicious green drink. Whether you're home-bound or on the go, you can easily create green drinks like smoothies, juices, and shakes that pack a ton of vitamins and nutrients in tasty combinations. And since making these drinks doesn't require expensive ingredients, opting for these healthy produce-packed drinks may be easier than you think. While you could certainly shop for the most expensive, powerful machines on the market, inexpensive countertop blenders and juicers work perfectly for these recipes.

You'll even find yourself saving money and time, since planning and shopping for specific ingredients can be far more inexpensive and efficient than "loading up" on expensive varieties of vegetables, fruits, and additions you may not even use. And you'll be pleasantly surprised by how quickly and easily you can prep, create, and clean up. The entire process can be as quick as a minute or two with planning and preparing ahead of time. Once you understand the process, you'll quickly see that the time you spend planning your week, shopping, preparing the foods once they're purchased, and actually creating the drinks is far less than it might seem at first. Best of all, you'll quickly figure out the easiest way to prep, store, and plan, and the entire process will fit seamlessly into your lifestyle.

The most common fear that holds people back from trying a healthy venture (like creating green drinks) is the fear that they'll somehow mess up the process and have disastrous results. You can (and will!) surprise yourself with how easily you can create delicious drinks that not only taste great, but make you feel great, too! The recipes included in this book will provide you with hundreds of combinations you can use to satisfy every taste and craving you may have. Within these pages you'll find the proper tips, recipes, and instructions to create delicious, nutritious green drinks that you can simply and easily add into your everyday life. You'll improve your life as a result.

CHAPTER 1

Green Drink Basics

Although the value of a diet rich in greens, fruits, and vegetables has been well known for quite some time, drinks of the green variety have not been common until just recently. With well-known health professionals like Dr. Oz praising and promoting green smoothies and juicing, sipping greens has gone from a mystifying or questionable notion to a widely accepted way of improving your health simply, easily, and deliciously. And let's not forget their plentiful benefits. Whether you find yourself trying to cure or calm an illness, lose weight, feel great, or live healthier, you may be surprised how easily green drinks will fit into your lifestyle and help you achieve your health goals.

What Are Green Drinks?

A green drink can be described as a drink comprised of a number of ingredients, with some (if not all) being greens. Green smoothies, juices, and an assortment of other green concoctions can be created using a variety of delicious fruits and vegetables that, when combined, produce healthy green drinks. While there are many fruit and vegetable combinations that can target specific needs or areas of the body and brain, the main reason most people consume green drinks is to eat more vegetables and fruits on a daily basis.

If you can drink just one of the juices or smoothies in this book per day, you'll find you'll live a healthier and happier lifestyle as a result of this major nutritional shift in your daily life. Adding these green drinks into your average day doesn't require any extra time, money, or hassle. It takes only minutes to prepare, combine, and enjoy these green treats, and requires only the simplest of tools and the vegetables and fruits of your choosing. The entire process is easy to understand and fits with any schedule—no matter how hectic.

Green drinks have received ringing endorsements from Dr. Oz as well as celebrity chef Rachael Ray. TV host Montel Williams drinks them daily, and socialite Nicole Richie has also been spotted sipping green smoothies. From children to adults and pregnant women to raw-food enthusiasts, everyone seems to be including green drinks in their diets. Those who want to boost their metabolism and those who suffer from serious ailments can all benefit from green drinks. You can mix, match, and manipulate fruit and vegetable combinations to create any type of green drink that you want.

The History of Juicing

Juicing is a delicious way to replenish the body's minerals and vitamins. Whether you're looking for a jumpstart in the morning, a healthy pre- or post-workout drink, or a way to satisfy a craving for a sweet or salty treat, juicing can be an ideal answer for almost any occasion.

The first written words on juicing are found in the Dead Sea Scrolls, which date from before 150 B.C. to about 70 A.D. History shows that succulent fruits that were especially easy to find, such as lemons, oranges, and pomegranates, have been made into beverages by many different cultures for many years. Island cultures created nutritious drinks from tropical fruits. For example, in Peru, passion fruit was smashed and combined with water to produce a refreshing drink.

The Need for Juicing in the Twentieth Century

The biggest advocate of juicing in the twentieth century was Dr. Norman W. Walker, an English researcher and author. His book *Raw Vegetable Juices*, published in 1936, introduced juicing to the modern age.

Today, the benefits of fresh juice are more important than ever. The modern diet has strayed dramatically from the natural diet that our ancestors followed. Commercial farming methods have robbed the soil of important mineral contents, resulting in fruits and vegetables that are severely lacking in vitamins and minerals.

The late Dr. Linus Pauling, winner of two Nobel Prizes, attributed most disease, illness, and ailments to mineral deficiencies in the diet and soil. He claimed that the increasing incidence of disease could be blamed in part on the adoption of commercial farming procedures in the United States, which rob the soil and produce of mineral content.

Pauling charged that crops are raised in toxic soil laced with commercial crop fertilizers that contain petroleum and other unhealthy chemicals, genetically altered foods are grown and harvested in unnatural settings, and farm animals are raised in unsanitary conditions and fed steroids to pump up their market weight. In addition, some scientists believe the world's seafood supply, once a reliable source of minerals, has become so contaminated by environmental poisons that some health experts advise against eating such popular seafood as tuna, shrimp, and scallops.

Over the past sixty years, there's been a sharp decline in the variety of foods that are being grown. Modern day agriculture emphasizes growing a handful of reliable and profitable crops over the smorgasbord of varieties grown by farmers in centuries past, which provided a fuller spectrum of vitamins and minerals. Today, the typical American eats fewer than twenty different kinds of food. In addition, modern food processing relies on overcooking, packaging and storage, and shipping procedures that transport food states, countries, and even continents away from where it was grown, thus robbing it of its nutritional value.

Juicing can help put nutrition back in your life. It condenses the nutrients of many different types of produce into one glass.

Green Smoothies and Nutrition

Green smoothies are smoothies with greens blended into them. They differ from juices in that they're a complete food—they still have fiber. Most people know that greens are very nutritious, but struggle to eat enough of them—they're not the easiest vegetables to prepare tastefully while maintaining all of the important vitamins and minerals your body requires. Steaming, sautéing, baking, and roasting vegetables causes them to lose the vitamins and minerals you're trying to consume. Greens can also be hard to digest—you may not get the full benefits from your average meal or salad containing greens because the greens themselves can be difficult to digest and tedious to chew to the point where digestion would be easy. Blended greens in smoothies have already been ripped apart and are effectively "predigested," allowing for almost immediate absorption.

The blending process used in green smoothies actually breaks down the cellulose in the greens, making the nutrients able to be absorbed 70 to 90 percent more than that of a traditional salad.

Although many people suffer from irregularity, few know about the power of the amount of fiber held in a serving of greens. A type of carbohydrate that resists the body's digestive enzymes and acids, soluble fiber forms a gel-like substance in the digestive tract that binds with cholesterol so it can't be reabsorbed by the body. Insoluble fiber (often referred to as "nature's broom") moves food through the digestive system more quickly, reducing instances of constipation. Increasing your daily intake of deep-green vegetables and certain fruits can make irregularity a thing of the past.

Green Smoothies Versus the Standard American Diet

When you take into consideration that the Standard American Diet is packed with high levels of sugars, sodium, saturated fats, and preservatives from the types of foods consumed and how those foods are prepared, the green smoothie can be a very important addition to any diet. Regular consumption of empty calories and dangerous additives can easily be changed, and consuming these nutrient-dense smoothies just once a day can reverse the adverse effects of such nutrient-deficient lifestyles. Between a skipped breakfast, a lunch on the run from a fast-food place, and a dinner made from ingredients packed with sodium, trans fats, and dangerous preservatives, the average consumer rarely fulfills the suggested serving sizes of fruits and vegetables in a normal day and ends up suffering from the symptoms and illnesses that result from important deficiencies. All of these ailments can be reversed and improved with green smoothies and their powerful ingredients.

Supplement Your Diet Naturally

Symptoms and illnesses that arise from a vitamin deficiency can only be cured by that particular vitamin. This makes deep-green vegetables a one-stop shop for ensuring you fulfill your body's needs for vitamins and negate any possible illnesses and symptoms that could arise from being deficient. Also, of the eight essential amino acids that you need for bodily functions such as muscle repair, manufacturing hormones, mental functions, sleep, memory, and physical and mental energy, your body does not produce any naturally, so you need to get them from the foods you consume.

How many essential amino acids do you think are in a processed and unidentifiable fast-food hamburger? Whatever the answer may be, it can't compare to the raw vegetables and raw fruits you'll be blending into your green smoothie. If you know you are lacking in vitamins, minerals, or amino acids, green smoothies are a great way to meet and exceed your dietary needs.

QUESTION

What are some of the benefits I'll receive from drinking green smoothies?
The vegetables, fruits, and herbs used in your green smoothies are rich in powerful antioxidants known for enhancing brain function, combating negative effects of stress, improving cardiovascular health, and reversing the aging process.

Of all of the vitamins and minerals absolutely required by the body, each green drink ingredient packs a powerful amount in order to keep your body and mind working at its fullest potential.

VITAMINS

- **Biotin.** Found in the deep-green leafy vegetables, biotin is responsible for cell growth, maintaining a steady blood sugar level, and the metabolism of fats and amino acids. It also strengthens hair and nails.
- **Carotene.** Vibrant orange and yellow vegetables and leafy greens get their color from this amazing vitamin that is a powerful antioxidant. It provides protection from free radicals and aids in cancer prevention. Important phytochemicals lutein, lycopene, and beta-carotene are released with the tearing of these vegetables and provide the body with enormous protection from illness and disease.
- **Vitamin A.** Carrots and dark-green and yellow vegetables hold this important vitamin known for its role in providing vision health and proper cell growth.
- **Vitamin B$_1$.** Also known as thiamine, B$_1$ aids in every process, including nervous system processes, muscle function, metabolism of carbohydrates, and the production of healthy digestive enzymes, as well as electrolyte flow. This vitamin can be found in oranges and certain citrus fruits.
- **Vitamin B$_2$.** Also known as riboflavin, this vitamin found mainly in broccoli and asparagus aids cells in their growth, maintains proper functioning, and produces energy.
- **Vitamin B$_3$.** Also known as niacin, this hormone-regulating vitamin assists the adrenal glands in production of sex- and stress-related hormones, lowers LDL ("bad" cholesterol) while raising HDL ("good"

cholesterol), and has been recently suggested to improve symptoms of arthritis.

- **Vitamin B$_5$.** Also known as pantothenic acid, this vitamin is responsible for synthesizing and metabolizing the fats, carbohydrates, and proteins for all necessary bodily functions.
- **Vitamin B$_6$.** Also known as pyridoxine, B$_6$ is found in peas, carrots, and spinach and is responsible for the synthesis of important neurotransmitters serotonin and norepinephrine.
- **Vitamin B$_{12}$.** Also known as cobalamin, this vitamin aids in blood formation and energy production and is necessary for the metabolism of every cell throughout the body.
- **Vitamin C.** Found in most citrus fruits and in vibrant-colored and deep-green vegetables, vitamin C is well known for its immune-boosting properties but is also necessary for iron absorption and supports the growth and repair of cartilage, collagen, muscle, and blood vessels.
- **Vitamin D.** Produced in our bodies as a result of exposure to the sun, helpful supplies of vitamin D from plant sources are needed in order to protect your body from autoimmune diseases, cancers, osteoporosis, and hypertension.
- **Vitamin E.** This fat-soluble antioxidant has been known for stimulating skin repair and strengthening cells, but it is absolutely necessary in removing free radicals from the body's systems. It is found in abundance in spinach, collards, and dandelion greens, as well as turnips and beets.
- **Vitamin K.** This fat-soluble compound is extremely helpful in blood clotting and is found in the deep-green leafy vegetables.

MINERALS

- **Boron.** Found in spinach, cabbage, and carrots, as well as apples, pears, and grapes, this mineral maintains the health of bones and teeth by metabolizing calcium, magnesium, and phosphorous. It has also been cited for building muscle and promoting mental clarity and brain functioning.
- **Calcium.** Although it's known for maintaining the strength of bones and teeth, calcium also plays a vital role in maintaining regularity of the heart and helping to metabolize iron efficiently. Found in kale,

broccoli, and collard greens, calcium is especially important for women who are pregnant, nursing, or menstruating.

- **Chromium.** This weight-loss helper is powerful in effective fatty-acid metabolism and works together with insulin to maintain the proper use of sugar in the body.
- **Copper.** Found in most green vegetables, copper is another mineral that aids in the absorption of iron, but also helps to maintain cardio-vascular health and can promote fertility in both men and women.
- **Iron.** Although all people require adequate amounts of iron found in dark-green vegetables, vegans and pregnant or menstruating women are in a different bracket, requiring much more. The reason iron is such a commodity for lifestyles requiring additional protein is that it is mainly responsible for strengthening the immune system, and it is found in great amounts in the proteins of red blood cells.
- **Magnesium.** Helpful in maintaining proper functioning of the muscles and the nervous system. Health problems resulting from low levels of magnesium include hypertension, diabetes, osteoporosis, and certain digestive disorders.
- **Potassium.** Working with sodium to maintain a proper balance of the body's water, potassium is mainly required for the metabolism of carbohydrates and the synthesis of proteins.
- **Selenium.** Found in deep-green vegetables (notably asparagus) and mushrooms, selenium is helpful in weight loss by stimulating the metabolism, and effective in disease prevention by acting as an anti-oxidant against free radicals that cause health issues like arthritis, cancer, and heart disease.
- **Sodium.** This mineral is important in maintaining proper muscle control and optimal nerve functioning, as well as correcting the body's distribution of fluid and maintaining proper pH balance.

Greens and Healing

When diagnosing patients with certain health problems, many doctors will recommend a change of diet. That changed diet usually includes an increase in fruits and vegetables with a decrease in refined carbohydrates and sugar intake. The studies, statistics, and testimonies of those that have introduced greens into their diet speak loudly in terms of the resulting physical and mental health improvements. Researchers at Harvard Medical School tracked the health of more than 22,000 physicians and found that those who ate at least two servings of vegetables daily reduced their risk of heart disease by almost 25 percent. At the University of California, Berkeley, researchers found that a high intake of fruits and vegetables also reduced the risk of cancer on an average of 50 percent. And a vegan diet rich in fruits and vegetables has reportedly reduced diabetes indicators and shown an increase in immune protection against arthritis.

Many people who add green drinks to their diet experience the benefits within a matter of days or a few short weeks. These benefits include more energy, mental clarity, better digestion, and clearer skin. Women and men have found their hair feels stronger, thicker, and more lustrous as a result of consuming important vitamins like calcium, magnesium, and biotin that are found in greens. Men and women have reported a sense of mental clarity that can be compared to "the clearing of a fog" when they started consuming green smoothies; almost every mineral, vitamin, and phytonutrient found in deep greens can aid in mental and physical processes.

Reduce Your Health Risks

From improved condition of hair, skin, and nails to a renewed mental clarity and increased stamina, green smoothies and juices combine the perfect ingredients to provide the essential vitamins, minerals, and nutrients to achieve almost any change desired. Vitamins necessary to sustain life and maintain healthy lifestyles can be found in deep greens and fruits. Folate (folic acid), found in many of the greens, is an important B vitamin needed especially by pregnant women in order to ensure the fetus is protected from spinal defects like spina bifida. The protein provided by vegetable sources far surpasses that of meats of any variety; a deep-green vegetable like broccoli can deliver a healthy dose of protein without the unhealthy saturated fats of an animal protein source.

ALERT

Vegetable juices and tonics found in the common marketplace can be packed with sodium and preservatives. By creating your own green smoothie, you know and control exactly what goes into every sip.

The powerful ingredients found in green drinks have alleviated conditions even as severe as osteoarthritis, osteoporosis, Alzheimer's, and various cancers. The phytochemicals found in these greens have been proven to have antioxidant activity that protects cells from oxidative damage and reduces the risks for certain cancers. If you like cabbage, you'll be pleased to learn that it contains indoles that stimulate enzymes that make estrogen less effective, and can reduce the risk of breast cancer!

Nutritional Benefits of Juicing

Freshly squeezed fruits and vegetables are the kings of the food kingdom, for several reasons. Fruits and vegetables provide a wealth of nutritional benefits that could never be squeezed into a vitamin supplement. Also, no other health food on earth can be so quickly digested and absorbed by the body.

Why Not Just Eat or Cook with Produce?

There's absolutely nothing wrong with eating fruits and vegetables or cooking them and enjoying them with meals. But there are several reasons why juicing is a more effective way of ensuring you get the most bang from your buck when you're dealing with fresh produce.

- Juicing filters out the fiber contained in fruits and vegetables and leaves you with a concentrated array of nutrients, making it an easier and convenient way to consume a greater volume of produce than you could ever comfortably consume in raw or cooked form.
- Unlike most forms of cooking, juicing does not destroy any of the nutrients in fruits and vegetables.
- Fresh produce doesn't contain any of the unhealthy fillers or ingredients that prepared produce may contain. You don't have to read any labels or do any guesswork to know your juice is 100 percent natural.
- Because juicing removes the fiber from produce, the result is juice that is almost completely self-digesting. The nutrients are absorbed almost immediately by your body.
- Juicing makes it easy to achieve what's sometimes called rainbow nutrition, or consuming the widest possible variety of fruits and vegetables every day. The color of each fruit or vegetable signals its unique

vitamins, minerals, trace minerals, antioxidants, anti-carcinogens, detoxifying agents, digestive aids, natural blood purifiers, blood thinners, immune stimulants, and memory enhancers.

- Juicing makes it easy to get the recommended five daily servings of fruits and vegetables for health and disease prevention.

According to the National Institutes of Health, most people get less than 75 percent of the recommended daily allowance (RDA) of essential nutrients. Because nearly all the necessary vitamins and minerals for health are found in fruits and vegetables, juicing is a fast, easy, delicious, and guaranteed way to cover your nutritional bases.

The Synergy Connection

Many nutrients need to work with other nutrients to enjoy maximum performance and really strut their nutritional stuff. For instance, vitamin E is most effective when it's combined with vitamin C and the mineral selenium, while beta-carotene boosts the benefits of zinc and many other nutrients.

Looking for fast energy? Fruits and vegetables have the highest rate of bioavailability of all foods. That means your body can make full use of the nutrients in juice within 45 minutes to 2 hours after you drink it. As a side bonus, juicing also helps reverse digestive problems caused by food additives, preservatives, overcooking, and processed foods.

Juicing for Enzyme Action

Fresh juice contains tons of enzymes—chemicals in fruits and vegetables that are catalysts for the biochemical reactions behind every function the body performs. Fruits and vegetables have digestive enzymes that help the body digest carbohydrates, fats, fiber, and proteins and convert large food chemicals into smaller ones that are more easily absorbed and used by the body.

Basic Ingredients for Green Drinks

The simplicity of green drinks is found in what is required to create one: a blender, a juicer, a knife for food prep, and the greens, fruits, and vegetables of your choosing. That's it! Whether you'd like to use your tried-and-true kitchen blender or juicer or you'd rather opt for a high-horsepower emulsifying machine, the choice is yours. A cutting board, peeler, and knife will help in cleaning and preparing your fruits and vegetables with ease and assist in quick clean up. In most cases, you may want to soak and rinse your greens in cold water, but rinsing by hand can be done just as easily. Salad spinners offer the option of spinning off any excess water from your greens.

FACT

In a fraction of the time required to make an entire meal, you can prep, blend, and enjoy a more nutritious green smoothie. Green smoothies can also cut down on the cost of preparing an entire meal.

Depending on the type, taste, or texture you desire, your ingredients will be the main priority throughout the drink-making process. The choice of greens, vegetables, and fruits that you'd like to combine in your drink is essential, and you can always stock up on any of the suggested additions you find appealing. Although certain fruits and vegetables may not be available locally or seasonally depending on the time of year, freezing is always an option that will allow you to enjoy your favorite ingredients year round.

Additional Ingredients

Soy and protein powders, spirulina, coconut milk, almond milk, rice milk, kefir, Greek-style yogurt, and cacao are tasty ingredients you can blend into your own green smoothies. These ingredients are widely available and can change the taste experience completely. The bottom line is that what you need in your pantry is what you would like in your green drink. Try one ingredient, or try them all—it's up to you!

Equipment for Green Smoothies

In order to prepare a green smoothie, all that's needed are the fruits and vegetables of your choosing (according to recipes that sound appetizing to you) and a high-speed blender capable of emulsifying the greens and additions. The blender needed for green smoothies can be completely based on your needs and choosing. In most reviews of blenders on the market today, green smoothie consumers compare them based upon a couple of major factors: power, noise, capacity, and ease of cleanup.

- **Power.** The power of your blender will determine how quickly and efficiently your smoothie and its ingredients can be liquefied and blended. If time or texture are of no importance, this factor may not require much attention.
- **Noise.** Noise can be of no importance or of the utmost importance when it comes to selecting the perfect blender. If you plan on blending your smoothie prior to the rest of your house waking, it might be smart to invest in a quieter version that will still get the job done nicely.
- **Capacity.** Capacity is extremely important, considering you will be putting cups of fruits and vegetables, along with other ingredients, into the same canister. You will need enough room for the blending to be efficient. Also, be sure to take into consideration that you will need enough room in your blender for the adequate amount of ingredients for your desired number of servings.
- **Ease of cleanup.** Although cleanup may also seem like a nonissue at first thought, consider your schedule or routine when making this purchase. Do you need it to be dishwasher safe? Will the blender require special tools for cleaning? Is there a recommended strategy to keep the blender clean while also ensuring a long lifespan?

The two most commonly used brands are Blendtec and Vitamix. Although these high-speed emulsifying machines come at a higher cost than your average blender, the quality, efficiency, and capabilities can make even those reluctant to purchase a new one consider making a swap. If you plan to use blenders for this precise purpose, more familiar brand names like KitchenAid, Black & Decker, and Krups also provide smoothie makers or blenders that will leave you delighted.

Types of Juicers

A juicer is a mechanical device that can be operated, either manually or electrically, to extract juice from vegetables, fruits, and leafy greens. There are different types depending on the fruit or the vegetable.

ESSENTIAL

Don't confuse a blender with a juicer; they are two different machines. A juicer has a mechanism that will separate the pulp from the juice, whereas a blender grinds the produce and the pulp has to be manually strained.

Centrifugal Versus Masticating Juicers

Centrifugal juicers are one of the oldest types and have a simple design with a shredder and a strainer. A spinning basket shreds the produce and then forces the juice through a fine strainer by centrifugal force. This process adds oxygen to the juices and makes them a little frothy.

In masticating juicers, the produce is squeezed through gears that crush the produce and force it through a fine strainer. The pulp is continuously extracted, and because the machine doesn't generate heat or friction, nutrients are preserved.

FACT

Both types of juicers work efficiently, so the best type is the one that works best for your needs. Although few stores will let you test-run a juicer before purchasing to ensure it's a good fit, you can find video demos and information online to help you make a decision.

Factors to Consider

Besides cost, there are other important factors to be considered before putting down money for a juicer:

- **Ease of use.** Look for an easy-to-use juicer that does not require much time and effort to operate and clean.
- **Reliability.** Buy a trusted brand that does not require you to replace parts often.
- **Horsepower.** Make sure your juicer has at least 0.5 horsepower to avoid burning out.
- **Multiple speeds.** Buy a quality juicer that has at least two speeds—high for harder jobs and slow for easier ones. Inexpensive juicers have only one high speed. In addition, make sure your machine has electronic circuitry that maintains blade speed during juicing.
- **Feed tube.** Look for a juicer with a large feed tube to avoid having to cut produce into teeny pieces. Also, make sure the tube is easy to use at your height.
- **Versatility.** Make sure your machine can handle tough, hard vegetables and fruits like carrots, pineapple skins, watermelon rinds, and beets, as well as delicate greens like lettuce, parsley, and herbs.
- **Output.** Check out how much juice your model can extract from the given quantity of food, choosing machines that remove at least 90 percent of the juice from the pulp. Some models yield more pulp than juice. Models that extract the pulp to an outside container leave less pulp behind than those that separate the pulp inside the machine.
- **Size.** Make sure you buy the right size juicer for your needs. If you plan to create juice just for yourself, choose a juicer with a beaker that holds a cup.
- **Continuous juicing.** Choose a machine that ejects pulp into a receptacle rather than a juicer that keeps the pulp in a center basket. Juicers with center baskets require that you stop the machine and wash out the basket frequently in order to continue juicing.
- **Simplicity.** Choose a juicer that has only a few parts to clean. The more parts a juicer has, and the harder and more complicated it is to wash, the longer it will take to clean and reassemble—and the less likely you'll be to want to use it again. Also, make sure all the washable parts of your juicer are dishwasher safe. In general, centrifugal juicers are easier to clean than masticating juicers.

- **Quality.** Make sure your juicer sits securely and solidly on your counter and doesn't jiggle around when you use it. You want to feed your body, not your floor!
- **Noise.** Choose a juicer that is quiet. Some brands are so loud you may need to wear earplugs to use them. In general, centrifugal juicers and more expensive models tend to be quieter than masticating models.

Juicy Truths and Myths

Before you delve into the details of juicing and invest in a juicer, take a moment to separate the truth from the bunk about juicing. Some claim juicing is a waste of time, energy, and money and that you're much better off just eating the whole fruit and skipping the juicing. The fact is that while fruits and vegetables are extremely nutritious when they are eaten raw and whole, the fiber they contain means the nutrients take longer to absorb and assimilate.

Most fruits and vegetables undergo a great deal of abuse before going into a can or bottle. When fruits and vegetables are frozen as concentrates, chemical processes destroy much of their nutrients and enzymes and make them a far cry from freshly made "living" juices.

According to the Department of Agriculture, 90 percent of the antioxidant action in fruit is in the juice, not the fiber. It's hard for most people to eat enough raw fruits and vegetables to equal what they'd get in a quart of juice. Remember that a quart of vegetable juice equals 5 pounds of tomatoes!

CHAPTER 2

Green Drinks for Weight Loss

In the past few years, there has been a growing interest in green drinks and their strong connection to successful, long-lasting weight loss. Smoothies, juicing, and green drinks have become all the rage in celebrity circles. Because of their popularity, seemingly every well-known personality is promoting his or her own "unique" way of losing weight with green drinks, but taking diet advice from svelte celebs who've never had a real weight problem is probably not such a great idea. First and foremost, the integration of green drinks in your daily diet is a powerful step toward weight loss and overall health, but it is only one aspect of a comprehensive weight loss program. You still have to exercise, you still have to eat the right kinds of foods, and above all, you must avoid the temptation to "binge" on the fattening stuff one day and then "purge" with a juice fast the next. The roller-coaster ride of healthy eating followed by poor eating, over and over again, is the sort of habit that can wreak havoc on your digestion and your metabolism, as well as decrease your chances of lasting weight-loss results.

You *Will* Lose Weight by Juicing Regularly

The good news is, by juicing only three or four times a week, you can expect to eliminate pounds of excess water weight and waste that may have been stored in the bowels over time. This further increases your energy levels because you are ridding your body of excess waste and adding quality nutrients that will help your body to metabolize food faster and more effectively. To take weight loss to the next level, though, you have to burn fat. If you're asking, "How do you do that?," the answer is three-fold: If you want to lose weight, you have to:

- take in fewer calories than your body needs,
- decrease your amount of body fat while increasing your amount of muscle mass,
- and keep yourself motivated and interested in your new and improved way of drinking your greens!

Creating a Caloric Deficit

In terms of your caloric intake and expenditure, consider this: The amount of calories your body needs to function normally depends on your metabolic rate, which is determined by a number of factors, such as your age, sex, amount and level of daily activity, and so forth. So let's say you need 2,000 calories a day. When you only consume 1,200 or 1,500, your body isn't getting enough fuel to have the energy to maintain your normal life, forcing your system to get the energy it needs from your stored fat cells. Your body requires a 3,500 caloric deficit in order to burn 1 pound, so if you were to consume 500 calories less than your caloric requirement each day for seven days, it would result in a 3,500 calorie difference each week, which is enough to help you lose a pound per week.

It's always a good idea to consult with your health practitioner to rule out any pre-existing conditions or health problems.

That can add up to a significant weight loss over time. Juice, smoothies, and drinks that are rich in fruits and vegetables are extremely low in calories, provide a host of essential nutrients, and can contain enough soluble fiber and simple sugars to help you feel full for extended periods of time. Green drinks are nutritional and easy-to-prepare meals or snack substitutes that are a delicious, low-calorie, healthy option to eliminate those 500 calories without even missing them!

Burning Fat and Building Muscle

In order to promote a healthy cycle of burning fat and building muscle, increasing your metabolism through regular exercise is a must. Between cardiovascular activity, strength training, and flexibility-focused exercise, the exercises you choose to engage in will help increase calorie burn and promote weight loss. The goal of exercise is to engage in activities where you use muscles to an extent that they are in need of repair following the bout of activity. The use of the muscles during the activity and the body's burning of calories during the repair process both require calories you either consume or have stored. Being smart about how you choose to provide your body with the "fuel" it needs to perform each of these processes can aid in achieving your weight-loss goals.

Because the body utilizes different nutrients for energy and repair, you can optimize your weight loss by consuming green drinks that contain foods that provide the exact nutrients your body needs for the processes it performs. Green drinks that contain a majority of complex carbohydrates will assist in the body's use of consumed nutrients and stored fat, and green drink varieties that are rich in protein will help the body repair itself after workouts. By selecting your nutrition appropriately, you can enjoy green drinks before and after exercise, promote fat burn and muscle gain, and achieve your weight-loss goals faster than you ever dreamed possible!

Which Fruits and Vegetables Are Best for Your Weight Loss?

Let's face it: No weight loss program is going to be effective if you don't like what you're supposed to be consuming. Bottom line: if you don't like it, you probably won't eat it. You know yourself and your likes and dislikes better than anyone else, so if you have reservations about a diet before even starting out, you may find comfort in the fact that by opting for a diet focused on green drinks, you have tasty options and tons of variety available. So when choosing fruits and vegetables for your weigh loss–focused green drinks, the first thing to consider is that it's important to choose what you like. If the mere idea of kale makes you turn up your nose, or kiwis give you the heebie-jeebies, then it doesn't make sense to include those things in your drink ingredients at the start. But, because all of the fruits and vegetables available have profound nutritional value in varying amounts, you should set a goal of including as many as possible as often as possible . . . even those you don't prefer at the start. A great idea is to find drink recipes that include your least favorite varieties in small amounts (that you may not even notice because of the overpowering flavors of the other ingredients) and increase their amounts gradually.

Keep in mind, though, that when it comes to weight loss, all fruits and vegetables are not necessarily created equal. Some have more nutrients per calorie than others, and selecting the right varieties can ensure your diet provides your body with what it needs.

The absolute best vegetables to help speed up weight loss are the deep green vegetables: chard, kale, bok choy, collard greens, spinach, cabbage, Brussels sprouts, and broccoli. Other helpful varieties with both nutrient values and diuretic properties are the lettuces, tomatoes, celery, and bell peppers.

By the same token, some fruits are considered better for weight loss than others. These include many of the superfoods, like oranges and apples. Taking the entire group into consideration, the real fruit stars of the weight loss team are the berries. Strawberries, raspberries, and blueberries top the list, followed by acai and goji berries. When choosing fruits for weight loss, always look for those with a high vitamin C content, such as kiwi or grapefruit, because vitamin C helps to flush your system of the waste that is produced as fat cells burn.

In Conclusion

When balancing your diet to maintain a caloric deficit and a proper proportion of the right nutrients to provide your body with what it needs when it needs it, keep in mind that variety can be the key to your success. Many well-meaning dieters have given into temptation just because they weren't giving their senses enough flavor, color, and delicious-smelling stimulation. Be sure to include foods that ward off sugar cravings, like rich fruits such as apples and bananas, and filling veggies with enough fiber to keep you feeling full, such as carrots and cabbage. Fortunately, nature has provided us with infinite combinations of produce, so feel free to experiment and explore those concoctions that are especially appealing to the nose, the eye, and the palate. Keeping yourself satisfied will keep you on the path to weight-loss success!

Best Produce for Weight Loss

1. Spinach
2. Kale
3. Apples
4. Watermelon
5. Broccoli
6. Beets
7. Citrus fruits (grapefruits, lemons, oranges)
8. Carrots
9. Sweet potatoes
10. Green tea

Green Drinks for Weight Loss

Watermelon Orange

Eating foods used as diuretics is helpful in managing water retention or bloat. Some of these foods are watermelon, garlic, cantaloupe, and dill.

INGREDIENTS | SERVES 1

1 cup chopped romaine lettuce

1 cup cubed watermelon

1 medium orange, peeled

1. Juice lettuce, watermelon, and orange.

2. Stir.

PER SERVING: Calories: 118 | Fat: 1 g | Protein: 2 g | Sodium: 5 mg | Fiber: 0 g | Carbohydrates: 29 g | Sugar: 23 g

Mini Melons

Watermelons are available in small individual sizes. They are about the size of a cantaloupe melon. You may want to use a melon baller, a small bowl-shaped tool, to cut rounds of melon. These can be placed on a skewer and used to decorate your juice.

Broccoli Cabbage Patch

Cabbage juice is good for weight loss, but it's best to mix it with something else so that it does not cause as much gas in your stomach. Cabbage is a cruciferous vegetable that contains some vitamin A and a good amount of vitamin C.

INGREDIENTS | SERVES 1

1 cup broccoli

¼ small head red cabbage

3 romaine lettuce leaves

1. Juice broccoli; set aside.

2. Juice cabbage and lettuce.

3. Stir all juices together.

PER SERVING: Calories: 101 | Fat: 1 g | Protein: 7 g | Sodium: 81 mg | Fiber: 0 g | Carbohydrates: 22 g | Sugar: 9 g

Green Juice

Cravings for sour foods can come from a lack of acetic acid. Green vegetables are high in chlorophyll and help with these types of cravings.

INGREDIENTS | SERVES 1

3 celery stalks, leaves intact
½ cucumber
1 medium red apple, cored
1 cup chopped spinach
1 cup beet greens

1. Juice ingredients in the order listed.

2. Stir together and serve.

PER SERVING: Calories: 152 | Fat: 1 g | Protein: 4 g | Sodium: 210 mg | Fiber: 0 g | Carbohydrates: 37 g | Sugar: 24 g

Skinny Dip

Citrus sometimes satisfies cravings for high fat foods. Lemon juice helps digestion, making sure that the liver rids itself of any impurities, which is essential to losing and keeping off excess weight.

INGREDIENTS | SERVES 1

½ cup chopped spinach
1 lemon, halved, rind intact
1 lime, halved, rind intact
1 cup sparkling water

1. Juice spinach, lemon, and lime together.

2. Add sparkling water to green lemon-lime juice.

3. Stir together and serve.

PER SERVING: Calories: 43 | Fat: 0 g | Protein: 2 g | Sodium: 15 mg | Fiber: 0 g | Carbohydrates: 14 g | Sugar: 3 g

Lemons

California is the leading producer of lemons in the United States. They are available year round. Make sure you juice a lemon immediately before you're going to use it. Lemons lose 20 percent of their vitamin C after eight hours at room temperature.

Apple Yammer

This juice is high in vitamins A and C. It's a great way to satisfy your sweet tooth while keeping things healthy.

INGREDIENTS | SERVES 1

1 cup chopped spinach
1 medium yam, cut into pieces
1 medium red apple, cored

1. Juice spinach, yam, and apple.

2. Stir together.

PER SERVING: Calories: 213 | Fat: 0 g | Protein: 3 g | Sodium: 97 mg | Fiber: 0 g | Carbohydrates: 52 g | Sugar: 24 g

Spinach Apple

Spinach is rich in iron and vitamins A, C, and E. It helps protect against osteoporosis. It is good for constipation and calcium absorption.

INGREDIENTS | SERVES 1

1 cup torn spinach leaves
1 medium red apple
¼ lemon, rind intact
1 celery stalk

1. Juice spinach, apple, lemon, and celery.

2. Stir together.

PER SERVING: Calories: 113 | Fat: 1 g | Protein: 2 g | Sodium: 58 mg | Fiber: 0 g | Carbohydrates: 29 g | Sugar: 20 g

Asparagus Carrot

Asparagus is a good source of vitamin E. It is a natural diuretic that is low in calories and high in vitamins and minerals.

INGREDIENTS | SERVES 1

1 cup chopped romaine lettuce
1 cup chopped asparagus
3 medium carrots, peeled

1. Juice romaine, asparagus, and carrots.

2. Stir together.

PER SERVING: Calories: 110 | Fat: 1 g | Protein: 5 g | Sodium: 133 mg | Fiber: 0 g | Carbohydrates: 24 g | Sugar: 12 g

Beet the Bloat

Beets are high in the vitamins, minerals, and antioxidants that promote your body's ability to function optimally. By combining beets with apples, lemon, ginger, and green tea, you can fuel your body with the nutrients it needs while optimizing its fat-burning potential.

INGREDIENTS | SERVES 3

1 cup chopped beet greens
1 beet, chopped
3 medium apples, peeled and cored
½ lemon, peeled
¼" ginger, peeled
2 cups green tea

1. Place beet greens, beet, apples, lemon, and ginger with 1 cup tea in a blender and blend until thoroughly combined.

2. Add remaining 1 cup tea, as needed, while blending until desired consistency is achieved.

PER SERVING: Calories: 95 | Fat: 0 g | Protein: 1 g | Sodium: 50 mg | Fiber: 4 g | Carbohydrates: 25 g | Sugar: 18 g

Green Tea Metabolism Booster

Green tea is packed with fat-burning catechin antioxidants that aid in weight loss. Using green tea instead of water in this smoothie amplifies the fat-burning properties of the vitamin- and mineral-rich greens and fruits.

INGREDIENTS | SERVES 3

1 cup watercress

1 lemon, peeled

2 cups cantaloupe, rind and seeds removed

1 cup raspberries

2 cups green tea

Making Quick Green Tea

Most people who are on the go prefer to make their green tea with the conveniently prepackaged tea bags. By purchasing quality green tea bags and using quality purified and filtered water, you can make your own fat-burning green tea on the go, at the office, or even in the car. Boil the water and pour it into a safe (preferably glass) container, steep the tea bag for the suggested amount of time to maximize antioxidant release and taste, and enjoy!

1. Place watercress, lemon, cantaloupe, raspberries, and 1 cup tea in a blender and blend until thoroughly combined.

2. Add remaining 1 cup tea, as needed, while blending until desired consistency is achieved.

PER SERVING: Calories: 64 | Fat: 1 g | Protein: 2 g | Sodium: 22 mg | Fiber: 4 g | Carbohydrates: 15 g | Sugar: 10 g

Slim Down Smoothie

This smoothie will satisfy any craving while delivering loads of vitamins and nutrients for optimizing your energy and stamina. It makes an amazing meal or snack that will energize your body and mind while keeping your diet on track.

INGREDIENTS | SERVES 3

1 cup chopped spinach
2 medium red apples, peeled and cored
2 medium pears, cored
½ lemon, peeled
¼" ginger, peeled
2 cups green tea

Benefits of Natural Carbs

The calories in fruits and vegetables are used in digestion and by body processes that function to perform normal activity, so there is virtually no waste of calories and none to be stored as fat. In addition, the carbohydrates of fruits and vegetables turn to sugars more slowly than refined carbohydrates, allowing them to burn fat without fluctuating blood sugar levels.

1. Place spinach, apples, pears, lemon, ginger, and 1 cup tea in a blender and blend until thoroughly combined.

2. Add remaining 1 cup tea, as needed, while blending until desired consistency is achieved.

PER SERVING: Calories: 125 | Fat: 0 g | Protein: 1 g | Sodium: 9 mg | Fiber: 6 g | Carbohydrates: 33 g | Sugar: 23 g

Colors of Success

By combining a variety of vibrant colors in your diet, you can ensure you're providing a variety of vitamins and minerals your body requires to run at its optimal level. The ingredients of this smoothie make a tasty treat for your eyes and your body.

INGREDIENTS | SERVES 5

1 cup beet greens
1 beet, chopped
3 medium carrots, peeled
2 medium apples, cored
1 banana, peeled
3 cups green tea

1. Place beet greens, beet, carrots, apples, banana, and 1½ cups tea in a blender and blend until thoroughly combined.

2. Add remaining 1½ cups tea, as needed, while blending until desired consistency is achieved.

PER SERVING: Calories: 83 | Fat: 0 g | Protein: 1 g | Sodium: 56 mg | Fiber: 4 g | Carbohydrates: 21 g | Sugar: 13 g

Cinch Pounds with Citrus

This sweet combination of greens and citrus makes for a refreshing snack for your body and mind. This smoothie stimulates your brain for improved mental clarity and focus, your body for more efficient metabolism, and your overall health with the abundance of vitamins and minerals.

INGREDIENTS | SERVES 3

1 cup watercress

1 medium grapefruit, peeled and seeded

½ pineapple, peeled and cored

1 medium orange, peeled

½ lemon, peeled

½ lime, peeled

2 cups green tea

1. Place watercress, grapefruit, pineapple, orange, lemon, lime, and 1 cup tea in a blender and blend until thoroughly combined.

2. Add remaining 1 cup tea, as needed, while blending until desired consistency is achieved.

PER SERVING: Calories: 125 | Fat: 0 g | Protein: 2 g | Sodium: 6 mg | Fiber: 5 g | Carbohydrates: 33 g | Sugar: 24 g

Vitamin C

Some restrictive diets can leave your body feeling fatigued and your mind fuzzy. With those side effects, it's no wonder so many people abandon their diet plans! With an increase in vitamin C in your daily diet, your body's metabolism of proteins, fats, and carbohydrates improves, making for wonderful effects in mental clarity, improved energy and stamina, and a better feeling of fullness from your foods. It also improves the body's ability to remove toxins and waste.

Apple Pie for Weight Loss

Even the most avid dieter who sticks to every aspect of her diet gets hit with cravings now and again. This smoothie will satisfy your taste buds' desire for delicious apple pie without the unhealthy sugars, fat, and lack of nutrition of the traditional treat.

INGREDIENTS | SERVES 3

1 cup watercress

3 medium Granny Smith apples, peeled and cored

½ lemon, peeled

1 teaspoon cloves

½" piece ginger, peeled

2 cups green tea

1. Place watercress, apples, lemon, cloves, ginger, and 1 cup tea in a blender and blend until thoroughly combined.

2. Add remaining 1 cup tea, as needed, while blending until desired consistency is achieved.

PER SERVING: Calories: 84 | Fat: 0 g | Protein: 1 g | Sodium: 7 mg | Fiber: 3 g | Carbohydrates: 22 g | Sugar: 17 g

A Smart Way to Satisfy Cravings

A smart suggestion for diet success is to consume water or healthy fruits and vegetables when cravings strike. Green smoothies are an excellent option because they provide a large dose of greens, fruits, and vegetables tailored to fit your craving. Sweet smoothies can provide the sugar you're craving, and the savory options work wonders in calming your desire for salt.

Gorgeous Greens for a Gorgeous Body

These gorgeous green fruits and veggies make a refreshing treat. Not only is this a filling smoothie option, but the ingredients offer balanced nutrition, vitamins, minerals, and antioxidants that will keep you moving throughout your day.

INGREDIENTS | SERVES 3

1 cup chopped spinach

2 Granny Smith apples, peeled and cored

2 celery stalks

1 medium cucumber, peeled

½ lime, peeled

2 cups green tea

1. Place spinach, apples, celery, cucumber, lime, and 1 cup tea in a blender and blend until thoroughly combined.

2. Add remaining 1 cup tea, as needed, while blending until desired consistency is achieved.

PER SERVING: Calories: 69 | Fat: 0 g | Protein: 1 g | Sodium: 31 mg | Fiber: 3 g | Carbohydrates: 17 g | Sugar: 12 g

Total Health Inside and Out

The natural nutrition found in greens and fruits can do wonders for your body on the inside and out! Consuming deep greens and vibrant fruits, hydrating with purified water, and exercising daily will help you feel and look great.

A Spicy Blue Blast

Antioxidant-rich blueberries and fat-burning blackberries pair up with soothing ginger for a refreshingly light smoothie that will make any diet more enjoyable! These sweet ingredients can even be enjoyed as a midnight snack without the guilt of the alternatives.

INGREDIENTS | SERVES 3

1 cup watercress
2 cups blueberries
1 cup blackberries
½" ginger, peeled
2 cups green tea

1. Place watercress, berries, ginger, and 1 cup tea in a blender and blend until thoroughly combined.

2. Add remaining 1 cup green tea, as needed, while blending until desired consistency is achieved.

PER SERVING: Calories: 78 | Fat: 1 g | Protein: 2 g | Sodium: 6 mg | Fiber: 5 g | Carbohydrates: 19 g | Sugar: 12 g

Magic Berries

Blueberries, blackberries, strawberries, and raspberries are superfoods disguised as sweet treats. These fat-burning fruits are low in calories and packed with antioxidants that promote weight loss, and supply quick energy that also allows you to burn fat fast. They are also rich in magnesium, one of the most important minerals when dieting, key to promoting energy regulation.

Minty Mango Metabolism Maximizer

The delightful flavors of watercress, mango, oranges, and green tea are intensified by the addition of mint in this recipe. This refreshing smoothie is sweet—but not too sweet.

INGREDIENTS | SERVES 3

1 cup watercress

1 cup chopped, pitted mango

2 medium oranges, peeled

¼ cup mint leaves

1 cup green tea

1. Place watercress, mango, oranges, mint, and ½ cup tea in a blender and blend until thoroughly combined.

2. Add remaining ½ cup tea, as needed, while blending until desired consistency is achieved.

PER SERVING: Calories: 81 | Fat: 0 g | Protein: 2 g | Sodium: 7 mg | Fiber: 4 g | Carbohydrates: 20 g | Sugar: 16 g

Protein-Packed Craving Calmer

With every ingredient contributing protein, this is one green drink that takes nutritious deliciousness to a whole new level!

INGREDIENTS | SERVES 2

1 cup chopped spinach

1 cup vanilla almond milk

3 tablespoons ground hemp seed

½ cup almonds

1 cup pitted dates

Combine all ingredients in a blender and blend until desired consistency is achieved.

PER SERVING: Calories: 529 | Fat: 24 g | Protein: 14 g | Sodium: 89 mg | Fiber: 13 g | Carbohydrates: 74 g | Sugar: 56 g

Coolest Cucumber

Keep it simple with just a few ingredients! This quick and easy green drink satisfies your cravings and dietary needs with every sip.

INGREDIENTS | SERVES 2

2 large English cucumbers
1 cup chopped spinach
1 cup pineapple chunks
1 cup coconut milk

Combine all ingredients in a blender and blend until desired consistency is achieved.

PER SERVING: Calories: 130 | Fat: 3 g | Protein: 3 g | Sodium: 41 mg | Fiber: 3 g | Carbohydrates: 26 g | Sugar: 16 g

Skinny Sweet Tropical Treat

Between the delicious sweetness of delightful citrus fruits and the filling fiber of luscious greens, this tropical treat provides everything you need for lasting fullness and taste bud satisfaction!

INGREDIENTS | SERVES 2

½ cup chopped romaine lettuce
½ mango, seeded and peeled
1 cup pineapple chunks
½ cup natural, unsweetened coconut
2 cups vanilla coconut milk

Combine all ingredients in a blender and blend until desired consistency is achieved.

PER SERVING: Calories: 235 | Fat: 12 g | Protein: 2 g | Sodium: 51 mg | Fiber: 4 g | Carbohydrates: 31 g | Sugar: 26 g

Cran-Orange Green Dream

The powerful tastes of cranberry and orange fill your cup with amazing deliciousness and provide your body with everything it needs to stay full longer and keep you feeling satisfied for sweets for hours!

INGREDIENTS | SERVES 2

2 cups cranberries
2 cups freshly squeezed orange juice
1 cup chopped spinach
2 medium oranges, peeled

1. Simmer cranberries and 1 cup orange juice in a medium saucepan over medium heat for 3 hours.

2. Remove from heat and allow to cool.

3. Combine all ingredients in a blender and blend until desired consistency is achieved.

PER SERVING: Calories: 226 | Fat: 1 g | Protein: 4 g | Sodium: 16 mg | Fiber: 9 g | Carbohydrates: 55 g | Sugar: 38 g

CHAPTER 3

Cleansing and Detox Drinks

Whether you prefer to cleanse and detoxify with clean nutrition on a regular monthly basis or prefer to perform your cleanings on a schedule more comparative to spring cleaning your house, there are plans and programs designed to fit your needs. Buying into fads, potions, and gimmicks that leave you tethered to your home (and your toilet!) or hovering somewhere between nauseated and faint throughout the day is not going to leave you feeling clean, energized, and rejuvenated. Opting for a natural green drink–based cleanse or detox will provide you with a simple do-it-yourself program that will fit your wants, fulfill your needs, and help you achieve success without any of the undesirable side effects those pills and potions provide.

What Is Cleansing and Detoxification?

Many people know that cleanses and detoxes are designed to help you lose weight by ridding your body of waste, but few can tell you how the process occurs, what's involved, and/or why there's a need to perform a detox or cleanse on your own. For clarification purposes, your body is eliminating toxins all the time; it's a normal physical process to eliminate or neutralize toxins through your organs, including the colon, liver, kidneys, lungs, lymph glands, and even your skin. While these natural metabolic processes are continually disposing of toxic matter, you can aid in the processes by minimizing your intake of unnatural foods, maximizing the amount of quality nutritional foods you consume, and increasing the amount of water you consume daily. Adhering to a simple detoxifying cleanse of green drinks for one day, or a number of days, will ensure you maximize the benefits of a clean body free of waste and toxins that would otherwise be weighing you down (literally!).

Helping the Body Remove Toxins

Why should you remove toxins if your body already does it naturally? Because people are exposed to more environmental toxins than ever before. Chemicals in the air you breathe, pesticides in the foods you eat, pollutants in the water you drink, and increased exposure to synthetic substances from almost every surface you touch can wreak havoc on your body. With the constant overload of toxic elements, the body's systems can easily become compromised, which can lead to reduced energy levels and a weakened immune system. Unhealthy living habits such as not getting enough exercise or sleep, experiencing high levels of stress, consuming a diet low in nutrients and rich in toxins, and even not drinking enough water can all adversely affect the body's efficiency at eliminating toxins.

While a number of experts insist that there is no scientific evidence to support the notion that more stringent detox regimens, cleanses, and fasts yield miraculous results, even the most skeptical agree that there are certain processes anyone can do to help speed up the body's elimination systems. . . . And one of those is consuming green drinks regularly.

So again, while integrating green drinks isn't exactly like waving a magic wand that will restore good health and vitality and eliminate all your bad habits, it can play a valuable role in keeping the body operating at maximum efficiency . . . so, it's pretty darn close!

Seven Signs You Need to Detox

Many doctors recommend that everyone detox at least once a year. So many people find themselves feeling overweight, overtired, overstressed, or overwhelmed with their current "less-than-ideal" diet and choose to hit the restart button on their health by doing a cleanse. If you find yourself suffering from constant fatigue, frequent illness, or just an overall desire to get into a healthier groove, a detoxifying cleanse of green drinks may be the right prescription for you. For a better idea of other warning signs to look for, here is a brief list of symptoms that may indicate your body needs a little "out with old and in with the new" diet:

- Lack of energy, sluggishness, confusion, or fatigue that has no obvious explanation
- Irritated skin, rashes, or complexion upsets
- Eruptions of herpes, shingles, psoriasis, or eczema
- Menstrual difficulties
- Bowel irregularity
- Disruption in focus and a feeling of mental "fogginess"
- Distended stomach

Make the Choice to Live Clean and Start Today

Many people find detoxifying cleanses based on green drinks to be easy to stick to. Since they don't have harsh side effects and the results are better than many expect (who doesn't enjoy a slimmer waistline and more energy?), starting off your cleansing regime with simple green drinks may be the beginning of a routine you engage in on a regular basis. You can choose to do a short fast or just take a few days to refuel and reboot with healthy foods and nutrients. Either option will get you moving in the right direction toward better health and a happier life.

While many people wait until after the holidays, the start of the new year, or a few weeks before a big event or bikini season to start their cleanse, don't wait—start living a healthier, cleaner life today!

Best Produce for Cleansing and Detox

1. Apples
2. Carrots
3. Ginger
4. Cranberries
5. Berries
6. Bananas
7. Cantaloupes and watermelons
8. Beets
9. Green tea
10. Spinach

Cleansing and Detox Drinks

Cleansing Cranberry

If you're looking for a sweet and tangy treat, urinary tract infection relief, or both, this smoothie is for you. The combination of cranberries, cucumber, lemon, and ginger give this smoothie the power to cleanse your body in no time.

INGREDIENTS | SERVES 4

1 cup watercress

2 pints cranberries

2 medium cucumbers, peeled

½ lemon, peeled

½" ginger, peeled

2 cups purified water

The Cleansing Power of Cranberries

Cranberries are packed with powerful anti-oxidants and an abundance of vitamins, minerals, and phytochemicals. Not only do these bright red berries promote health in almost every area of the body, but they also do wonders for cleansing bad bacteria out of the urinary tract while promoting bladder health. Most store-bought cranberry juices contain mixtures of sugars and other juices.

1. Place watercress, cranberries, cucumbers, lemon, ginger, and 1 cup purified water in a blender and blend until thoroughly combined.

2. Add the remaining 1 cup water while blending, as needed, until desired texture is achieved.

PER SERVING: Calories: 62 | Fat: 0 g | Protein: 1 g | Sodium: 8 mg | Fiber: 6 g | Carbohydrates: 15 g | Sugar: 6 g

Ginger and Apple Cleansing Blend

With loads of fiber from the spinach and apples, ginger makes a star-studded appearance as a lightly spicy and aromatic addition in this recipe. It will keep your detox on track with a delightfully sweet twist.

INGREDIENTS | SERVES 3

1 cup chopped spinach
3 medium apples, peeled and cored
½" ginger, peeled
2 cups purified water

The Importance of Fiber in Cleansing

Apples are sometimes referred to as "nature's scrub brushes" because of the powerful amount of fiber they contain. Found in deep greens, vegetables, and fruits, fiber plays an important role in helping your body rid itself of waste products that may be causing irregularity. The indigestible fibers that pass through the digestive system literally sweep lingering waste with them as they leave the body. When it comes to cleansing your body, moving the waste out is an important factor.

1. Place spinach, apples, ginger, and 1 cup water in a blender and blend until thoroughly combined.

2. Add remaining 1 cup water while blending, as needed, until desired texture is achieved.

PER SERVING: Calories: 81 | Fat: 0 g | Protein: 1 g | Sodium: 8 mg | Fiber: 2 g | Carbohydrates: 21 g | Sugar: 16 g

Alcohol Recovery Recipe

Although this smoothie may not relieve that pounding headache, it will definitely assist your liver in flushing out the toxins caused by alcohol consumption.

INGREDIENTS | SERVES 3

1 cup chopped spinach

3 medium carrots, peeled

2 medium apples, peeled and cored

1 beet, chopped

2½ cups purified water

Combating the Effects of Alcohol

Because alcohol can really do a number on your liver, it is important to supply your body with the best foods to maintain your liver's optimal functioning following heavy alcohol consumption. Spinach, carrots, apples, beets, lemon, wheatgrass, and grapefruit have shown to be true super-foods when it comes to purging the liver of harmful toxins. In addition, they are also high in vitamin C and promote health while minimizing feelings of moodiness and depression.

1. Place spinach, carrots, apples, beet, and 1¼ cups water in a blender and blend until thoroughly combined.

2. Add remaining 1¼ cups water while blending, as needed, until desired texture is achieved.

PER SERVING: Calories: 91 | Fat: 0 g | Protein: 2 g | Sodium: 71 mg | Fiber: 4 g | Carbohydrates: 23 g | Sugar: 16 g

Broccoli for Bladder Health

Broccoli can aid in promoting bladder health because of its vitamins, minerals, and phytochemicals, which far exceed those contained in other fruits and veggies.

INGREDIENTS | SERVES 3

1 cup watercress

1 cup broccoli spears

3 medium red Gala apples, peeled and cored

2 cups purified water

The Important Vitamins and Minerals in Broccoli

Broccoli probably isn't the superfood that comes to mind when you think of cleansing, but this super veggie provides far more vitamins and nutrients than you would think. A single serving of broccoli includes the important vitamins A, B, C, and K along with fiber, zinc, folic acid, magnesium, iron, and beta-carotene.

1. Place watercress, broccoli, apples, and 1 cup water in a blender and blend until thoroughly combined.

2. Add remaining 1 cup water while blending, as needed, until desired texture is achieved.

PER SERVING: Calories: 89 | Fat: 0 g | Protein: 2 g | Sodium: 15 mg | Fiber: 3 g | Carbohydrates: 23 g | Sugar: 17 g

The Bright Bloat Beater

With important vitamins and minerals from the watercress, antioxidants from the blueberries, potassium from the bananas, and vitamin C from the lemon, this smoothie is helpful in fighting free radicals and promoting overall health.

INGREDIENTS | SERVES 3

1 cup watercress
2 cups blueberries
2 bananas, peeled
½ lemon, peeled
2 cups purified water

1. Place watercress, blueberries, bananas, lemon, and 1 cup water in a blender and blend until thoroughly combined.

2. Add remaining 1 cup water while blending, as needed, until desired texture is achieved.

PER SERVING: Calories: 129 | Fat: 1 g | Protein: 2 g | Sodium: 7 mg | Fiber: 5 g | Carbohydrates: 33 g | Sugar: 20 g

The Spicy Savior

The ginger in this recipe is what gives this smoothie its spicy zing! The watercress, carrots, broccoli, and ginger all combine for a filling meal replacement in any detox diet.

INGREDIENTS | SERVES 3

1 cup watercress
1 cup broccoli spears
3 medium carrots, peeled
½" ginger, peeled
2 cups purified water

1. Place watercress, broccoli, carrots, ginger, and 1 cup water in a blender and blend until thoroughly combined.

2. Add remaining 1 cup water while blending, as needed, until desired texture is achieved.

PER SERVING: Calories: 38 | Fat: 0 g | Protein: 2 g | Sodium: 57 mg | Fiber: 3 g | Carbohydrates: 8 g | Sugar: 3 g

Sweet and Spicy Spinach Smoothie

Combining spinach with sweet apples and bananas and slightly spicy ginger can make even the most devout spinach skeptic enjoy this nutritious green veggie as a part of a detox diet.

INGREDIENTS | SERVES 3

1 cup chopped spinach

3 medium apples, cored and peeled

2 bananas, peeled

½ lemon, peeled

2 cups purified water

1. Place spinach, apples, bananas, lemon, and 1 cup purified water in a blender and blend until thoroughly combined.

2. Add remaining 1 cup purified water while blending, as needed, until desired texture is achieved.

PER SERVING: Calories: 152 | Fat: 1 g | Protein: 2 g | Sodium: 9 mg | Fiber: 5 g | Carbohydrates: 40 g | Sugar: 26 g

Fabulous Fiber Flush

Kale provides vitamins A and K. Combined with the iron- and folate-rich broccoli, pectin-providing apples, and beta-carotene-filled carrot, the kale makes this smoothie a completely fiber-filled one.

INGREDIENTS | SERVES 3

2 large kale leaves

1 cup chopped broccoli

2 medium apples, peeled and cored

1 medium carrot, peeled

½ lemon, peeled

2 cups purified water

1. Place kale, broccoli, apples, carrot, lemon, and 1 cup water in a blender and blend until thoroughly combined.

2. Add remaining 1 cup water while blending, as needed, until desired texture is achieved.

PER SERVING: Calories: 95 | Fat: 1 g | Protein: 3 g | Sodium: 41 mg | Fiber: 3 g | Carbohydrates: 22 g | Sugar: 13 g

Carrot Cleanser

This simple recipe takes little time to make and tastes absolutely delicious! The carrots and lemon do a complementary balancing act that provides a sweet and tangy twist.

INGREDIENTS | SERVES 3

1 cup chopped spinach
4 medium carrots, peeled
1 lemon, peeled
2 cups purified water

Carrots as Superfoods

Harnessing the powerful vitamins and minerals contained in carrots while you're on a detoxifying cleanse can help in many ways. The beta-carotene that gives carrots their vibrant color is not only important for eye health, but is also a strong cancer-fighting antioxidant that protects cells against harmful free radicals and promotes optimal cell functioning. Carrots also lower the risk of heart disease, cancers, and type 2 diabetes and provide sound nutrition for pregnancy and night vision.

1. Place spinach, carrots, lemon, and 1 cup water in a blender and blend until thoroughly combined.

2. Add remaining 1 cup water while blending, as needed, until desired texture is achieved.

PER SERVING: Calories: 41 | Fat: 0 g | Protein: 1 g | Sodium: 64 mg | Fiber: 3 g | Carbohydrates: 10 g | Sugar: 4 g

Colorful Cleansing Combo

This colorful combination of vegetables makes a visually and palate-pleasing creation. The ingredients provide a wealth of vitamins and minerals that will cleanse while optimizing digestive health and comfort.

INGREDIENTS | SERVES 3

1 cup watercress

3 medium carrots, peeled

1 medium cucumber

1 beet, chopped with greens removed

2 cups purified water

Taste the Rainbow for Optimal Health

It may be difficult to figure out which food group is best for your body and promotes its ideal functioning. The answer is   all of them! The easiest route to achieving optimum health is to taste the rainbow: Eat a variety of different foods with vibrant colors. By consuming a variety of fruits and vegetables with color, you can ensure your body is receiving abundant vitamins and nutrients. With variety comes the added benefit of never becoming tired of the same old fruit or veggie.

1. Place watercress, carrots, cucumber, beet, and 1 cup water in a blender and blend until thoroughly combined.

2. Add remaining 1 cup water while blending, as needed, until desired texture is achieved.

PER SERVING: Calories: 53 | Fat: 0 g | Protein: 2 g | Sodium: 70 mg | Fiber: 3 g | Carbohydrates: 12 g | Sugar: 6 g

Apple Broccoli Detox Blend

Packed with fiber, vitamins, minerals, and phytochemicals that will clear out your digestive system, optimize brain functioning and mental clarity, and revitalize your body's many systems of operation, this recipe is a must-have for detox!

INGREDIENTS | SERVES 3

1 cup chopped romaine lettuce
2 medium apples, peeled and cored
1 cup broccoli
1 medium orange, peeled
⅛ cup parsley
2 cups purified water

1. Place romaine, apples, broccoli, orange, parsley, and 1 cup water in a blender and blend until thoroughly combined.

2. Add remaining 1 cup water while blending, as needed, until desired texture is achieved.

PER SERVING: Calories: 87 | Fat: 0 g | Protein: 2 g | Sodium: 13 mg | Fiber: 4 g | Carbohydrates: 22 g | Sugar: 16 g

Cleanse Your Body with Sweet Citrus

Vitamin C does more than prevent illness; it also promotes great health! This delicious combination of citrus fruits, watercress, and ginger is a tasty way to detoxify your body and promote health.

INGREDIENTS | SERVES 5

1 cup watercress
2 cups pineapple chunks
1 medium orange, peeled
2 medium apples, peeled and cored
½" ginger, peeled
2 cups purified water

1. Place watercress, pineapple, orange, apples, ginger, and 1 cup water in a blender and blend until thoroughly combined.

2. Add remaining 1 cup water while blending, as needed, until desired texture is achieved.

PER SERVING: Calories: 78 | Fat: 0 g | Protein: 1 g | Sodium: 4 mg | Fiber: 2 g | Carbohydrates: 20 g | Sugar: 16 g

The Deep Colors of Detox

The vibrant colors of the kale, carrot, tomato, celery, and cucumber combine with potent garlic to develop a savory, delicious smoothie. This treat provides a variety of vitamins and minerals and satisfies multiple vegetable servings in just one drink.

INGREDIENTS | SERVES 3

2 kale leaves
1 medium cucumber, peeled
2 celery stalks
1 medium carrot, peeled
1 medium tomato
1 clove garlic
2 cups purified water

1. Place kale, cucumber, celery, carrot, tomato, garlic, and 1 cup water in a blender and blend until thoroughly combined.

2. Add remaining 1 cup water while blending, as needed, until desired texture is achieved.

PER SERVING: Calories: 51 | Fat: 1 g | Protein: 3 g | Sodium: 56 mg | Fiber: 2 g | Carbohydrates: 10 g | Sugar: 3 g

A Fruity Flush

This is an easy and delicious way to satisfy cravings and fruit and vegetable servings in the same smoothie.

INGREDIENTS | SERVES 3

1 cup watercress
1 medium cucumber, peeled
½ cantaloupe, rind and seeds removed
1 medium pear, cored
1 banana, peeled
2 cups purified water

1. Place watercress, cucumber, cantaloupe, pear, banana, and 1 cup water in a blender and blend until thoroughly combined.

2. Add remaining 1 cup water while blending, as needed, until desired texture is achieved.

PER SERVING: Calories: 109 | Fat: 1 g | Protein: 2 g | Sodium: 22 mg | Fiber: 4 g | Carbohydrates: 27 g | Sugar: 19 g

Refreshing Reprieve

Refreshing flavors can keep a detoxifying diet on track. This smoothie helps calm cravings for sweets or salty foods and can keep your focus on your health rather than the unhealthy alternatives.

INGREDIENTS | SERVES 3

1 cup chopped romaine lettuce

1 apple, peeled and cored

1 cucumber, peeled

1 celery stalk

1 carrot, peeled

1 clove garlic

2 cups purified water

1. Place romaine, apple, cucumber, celery, carrot, garlic, and 1 cup water in a blender and blend until thoroughly combined.

2. Add remaining 1 cup water while blending, as needed, until desired texture is achieved.

PER SERVING: Calories: 48 | Fat: 0 g | Protein: 1 g | Sodium: 27 mg | Fiber: 2 g | Carbohydrates: 11 g | Sugar: 8 g

Berry-Banana Blast for Bladder Health

This drink combines the powerful antioxidants of berries with the flushing power of fiber-rich bananas. You can whip up this cleansing combination of delicious fruits for a naturally potent cleanse that will keep you feeling fit and free.

INGREDIENTS | SERVES 2

1 cup chopped spinach

1 cup blueberries

1 cup strawberries, tops removed

1 cup cranberries

1 large banana, peeled

1 cup water

1. Combine spinach, berries, and banana in blender.

2. Blend until macerated and thoroughly combined.

3. Add water, as needed, until desired consistency is achieved.

PER SERVING: Calories: 151 | Fat: 1 g | Protein: 2 g | Sodium: 15 mg | Fiber: 8 g | Carbohydrates: 38 g | Sugar: 21 g

Mega Melon Mending Juice

Great for detoxification purposes, melons provide a plethora of essential nutrients with the added benefit of much-needed natural juices.

INGREDIENTS | SERVES 2

1 cup chopped romaine lettuce

1 cup cubed watermelon, rind and seeds removed

1 cup cubed honeydew melon, rind and seeds removed

1 cup cubed cantaloupe, rind and seeds removed

1 cup ice

1. Combine all ingredients, except ice, in a blender and blend until completely liquefied.

2. Add ice to blender.

3. Blend melon mixture and ice until thoroughly combined and desired consistency is achieved.

PER SERVING: Calories: 84 | Fat: 0 g | Protein: 2 g | Sodium: 30 mg | Fiber: 2 g | Carbohydrates: 21 g | Sugar: 18 g

Cleansing Cucumber Citrus

Combine the natural powers of the nutrients in grapefruit and cucumbers, and what do you get? A mix of immunity-boosting vitamins and cleansing minerals, that's what.

INGREDIENTS | SERVES 2

1 cup chopped spinach

2 medium cucumbers, peeled

1 medium grapefruit, peeled and seeded

1 cup ice (optional)

1. Combine spinach, cucumbers, and grapefruit in a blender.

2. Blend thoroughly and add ice until desired consistency is achieved.

PER SERVING: Calories: 69 | Fat: 1 g | Protein: 2 g | Sodium: 16 mg | Fiber: 3 g | Carbohydrates: 15 g | Sugar: 12 g

Sweet Beets with Apples and Ginger Juice

Juice your way to a clean day with this trifecta of fruits and roots! Naturally nutritious, this zippy sweet treat will keep you clean and detoxified with a pep in your step.

INGREDIENTS | SERVES 1

2 medium red apples, cored
1 beet, greens removed
1" ginger, peeled

1. Juice apples, beet, and ginger.

2. Stir well.

PER SERVING: Calories: 231 | Fat: 1 g | Protein: 2 g | Sodium: 69 mg | Fiber: 0 g | Carbohydrates: 60 g | Sugar: 43 g

Green Tea Citrus Flush

The antioxidant-rich green tea in this recipe gets a natural boost of flavor and nutrition with the vitamin C of citrus fruits.

INGREDIENTS | SERVES 2

1 cup chopped spinach
2 cups prepared organic green tea
½ lemon, peeled and seeded
½ medium pink grapefruit, peeled and seeded
1 medium orange, peeled

1. Combine spinach, tea, lemon, grapefruit, and orange in a blender.

2. Blend until thoroughly combined.

PER SERVING: Calories: 61 | Fat: 0 g | Protein: 1 g | Sodium: 12 mg | Fiber: 3 g | Carbohydrates: 15 g | Sugar: 11 g

CHAPTER 4

Drinks for Healthy Hair, Skin, and Nails

It seems like the constant slew of commercials and advertisements promoting the latest and greatest pills, potions, and products for supple skin, lustrous hair, and beautiful nails are unavoidable. Every year, people spend a fortune on products that will help them achieve aesthetic perfection, but the real secret to getting and maintaining lasting beauty lies right in your own refrigerator! Beauty may be only skin deep, but it begins on the inside—with a healthy diet of fruits and vegetables that provide your skin, hair, and nails with the natural vitamins and minerals they need to thrive. The nutrients that will promote great-looking hair, skin, and nails are simply a sip away!

Why Nutrition Matters

The healthy skin, hair, and nails that are so sought after are literal extensions of the healthy body that produces them. Without question, the quality of the nutrients you choose to provide your body with will help or hinder the production and renewal of the cells that make up your skin, hair, and nails. With a healthy diet focused on foods loaded with the nutrients that allow skin to remain hydrated, hair to remain shiny and thick, and nails that resist damage and breaking, you can save yourself the time and money and forgo the products and services that fall flat on promises.

Keratin: The Magic Protein

The fact is, your skin, hair, and nails are some of the most powerful indicators of your overall health. That's because they have a common building block, a protein called keratin. As keratin cells naturally push upward through the skin, they die and then harden, turning into your hair and nails, or are "shed" as the skin cells are replaced. Healthy bodies with adequate amounts of keratin will produce smooth nails without ridges; thick, strong hair that isn't prone to falling out or breakage; and a clear, glowing complexion. On the contrary, a deficiency in this protein will show itself with problems in these exact areas such as brittle nails; thinning, lackluster hair; and a complexion riddled with unattractive issues such as acne, discoloration, etc. Take into consideration, too, that many beauty product manufacturers are turning to "nature's medicine chest" and including vitamins, natural oils, fruit acids, and nutrients in their cosmetics. While many of these increasingly "natural" products may be beneficial to some extent, it only makes sense to begin your beauty regime in your kitchen at home . . . from the inside out.

The Best Nutrients for Healthy Skin, Hair, and Nails

Here are some of the most important nutrients for a glowing complexion, beautiful hair, and strong, healthy nails:

- **Selenium** plays a key role in skin cancer prevention and protects skin from sun damage. If you're a sun worshipper, selenium could help reduce your chance of burning. Pumpkins are a good source of selenium.
- **Silica** is a trace mineral that strengthens the body's connective tissues and is found in cucumbers. Too little silica can result in reduced skin elasticity and slower healing of wounds.
- **Zinc** controls the production of oil in the skin and may also help control some of the hormones that create acne. It clears skin by taming oil production and controlling the formation of acne lesions and is found in spinach, grapes, and garlic.
- **Calcium** strengthens not just nails but bones and connective tissues as well. Oranges and tangerines are rich in calcium.
- **Essential fatty acids**, also called omega acids, moisturize and maintain the skin's flexibility. Without enough of them, the skin produces a more irritating form of sebum, or oil, which dries the skin and clogs pores, causing acne and inflammation. Avocados are a rich source of these nutrients.
- **Vitamin C** reduces damage caused by free radicals, a harmful byproduct of sunlight, smoke, and pollution that destroys collagen and elastin (fibers that support your skin structure) and results in wrinkles and other signs of aging. Citrus fruits are a well-known source of vitamin C as are many other fruits and vegetables
- **Vitamin E** helps reduce sun damage, wrinkles, and uneven textures caused by sun damage. Strawberries and lettuce both contain vitamin E.
- **Vitamin B** complex, especially biotin, is the nutrient that forms the basis of skin, nail, and hair cells. Without enough B vitamins, dermatitis and hair loss can occur. Apples, Swiss chard, and papaya are all excellent sources of B-complex vitamins.
- **Vitamin A** is necessary for the maintenance and repair of skin tissue. Look for it in raspberries, kale, and cherries.

A Beautiful Diet

Knowing that your body will be using the nutrients from your diet in order to produce your hair, skin, and nails, you can now take control of their quality by opting for nutrient-rich foods that provide all they need and more. Creating green drinks that combine deep green vegetables with antioxidant-rich fruits will provide your body with the adequate nutrition it needs to fight off and repair cell damage and rejuvenate the cells that produce and maintain the beautiful hair, skin, and nails you've always wanted.

Best Produce for Healthy Hair, Skin, and Nails

1. Cucumbers
2. Celery
3. Pears
4. Peaches
5. Nectarines
6. Apples
7. Berries
8. Kale
9. Spinach
10. Citrus fruits

Drinks for Healthy Hair, Skin, and Nails

Skin-Saving Vitamin C Blast

When you're feeling dried out, tired, or just down, vitamin C–rich smoothies like this one can give you automatic energy that will pick you up and keep you going. Staying focused on your weight-loss goals is a lot easier when you feel refreshed.

INGREDIENTS | SERVES 3

1 cup watercress
½ cantaloupe, rind and seeds removed
1 cup strawberries, tops removed
1 medium orange, peeled
½ lemon, peeled
1 cup green tea

Vitamin C Deficiencies

Even though orange juice, fresh produce, and affordable fruits and vegetables packed with vitamin C are readily available and accessible to Americans, most don't get the recommended daily value of 60 mg per day. Although multivitamins and vitamin C pill alternatives provide loads of vitamin C, the fresh sources of this important vitamin are a healthier, more refreshing option that can give you the added benefits of extra vitamins and minerals.

1. Place watercress, cantaloupe, strawberries, orange, lemon, and ½ cup tea in a blender and blend until thoroughly combined.

2. Add remaining green tea, as needed, while blending until desired consistency is achieved.

PER SERVING: Calories: 72 | Fat: 0 g | Protein: 2 g | Sodium: 20 mg | Fiber: 3 g | Carbohydrates: 18 g | Sugar: 14 g

Spicy Skin Saver

Spicy and sweet, this green drink's delicious ingredients promote supple skin.

INGREDIENTS | SERVES 2

1 cup arugula

1 cup red grapes

2 medium pears, peeled and cored

2 medium red apples, peeled and cored

1" ginger, peeled

2 cups water

Combine all ingredients in a blender and blend until desired consistency is reached.

PER SERVING: Calories: 215 | Fat: 1 g | Protein: 2 g | Sodium: 6 mg | Fiber: 8 g | Carbohydrates: 57 g | Sugar: 41 g

Reverse Time with Raspberries

Packed with powerful antioxidants, this quickly whipped up green drink will reverse the aging process of everything from your skin to your nails, deliciously!

INGREDIENTS | SERVES 2

1 cup spinach

2 pints raspberries

1" ginger, peeled

½ lemon, peeled and seeded

2 cups chamomile tea

1 teaspoon organic maple syrup

Combine all ingredients in a blender and blend until desired consistency is reached.

PER SERVING: Calories: 150 | Fat: 2 g | Protein: 4 g | Sodium: 18 mg | Fiber: 17 g | Carbohydrates: 35 g | Sugar: 14 g

De"light"ful Double-Duty

Light yet satisfying, this tropical combination of hydrating ingredients will provide your body and brain with the perfect combination of vitamins and minerals for beauty on both the inside and out!

INGREDIENTS | SERVES 2

1 cup chopped romaine lettuce

1 cup pineapple chunks

1 green apple, cored and peeled

1 medium orange, peeled

½ lime, peeled and seeded

2 cups vanilla coconut milk

Combine all ingredients in a blender and blend until desired consistency is reached.

PER SERVING: Calories: 211 | Fat: 5 g | Protein: 2 g | Sodium: 48 mg | Fiber: 5 g | Carbohydrates: 41 g | Sugar: 32 g

Soothe Away Sun Damage

Sunburns are no fun! Reverse the sun's damage and its hurtful consequences by sipping this simple sweetness in a cup.

INGREDIENTS | SERVES 2

½ cup watercress

2 medium green apples, peeled and cored

2 large English cucumbers

1 celery stalk

2 cups plain coconut milk

1 teaspoon organic maple syrup

Combine all ingredients in a blender and blend until desired consistency is reached.

PER SERVING: Calories: 215 | Fat: 6 g | Protein: 3 g | Sodium: 71 mg | Fiber: 4 g | Carbohydrates: 41 g | Sugar: 30 g

Nourish Those Nails

Providing enough silica in your diet is a cinch with simple smoothies like this one. Rich with ingredients that pack protein and hydrating silica, this smoothie is a must-have for anyone struggling with brittle nails.

INGREDIENTS | SERVES 2

1 cup chopped iceberg lettuce

2 medium cucumbers

2 celery stalks

½ cantaloupe, rind and seeds removed

2 cups almond milk

1 cup ice

Combine all ingredients in a blender and blend until desired consistency is reached.

PER SERVING: Calories: 193 | Fat: 3 g | Protein: 5 g | Sodium: 214 mg | Fiber: 5 g | Carbohydrates: 40 g | Sugar: 32 g

Skin Repair Salad in a Cup

Sometimes it's just easier to sip your salad. Whip up this easy green drink for a salad on-the-go that will make your skin feel refreshed, your tummy full, and your whole body energized.

INGREDIENTS | SERVES 2

1 cup chopped spinach

1 English cucumber, peeled

1 celery stalk

1 Roma tomato

1½ cups water

Combine all ingredients in a blender and blend until desired consistency is reached.

PER SERVING: Calories: 24 | Fat: 0 g | Protein: 1 g | Sodium: 31 mg | Fiber: 2 g | Carbohydrates: 5 g | Sugar: 3 g

Lusciousness Sipped

Beauty begins on the inside, because the damage to our body's cells shows in our skin, nail, and hair quality first. Reverse aging, and return lusciousness to your outside by repairing the inside first!

INGREDIENTS | SERVES 2

1 cup chopped romaine lettuce

1 cup pineapple chunks

1 English cucumber

1 cup blueberries

1 cup vanilla coconut milk

Combine all ingredients in a blender and blend until desired consistency is reached.

PER SERVING: Calories: 154 | Fat: 3 g | Protein: 2 g | Sodium: 29 mg | Fiber: 4 g | Carbohydrates: 32 g | Sugar: 23 g

Pineapple Grapefruit Smoothie

Rescuing your body from all of the daily environmental damage it encounters is as simple as sipping this vitamin C–packed smoothie.

INGREDIENTS | SERVES 2

½ cup watercress

1 cup pineapple chunks

½ medium pink grapefruit, peeled and seeded

1 medium orange, peeled

1 cup plain coconut milk

1 cup ice

Combine all ingredients in a blender and blend until desired consistency is reached.

PER SERVING: Calories: 135 | Fat: 3 g | Protein: 2 g | Sodium: 27 mg | Fiber: 4 g | Carbohydrates: 28 g | Sugar: 22 g

Green Goddess

If the flavor of this kale-based juice seems too intense, add distilled water or half a container of plain 6-ounce yogurt.

INGREDIENTS | SERVES 1

2 medium apples, cored
2 medium carrots, trimmed
2 medium pears, cored
½ large cucumber
6–8 leaves fresh kale

1. Process the apples and carrots through an electronic juicer according to the manufacturer's directions.

2. Add the pears, followed by the cucumber.

3. Roll the kale leaves together to compress and add to the juicer.

4. Stir or shake the mixture to combine ingredients.

PER SERVING: Calories: 662 | Fat: 5 g | Protein: 22 g | Sodium: 247 mg | Fiber: 0 g | Carbohydrates: 157 g | Sugar: 81 g

The Anti-Aging Body Booster

Cherries contain lutein. Lutein plus vitamins A and C up collagen production, which results in stronger bones and younger-looking skin.

INGREDIENTS | SERVES 1

1 cup chopped spinach
1 medium apple, cored
2 medium pears, cored
½ cup Bing or Queen Anne cherries, pitted

1. Process the spinach and apple through an electronic juicer according to the manufacturer's directions.

2. Add the pears, followed by the cherries.

3. Whisk the juice to combine ingredients and enjoy.

PER SERVING: Calories: 353 | Fat: 1 g | Protein: 3 g | Sodium: 29 mg | Fiber: 0 g | Carbohydrates: 93 g | Sugar: 64 g

Antioxidants Anyone?

Cherries are extraordinarily high in the nutrients necessary to help the body destroy free radicals. Data from the USDA's 2007 Oxygen Radical Absorbance Capacity table gives sweet cherries a total ORAC score of 3,365 per 3.5 ounces.

Green Apple Grape Cocktail

Many lines of creams and cosmetics use grape-seed oils and extracts for their benefits to the skin, so if you happen to have seeded grapes on hand, don't hesitate to use them!

INGREDIENTS | SERVES 1

1 cup chopped romaine lettuce
2 medium red Gala or Fuji apples, cored
1 cup grapes, any variety

1. Process the romaine and apples through your electronic juicer according to the manufacturer's directions.

2. Add the grapes.

3. Mix the juice thoroughly to combine and serve alone or over ice.

PER SERVING: Calories: 259 | Fat: 1 g | Protein: 2 g | Sodium: 9 mg | Fiber: 0 g | Carbohydrates: 68 g | Sugar: 53 g

Apple Strawberry Temptation

Strawberries are known for their ability to fight free radicals and the environmental damage that comes from pollutants in the air and water.

INGREDIENTS | SERVES 1

1 cup chopped spinach
2 medium Gala apples, cored
2 medium Granny Smith apples, cored
1 cup strawberries, tops removed
¼ lemon, rind intact

1. Process the spinach and apples through your electronic juicer according to the manufacturer's directions.

2. Add the strawberries, followed by the lemon wedge.

3. Mix the juice thoroughly to combine and serve alone or over ice.

PER SERVING: Calories: 437 | Fat: 2 g | Protein: 4 g | Sodium: 33 mg | Fiber: 0 g | Carbohydrates: 114 g | Sugar: 83 g

Cucumber Complexion Tonic

Cucumbers are known to help the skin from becoming overly dry. Cucumbers contain silica, which helps improve the complexion.

INGREDIENTS | SERVES 1

1 cup chopped spinach
½ large cucumber, peeled
1 celery stalk, leaves intact
2 sprigs fresh baby dill, for garnish

1. Process the spinach and cucumber through your electronic juicer according to the manufacturer's directions.

2. Add the celery.

3. Mix the juice thoroughly to combine and add fresh sprigs of dill to the top of the drink for garnish.

PER SERVING: Calories: 30 | Fat: 0 g | Protein: 2 g | Sodium: 59 mg | Fiber: 0 g | Carbohydrates: 5 g | Sugar: 3 g

Pineapple Papaya Potion

For a clear complexion, use the leftover fruit pulp from this juice as a face mask. Leave it on for 10 minutes, or until slightly sticky, rinse well, and pat dry.

INGREDIENTS | SERVES 1

1 cup chopped romaine lettuce
1 cup pineapple chunks
½ cup strawberries, tops removed
½ papaya, seeds removed

Papaya
Papaya contains many of the same enzymes found in pineapple and holds many of the same benefits for the skin, so this recipe packs a double punch!

1. Process the romaine and pineapple chunks through your electronic juicer according to the manufacturer's directions.

2. Add the strawberries.

3. Add the papaya.

4. Stir or shake the juice thoroughly to combine and serve alone or over ice.

PER SERVING: Calories: 179 | Fat: 1 g | Protein: 3 g | Sodium: 18 mg | Fiber: 0 g | Carbohydrates: 45 g | Sugar: 32 g

Acne Blaster

Whether you're troubled by long-term acne problems or annoying little monthly breakouts, this one will help clear your skin fast!

INGREDIENTS | SERVES 1

2 medium carrots, trimmed

1 medium cucumber

1 cup spinach

1. Process the carrots through your electronic juicer according to the manufacturer's directions.

2. Add the cucumber, followed by the spinach.

3. Stir or shake the juice thoroughly to combine and serve alone or over ice.

PER SERVING: Calories: 102 | Fat: 1 g | Protein: 4 g | Sodium: 114 mg | Fiber: 0 g | Carbohydrates: 24 g | Sugar: 11 g

Clear Complexion Cocktail

This drink will help keep your skin clear of acne. Reducing junk foods and drinking healthy juice will be a step in the right direction, too.

INGREDIENTS | SERVES 1

2 medium red apples, cored

2 medium carrots, peeled

4 large kale leaves

1 cup spinach leaves

Vitamins C and E

According to *The Journal of Investigative Dermatology*, people who consumed vitamins C and E saw a reduction in sunburns caused by exposure to UVB radiation, as well as a reduction of factors linked to DNA damage within skin cells. Scientists believe these two antioxidant vitamins may help protect against DNA damage.

1. Process the apples through your electronic juicer according to the manufacturer's directions, followed by the carrots.

2. Add the kale and spinach.

3. Stir or shake the juice thoroughly to combine and serve alone or over ice.

PER SERVING: Calories: 378 | Fat: 4 g | Protein: 14 g | Sodium: 213 mg | Fiber: 0 g | Carbohydrates: 86 g | Sugar: 44 g

Prickly Pear Cocktail

Prickly pears are also known as cactus pears. These small, egg-shape fruits contain edible seeds and are rich in a wide variety of phytonutrients and vitamin C. Be sure to peel your pears before you use them, as the rind is not digestible.

INGREDIENTS | SERVES 1

2 prickly pears, peeled
1 cup chopped spinach
3 medium carrots, trimmed
1 cup red grapes

Beautiful Beta-Carotene
Vitamin A in the form of beta-carotene is a pigment that protects the health of your eyes and skin.

1. Process the prickly pears through your electronic juicer according to the manufacturer's directions.

2. Add the spinach and carrots, followed by the grapes.

3. Stir or shake the juice thoroughly to combine and serve immediately.

PER SERVING: Calories: 228 | Fat: 2 g | Protein: 5 g | Sodium: 162 mg | Fiber: 0 g | Carbohydrates: 54 g | Sugar: 24 g

Raspberry Peach Passion

So good tasting, you'll want some every day! Passion fruit is rich in fiber, potassium, and vitamins A and C.

INGREDIENTS | SERVES 1

2 large peaches, pitted
1 cup chopped romaine lettuce
1 cup raspberries
1 cup passion fruit pulp

A Passion for Passion Fruit
Choose fruits that are well ripened, plump, and heavy for their size. Fruits with a lightly wrinkled skin are actually more flavorful. Scoop out the pulp and discard the tough shell.

1. Process the peaches through your electronic juicer according to the manufacturer's directions.

2. Add the romaine and raspberries, followed by the passion fruit.

3. Stir or shake the juice thoroughly to combine ingredients and serve over ice.

PER SERVING: Calories: 437 | Fat: 3 g | Protein: 10 g | Sodium: 71 mg | Fiber: 0 g | Carbohydrates: 105 g | Sugar: 62 g

Peach Perfection

Peaches are a wonderful source of vitamin E, which is especially beneficial for the skin.

INGREDIENTS | SERVES 1

2 medium peaches, pitted
½ cup watercress
2 apricots, pitted
½ cup green grapes

All about Apricots

These much-prized fruits were first brought to Europe by Greeks, who called them "golden eggs of the sun." Sun-dried organic fruits have more concentrated nutrient values than fresh ones, although they have less vitamin C content.

1. Process the peaches through your electronic juicer according to the manufacturer's directions.

2. Add the watercress and apricots, followed by the grapes.

3. Stir or shake the juice thoroughly to combine the ingredients and serve.

PER SERVING: Calories: 183 | Fat: 1 g | Protein: 4 g | Sodium: 9 mg | Fiber: 0 g | Carbohydrates: 45 g | Sugar: 39 g

Green Nectarine Juice

Like their close cousin the peach, nectarines originated in China. From there, they spread to central Asia, Persia, and Europe through ancient silk routes.

INGREDIENTS | SERVES 1

4 medium nectarines, pitted
1 medium carrot, trimmed
½ cup chopped spinach
1 medium orange, peeled

1. Process the nectarines through your electronic juicer according to the manufacturer's directions.

2. Add the carrot and spinach, followed by the orange.

3. Stir or shake the juice thoroughly to combine the ingredients and serve.

PER SERVING: Calories: 320 | Fat: 2 g | Protein: 7 g | Sodium: 54 mg | Fiber: 0 g | Carbohydrates: 77 g | Sugar: 57 g

CHAPTER 5

Drinks for Longevity and Anti-Aging

No doubt about it: people are obsessed with youth. But the desire to stay youthful isn't just about vanity or hating those wrinkles and gray hair. If you love life, it only stands to reason that you want to extend it for as long as possible, enjoying all the benefits of good health, optimum energy, and sharpness of mind along the way. Current studies indicate that people are living longer than ever before, and that's partly due to advances in traditional medicine and cures for many diseases. Longer lifespans are also due to an increased public awareness of what it takes to stay healthy and prevent disease, too. Good eating habits, regular exercise, and creating a healthier, more sustainable environment all play a big role in extending your lifespan. But whether you're concerned about living to be 100 or trying to live every moment to its absolute fullest, nutrition can be the key!

Aging Gracefully

Just how well or how fast you age can have a lot to do with genetics, but perhaps more to do with lifestyle and diet. It's a simple law of physics: Objects at rest tend to stay at rest; objects in motion tend to stay in motion. The same holds true of people. Active types tend to stay active longer, while more sedentary types tend to be less likely to motivate themselves off the couch and into a yoga class. Other factors that can affect aging include stress, environmental exposure, disease, smoking, excess alcohol, and overexposure to the sun.

Yet experts agree that the two factors critical to increased longevity and staving off some of the more unpleasant effects of Father Time are diet and exercise. And that's where green drinks come in.

Green Drinks and Longevity

Anyone who enjoys green drinks on a regular basis is almost certainly aware of their ability to remove toxins, increase energy and immunity, and improve overall health. But when it comes to longevity, the picture gets even brighter.

According to research compiled by the North Carolina Research Campus, the American Dietetic Association, the American Cancer Foundation, and the American Diabetes Association, there are almost as many reasons to partake in drinks of the green variety for longevity and anti-aging as there are fruits and vegetables to blend into them!

- Fresh green drinks contain proteins, carbohydrates, essential fatty acids, vitamins, and minerals in a form your body can easily absorb.
- Fresh fruits and vegetables are rich in potassium and low in sodium, which helps promote cardiovascular health and prevent cancer.
- The enzymes in fruits and vegetables are essential for digestion and the rapid absorption of nutrients in your food.
- The juice and fiber of fruits and vegetables are loaded with powerful antioxidants called carotenes, found in dark leafy green vegetables and red, purple, and yellow-orange fruits and vegetables, all of which neutralize cancer-causing free radicals and promote longevity.

- The bio-availability of green drinks' nutrition is perfect as you get older, because it's easier on digestion. When you add the process of creating green drinks to your daily routine, it makes you more aware of your health choices. Increased levels of energy mean you'll be more likely to exercise and maintain muscle tone.

ESSENTIAL

There's also a subtler psychological effect that occurs when you begin to incorporate healthier habits like juicing. Chances are, taking the initiative to start including a vibrant glass of fresh-pressed juice or whipped smoothie in your daily diet is going to help you feel better, making you want to do what your body needs to be better. Those healthy and successful feelings are going to help motivate you even more to continue on the right path to optimize your health . . . and the cycle of "quality nutrition, better health, better life" will continue for the rest of your life!

Fresh fruits and vegetables in green drinks also help maintain and protect the skin, regulate metabolism, prevent high blood pressure, ease conditions such as arthritis, prevent the buildup of plaque in the arteries, and add calcium, a vital mineral for maintaining bones and teeth. This high-powered liquid nutrition also helps with hydration, which is always important, but especially so as you age. Green drinks can help counter the negative side effects of prescription medication and even help improve memory and brain function. Further, as appetites decrease, consuming green drinks regularly is a way to give the body those essential fruit and vegetable nutrients you may not be motivated to eat otherwise.

Great Veggies for Longevity

According to the North Carolina Research Center, headed by the former CEO of Dole, the following are the best juicing and smoothie vegetables to stay younger and healthier longer.

- **Spinach** helps with mental alertness and reduces the risk of certain cancers, including cancer of the liver, ovaries, colon, and prostate. It also contains vitamins A, B, C, D, and K.
- **Red bell peppers** help prevent sun damage, build cardiovascular health, and may decrease the risk of certain cancers, including lung, prostate, ovarian, and cervical cancer.
- **Broccoli** decreases the risk of certain cancers, including prostate, bladder, colon, pancreatic, gastric, and breast cancer; helps offset type 2 diabetes; and helps protect against brain injuries.
- **Carrots** battle cataracts and offer protection against certain cancers. They also provide vitamins A, B, and C, as well as calcium, potassium, and sodium.
- **Cauliflower** helps inhibit the growth of breast cancer cells, protects against prostate cancer, and stimulates the body's detox systems. Cauliflower contains the compound allicin, which helps reduce the risk of stroke and improves heart health. Allicin also helps detoxify the blood and liver.
- **Cucumber** is rich in silica, which strengthens connective tissue of muscles, tendons, ligaments, cartilage, and bone. Cucumber juice and pulp also promotes strong, lustrous hair, glowing skin, and strong nails.
- **Artichokes** aid blood clotting and reduce bad cholesterol. Artichokes are high in vitamin C and fiber.
- **Arugula** is good for the eyes and reduces the risk of fracture. High in beta-carotene, the antioxidant that fights heart disease, arugula is also high in vitamin C, folic acid, potassium, and fiber.
- **Asparagus** helps promote healthy bacteria in the digestive system and builds a healthy heart. Asparagus is rich in vitamins A and B_1.
- **Green cabbage** helps with blood clotting and reduces the risk of certain cancers, including prostate, colon, breast, and ovarian cancer. Cabbage contains the nitrogenous compound indoles, which helps lower blood pressure, and has more nutrients that protect against cancer than any other vegetable. According to research conducted at Stanford University, cabbage juice can completely restore the gastrointestinal tract and heal ulcers in seven days.

- **Kale** helps regulate estrogen levels, prevent sun damage to the eyes, and build bone density.
- **Sweet potatoes** reduce the risk of stroke and cancer and offer protection against macular degeneration.
- **Mushrooms** help decrease the risk of certain cancers, including colon and prostate. They also lower blood pressure and enhance the body's natural detox systems.
- **Butternut squash** helps fight wrinkles, promote good night vision, and build a healthy heart.

Best Produce for Longevity

1. Pineapples
2. Mangoes
3. Carrots
4. Spinach
5. Kale
6. Celery
7. Apples
8. Figs
9. Cauliflower
10. Peppers

Drinks for Longevity and Anti-Aging

Pineapple Anti-Arthritis Blend

This vitamin-packed smoothie does a world of good for preventing discomfort associated with everything from the common cold to arthritis. Sweet, satisfying, and full of fruits and veggies, this is one smoothie that does it all!

INGREDIENTS | SERVES 3

1 cup watercress
1 pint blueberries
2 cups pineapple chunks
¼" ginger, peeled
2 cups chamomile tea

Pineapple Prevention

Did you know that every bite of pineapple has vitamins and enzymes that can drastically reduce the discomfort associated with common ailments? The vitamin C content and the enzyme bromelain are responsible for the major health benefits offered up by this super fruit. Those suffering from asthma, arthritis, angina, and indigestion can find extra relief from indulging in one of nature's most delightfully sweet treats.

1. Place watercress, blueberries, pineapple, ginger, and 1 cup tea in a blender and blend until thoroughly combined.

2. Add remaining 1 cup tea, as needed, while blending until desired consistency is achieved.

PER SERVING: Calories: 113 | Fat: 0 g | Protein: 1 g | Sodium: 6 mg | Fiber: 4 g | Carbohydrates: 29 g | Sugar: 20 g

Fat-Burning Fuel

The refreshing combination of watermelon, raspberries, lime, crisp romaine, and calming chamomile will take your life to new heights by improving metabolism and promoting healthy brain function.

INGREDIENTS | SERVES 3

1 cup romaine lettuce

2 cups cubed watermelon, seeded

1 pint raspberries

½ lime, peeled

1 cup chamomile tea

1. Place romaine, watermelon, raspberries, lime, and ½ cup tea in a blender and blend until thoroughly combined.

2. Add remaining ½ cup tea, as needed, while blending until desired consistency is achieved.

PER SERVING: Calories: 80 | Fat: 1 g | Protein: 2 g | Sodium: 4 mg | Fiber: 6 g | Carbohydrates: 19 g | Sugar: 10 g

Ache Aid Smoothie

Reducing aches, pains, soreness, and stiffness can be as easy as blending this fruit, veggie, and herb smoothie!

INGREDIENTS | SERVES 3

1 cup watercress

2 cups cubed cantaloupe, rind and seeds removed

1 cucumber, peeled

2 tablespoons mint leaves

¼" ginger, peeled

1 cup chamomile tea

1. Place watercress, cantaloupe, cucumber, mint, ginger, and ½ cup tea in a blender and blend until thoroughly combined.

2. Add remaining ½ cup tea, as needed, while blending until desired consistency is achieved.

PER SERVING: Calories: 48 | Fat: 0 g | Protein: 2 g | Sodium: 25 mg | Fiber: 2 g | Carbohydrates: 11 g | Sugar: 9 g

Mango Strawberry Disease Fighter

In this drink, mangoes, strawberries, lemon, sweet romaine, and soothing chamomile combine to fight illness.

INGREDIENTS | SERVES 3

1 cup romaine lettuce

2 cups mangoes, peeled and seeded

1 pint strawberries, tops removed

½ lemon, peeled

2 cups chamomile tea

Food Combining for Optimal Benefits

When you're looking for the benefits from fruits and vegetables, how can you possibly decide which is the best? With the varied vitamin and mineral contents in different fruits and vegetables, there's no one "best." Your best bet would be to include as much nutrition from fruits and vegetables in as wide a variety as possible; the benefits to your immune system, major bodily functions, brain chemistry, and mental processes are innumerable.

1. Place romaine, mangoes, strawberries, lemon, and 1 cup tea in a blender and blend until thoroughly combined.

2. Add remaining 1 cup tea, as needed, while blending until desired consistency is achieved.

PER SERVING: Calories: 104 | Fat: 1 g | Protein: 2 g | Sodium: 5 mg | Fiber: 4 g | Carbohydrates: 26 g | Sugar: 20 g

Smart Start

This smoothie is the perfect way to start your day! Loaded with vitamin- and mineral-rich fruits and greens, this recipe's nutrition and sustaining benefits will last throughout your day.

INGREDIENTS | SERVES 5

1 cup chopped spinach
2 medium apples, peeled and cored
2 medium pears, peeled and cored
2 bananas, peeled
¼" ginger, peeled
2 cups chamomile tea

1. Place spinach, apples, pears, bananas, ginger, and 1 cup tea in a blender and blend until thoroughly combined.

2. Add remaining 1 cup tea, as needed, while blending until desired consistency is achieved.

PER SERVING: Calories: 116 | Fat: 0 g | Protein: 1 g | Sodium: 7 mg | Fiber: 4 g | Carbohydrates: 30 g | Sugar: 19 g

Very Green Smoothie

This smoothie combines a variety of greens for the very best benefits. Spinach, kale, and wheatgrass are packed with vitamins and minerals that work hard to maintain your health.

INGREDIENTS | SERVES 3

1 cup chopped spinach
2 kale leaves
1 cup wheatgrass
1 celery stalk
½ lemon, peeled
1 clove garlic
2 cups chamomile tea

1. Place spinach, kale, wheatgrass, celery, lemon, garlic, and 1 cup tea in a blender and blend until thoroughly combined.

2. Add remaining 1 cup tea, as needed, while blending until desired consistency is achieved.

PER SERVING: Calories: 240 | Fat: 1 g | Protein: 16 g | Sodium: 53 mg | Fiber: 17 g | Carbohydrates: 32 g | Sugar: 1 g

Root Veggie Variety

Root vegetables are packed with especially high levels of minerals that promote eye health and offer protection against a number of cancers. Drink up to promote the best defense against serious illnesses.

INGREDIENTS | SERVES 3

1 cup chopped romaine lettuce

1 turnip, peeled and cut to blender capacity

3 carrots, peeled

1 medium apple, peeled and cored

2 cups purified water

1. Place romaine, turnip, carrots, apple, and 1 cup water in a blender and blend until thoroughly combined.

2. Add remaining 1 cup water, as needed, while blending until desired consistency is achieved.

PER SERVING: Calories: 65 | Fat: 0 g | Protein: 1 g | Sodium: 71 mg | Fiber: 3 g | Carbohydrates: 16 g | Sugar: 10 g

Maximize Your Root Veggie's Potential

One of the many reasons raw-food enthusiasts adopt and adhere to the raw food diet is the dramatic drop in vitamins, minerals, and nutrients when produce is heated above a certain temperature. Most people prefer to have their root vegetables steamed, mashed, baked, or roasted, which may taste great, but the scorching heat also scorches a large percentage of the nutrient content. Blending these veggies in a green smoothie is a delicious way to enjoy these superfoods with all of the nutrition nature intended.

Memory Maintainer

Protecting your brain was never this delicious! The vitamins, minerals, and antioxidants that promote optimal functioning of your mental processes also prevent the brain's deterioration from illness and disease.

INGREDIENTS | SERVES 3

1 cup chopped romaine lettuce

½ cup chopped broccoli

½ cup chopped cauliflower

1 medium tomato

1 clove garlic

2 cups purified water

1. Place romaine, broccoli, cauliflower, tomato, garlic, and 1 cup water in a blender and blend until thoroughly combined.

2. Add remaining 1 cup water, as needed, while blending until desired consistency is achieved.

PER SERVING: Calories: 21 | Fat: 0 g | Protein: 1 g | Sodium: 13 mg | Fiber: 2 g | Carbohydrates: 4 g | Sugar: 2 g

Colorful Combo for Cancer Prevention

Combining for a sweet, down-to-earth flavor, the fruits and vegetables with dark leafy greens and chamomile make an intoxicating blend for your mind and body's total health.

INGREDIENTS | SERVES 3

1 cup chopped romaine lettuce

2 cups cubed cantaloupe, rind and seeds removed

2 medium carrots, peeled

1 cup pineapple chunks

1 beet, chopped

2 cups chamomile tea

1. Place romaine, cantaloupe, carrots, pineapple, beet, and 1 cup tea in a blender and blend until thoroughly combined.

2. Add remaining 1 cup tea, as needed, while blending until desired consistency is achieved.

PER SERVING: Calories: 96 | Fat: 0 g | Protein: 2 g | Sodium: 69 mg | Fiber: 4 g | Carbohydrates: 23 g | Sugar: 18 g

Mental Makeover

Hate forgetting things? Feel like you have absentmindedness a little too often? This smoothie is designed to get your brain back on track with rich sources of vitamins and minerals that stimulate and rejuvenate brain functions.

Ingredients | Serves 3
1 cup chopped spinach
2 medium cucumbers, peeled
2 celery stalks
1 medium tomato
2 cups chamomile tea

The Many Hats of Spinach

In addition to being a rich source of iron and folate (which actually aids in iron absorption), this amazing veggie holds a wealth of vitamins A, B, C, D, and K, which provide cancer-fighting power against liver, ovarian, colon, and prostate cancers. By including just 1 cup of this powerful veggie in your daily diet (raw), you can satisfy over 180 percent of your daily value for vitamin K and almost 400 percent of your vitamin A intake!

1. Place spinach, cucumbers, celery, tomato, and 1 cup tea in a blender and blend until thoroughly combined.

2. Add remaining 1 cup tea, as needed, while blending until desired consistency is achieved.

PER SERVING: Calories: 32 | Fat: 0 g | Protein: 2 g | Sodium: 36 mg | Fiber: 2 g | Carbohydrates: 6 g | Sugar: 3 g

Chamomile Cancer Preventer

Protect yourself by arming your body's defenses with great nutrition that will not only create energy, focus, and total health, but will be a strong preventive against cancers, too.

INGREDIENTS | SERVES 3

½ cup chopped romaine lettuce

½ cup chopped spinach

½ cup chopped broccoli

½ cup chopped cauliflower

2 medium carrots, peeled

1 celery stalk

1 clove garlic

2 cups chamomile tea

1. Place romaine, spinach, broccoli, cauliflower, carrots, celery, garlic, and 1 cup tea in a blender and blend until thoroughly combined.

2. Add remaining 1 cup tea, as needed, while blending until desired consistency is achieved.

PER SERVING: Calories: 34 | Fat: 0 g | Protein: 2 g | Sodium: 55 mg | Fiber: 2 g | Carbohydrates: 7 g | Sugar: 3 g

Antioxidant Assist

No matter how healthy your body may feel, there's always room for some assistance by antioxidants. Warding off illness and preventing degeneration of your body's processes are the main responsibilities of these powerful nutrients.

INGREDIENTS | SERVES 3

½ cup chopped arugula

½ cup chopped spinach

½ cup chopped asparagus

½ cup chopped broccoli

1 clove garlic

2 cups chamomile tea

1. Place arugula, spinach, asparagus, broccoli, garlic, and 1 cup tea in a blender and blend until thoroughly combined.

2. Add remaining 1 cup tea, as needed, while blending until desired consistency is achieved.

PER SERVING: Calories: 15 | Fat: 0 g | Protein: 1 g | Sodium: 12 mg | Fiber: 1 g | Carbohydrates: 3 g | Sugar: 1 g

Cauliflower to the Rescue Smoothie

This sweet veggie smoothie makes a grand impact on brain and heart health.

INGREDIENTS | SERVES 3

1 cup chopped romaine lettuce

1 cup cauliflower florets

2 medium carrots, peeled

1 medium apple, peeled and cored

2 cups chamomile

Ever Heard of Allicin?

Packed with important nutrition that satisfies daily dietary needs, this stark white veggie has a powerful secret weapon, too. Cauliflower provides allicin, an important compound that actually reduces the risk of stroke and heart disease while detoxifying the blood and liver. With abilities like that, this veggie is a must-have in any disease-preventing diet.

1. Place romaine, cauliflower, carrots, apple, and 1 cup tea in a blender and blend until thoroughly combined.

2. Add remaining 1 cup tea, as needed, while blending until desired consistency is achieved.

PER SERVING: Calories: 55 | Fat: 0 g | Protein: 1 g | Sodium: 41 mg | Fiber: 3 g | Carbohydrates: 13 g | Sugar: 8 g

Carotenes Against Cancer

The potent healing powers of beta-carotenes are unleashed in this delicious blend of carrots and sweet potatoes. With this satisfying treat for any sweet tooth, you'll be protecting your health with each delicious sip!

INGREDIENTS | SERVES 3

1 cup chopped romaine lettuce
3 medium carrots, peeled
1 cup chopped sweet potato
¼" ginger, peeled
2 cups chamomile tea

1. Place romaine, carrots, sweet potato, ginger, and 1 cup tea in a blender and blend until thoroughly combined.

2. Add remaining 1 cup tea, as needed, while blending until desired consistency is achieved.

PER SERVING: Calories: 68 | Fat: 0 g | Protein: 1 g | Sodium: 69 mg | Fiber: 3 g | Carbohydrates: 16 g | Sugar: 5 g

Youth Juice

This recipe helps restore energy and packs a real nutritional punch. The parsley adds not only necessary chlorophyll but also great flavor for those who may not take to the taste of cauliflower.

INGREDIENTS | SERVES 1

1 cup chopped spinach
4 medium carrots, trimmed
1 cup cauliflower florets
½ cup parsley

Cauliflower Power

Cauliflower is packed with boron, which contributes to proper brain function, helps to lower cholesterol levels in the blood, helps prevent arthritis, and protects against fungal infections.

1. Process the spinach and carrots through an electronic juicer according to the manufacturer's directions.

2. Add the cauliflower florets.

3. Roll the parsley leaves into a ball to compact them, and process.

4. Whisk the ingredients thoroughly to combine and enjoy.

PER SERVING: Calories: 143 | Fat: 1 g | Protein: 6 g | Sodium: 239 mg | Fiber: 0 g | Carbohydrates: 31 g | Sugar: 14 g

Apple Celery Cucumber Cocktail

Sip this drink at bedtime to ease inflammation, prevent stiff joints, and promote a good night's sleep.

INGREDIENTS | SERVES 2

2 medium apples, cored and sliced

1 cup chopped romaine lettuce

4 celery stalks, with leaves

1 medium cucumber, cut into chunks

Make the Connection

Cucumber juice is rich in silica, which strengthens connective tissue of muscles, tendons, ligaments, cartilage, and bone.

1. Process the apple slices through the feed tube of an electronic juicer according to the manufacturer's directions.

2. Add the romaine and celery stalks one or two at a time.

3. Add the cucumber chunks.

4. Whisk the juice together to blend and serve immediately.

PER SERVING: Calories: 134 | Fat: 1 g | Protein: 2 g | Sodium: 71 mg | Fiber: 0 g | Carbohydrates: 34 g | Sugar: 23 g

Pepper Juice

Bell peppers come in an array of colors: red, green, yellow, orange, and even purple. Each contains different levels of the pepper's basic nutrients, so mix it up and enjoy.

INGREDIENTS | SERVES 1

½ red bell pepper, cored and seeded

½ green bell pepper, cored and seeded

½ yellow bell pepper, cored and seeded

3 medium tomatoes

2 celery stalks, with leaves

1 cup chopped spinach

½ cup parsley

½ lemon, peeled

Ring the Bell

Bell peppers are packed with vitamin C and contain other nutrients that have been shown to be essential in preventing heart attacks and stroke.

1. Process the pepper sections through an electronic juicer according to the manufacturer's directions.

2. Add the tomatoes, followed by the celery and spinach.

3. Roll the parsley into a ball to compress and add to the juicer, followed by the lemon.

4. Whisk the juice to combine and serve in a chilled glass or over ice.

PER SERVING: Calories: 161 | Fat: 2 g | Protein: 8 g | Sodium: 130 mg | Fiber: 0 g | Carbohydrates: 35 g | Sugar: 16 g

Eye Health Juice

When carrots are eaten raw, you only absorb 1 percent of the carrot's available beta-carotene. When you juice your carrots, that amount is increased by almost a hundredfold. Plus, the sweet potato included in this recipe is rich in vitamin B_6, which has been shown to be essential in the maintenance of healthy blood vessels.

INGREDIENTS | SERVES 1

4 medium carrots, trimmed

1 sweet potato, peeled and cut into chunks

1 cup chopped spinach

1 cup pineapple chunks

2 medium oranges, peeled

Feeling Ravaged by Time?

The nutrients in fresh fruit and vegetable juice are also responsible for reducing or eliminating high cholesterol, carpal tunnel, constipation, gallstones, glaucoma, hypertension, indigestion, insomnia, kidney stones, macular degeneration, menopause, osteoporosis, prostate enlargement, psoriasis, and varicose veins.

1. Process the carrots, one at a time, through an electronic juicer according to the manufacturer's directions.

2. Add sweet potato to the juicer.

3. Add the spinach and pineapple chunks, followed by the orange.

4. Whisk the juice together to combine and serve immediately.

PER SERVING: Calories: 431 | Fat: 2 g | Protein: 8 g | Sodium: 265 mg | Fiber: 0 g | Carbohydrates: 105 g | Sugar: 59 g

Super Carotene Combo

Carotene is especially helpful for the eyes, but it also helps the liver. In addition to providing a great energy boost, it's also believed to be especially helpful in preventing the onset of type 2 diabetes.

INGREDIENTS | SERVES 1

3 medium carrots, trimmed

½ large cantaloupe, peeled, seeded, and cut into chunks

1 cup chopped romaine lettuce

1 medium sweet potato, peeled and cut into chunks

1 tablespoon fresh mint leaves

Mint and Melon

This classic combination of flavors is the perfect summertime refreshment. Not only do fresh mint leaves add wonderful flavor, but they also add chlorophyll and a touch of green goodness to this bright orange juice. Garnish with additional mint leaves for extra eye appeal.

1. Process the carrots through an electronic juicer according to the manufacturer's directions.

2. Add the cantaloupe to the juicer, followed by the romaine.

3. Add the sweet potato.

4. Roll the mint leaves into a ball to compress and add to the juicer.

5. Whisk the juice together and serve over ice, if desired.

PER SERVING: Calories: 336 | Fat: 1 g | Protein: 8 g | Sodium: 268 mg | Fiber: 0 g | Carbohydrates: 79 g | Sugar: 47 g

Fig Smoothie

If you're fortunate enough to have fresh figs, you already know how delightful they can be. If you have a masticating juicer, use a wider mesh net attachment to allow some fiber to pass through. Alternatively, for a thicker smoothie texture, process the figs in a blender to purée, then add to the juice.

INGREDIENTS | SERVES 1

10 figs, halved
3 medium carrots, trimmed
1 small sugar beet
1 cup beet greens
2 celery stalks, with leaves
2 medium apples, cored
1 medium cucumber, sliced
½ lemon, peeled

Health Benefits of Figs

Figs are high in potassium, and are important for lowering high blood pressure (hypertension) and controlling blood sugar levels in diabetics.

1. Process the figs in a masticating juicer or blender until smooth.

2. Process the carrots, beet, and beet greens through an electronic juicer according to the manufacturer's directions.

3. Add the celery, apples, and cucumber to the juicer, followed by the lemon.

4. Whisk or blend the ingredients together and enjoy.

PER SERVING: Calories: 744 | Fat: 3 g | Protein: 11 g | Sodium: 355 mg | Fiber: 0 g | Carbohydrates: 189 g | Sugar: 141 g

CHAPTER 6

Drinks for Happiness and Mental Stability

The vitamins, minerals, antioxidants, and phytochemicals in fruits and vegetables are natural mood stabilizers that have been shown to alleviate a host of emotional and mental issues, including depression, panic attacks, stress, migraines, attention deficit disorder, and tinnitus—even Alzheimer's disease has been shown to improve with quality adequate nutrition. Nutritional deficiencies can set off or exacerbate existing conditions, and consuming green drinks is a delicious, natural way to remedy those deficiencies by providing a condensed form of the essential nutrients needed for mental and emotional health.

Nutrients That Enhance Mental Health and Wellness

Feeling down, depressed, or anxious? Before deciding to treat the problem with antidepressants or other powerful prescription drugs, you may want to give the friendly produce in your refrigerator's crisper bin a chance. New studies show that fresh fruits and vegetables contain powerful mood elevators that promote mental and emotional health without the side effects of medication.

Those Wonderful B Vitamins

Vitamin B deficiencies have long been linked to depression and anxiety because vitamin B helps to metabolize neurotoxins that may be linked to anxiety problems. It can help with severe forms of depression, too.

Here's how vitamin B can help combat anxiety:

- Thiamine, or B_1, reduces feelings of irritability and mental confusion. A deficiency of B_1 can lead to fatigue, irritability, depression, anxiety, loss of appetite, insomnia, and memory impairment. Thiamine also helps to temporarily correct some complications of metabolic disorders associated with genetic diseases.
- B_{12} is important in the formation of red blood cells. Deficiencies of B_{12} vitamin can cause mood swings, paranoia, irritability, confusion, and hallucinations. The vitamin is most active against depression. Because the human body stores several years' worth of vitamin B_{12}, nutritional deficiency is extremely rare, although inability to absorb vitamin B_{12} from the intestinal tract can be caused by pernicious anemia. In addition, strict vegetarians or vegans who are not taking in proper amounts of B_{12} through diet or quality supplements may be prone to deficiency.
- Inositol is a compound found in vitamin B that has been proven to alleviate panic attacks.
- Pantothenic acid helps reduce stress by building the body's resistance to it.

- Niacin (vitamin B_3) has been shown to help reduce anxiety, depression, and insomnia and has a chemical composition similar to Valium, a benzodiazepine tranquilizer.
- Vitamin B_5 helps the body manufacture anti-stress hormones.
- Pyridoxine, or vitamin B_6, is another vitamin that helps diminish anxiety, especially in women.
- Folic acid is a B vitamin that is instrumental in keeping your blood healthy. A deficiency in folic acid causes a decrease in healthy red blood cells, which carry oxygen throughout your body. The result is lethargy and headaches, which may cause irritability and anxiety.

The Wonders of Vitamin C

Vitamin C is useful for regulating cortisol secretion in the body. Cortisol is necessary for the fight or flight response to stressful situations, but too much of it can be unhealthy. Cortisol is released by the adrenal glands and sends stress signals throughout the body and mind.

FACT

The daily recommended dosage for vitamin C is 60 milligrams, but you may need to take a much higher dose to reduce stress. In a study published in the *International Journal of Sports Medicine*, vitamin C was found to be most effective in regulating adrenal stress hormones at 1,500 milligrams per day in athletes.

Vitamin E to the Rescue

Psychological stress can result in oxidative stress; that's when free radicals accumulate in the body and result in cell damage. Vitamin E can help combat oxidative stress by working with vitamins B and C to repair and protect the nervous system. Vitamin E also supports a healthy immune system, which helps prevent mood swings. A vitamin E deficiency in the body can make stress quickly turn into more serious problems like depression. Oxidative stress can also lead to neuron damage and cancer, but vitamin E protects the body against this type of damage as well.

The Wonders of Vitamin D

Research published in Medical Hypotheses found that a deficiency of vitamin D increased anxiety and altered emotional behavior in mice. Another study found that a deficiency of vitamin D was also associated with depression and poor moods.

Minerals

Minerals help relieve anxiety and mineral deficiencies that are sometimes indirect causes of anxiety.

- **Magnesium:** Too little causes confusion, agitation, anxiety, and hallucinations.
- **Iron:** Transports life-sustaining nutrients throughout the body along with oxygen while removing carbon dioxide. Iron ensures a healthy immune system and creates energy. A deficiency in iron can cause a variety of health problems, including fatigue, irritability, and headaches.
- **Taurine:** A little-known amino acid that plays an essential role in metabolism and mental functioning. Studies also link taurine to the regulation of insulin in the body. In addition, taurine stimulates the body's immune system. Taurine has also been suggested as a potential treatment for epilepsy, cardiovascular disease, diabetes, alcoholism, cystic fibrosis, and Alzheimer's. Many vegetarians are deficient in this amino acid and should take a supplement to ensure a proper balance promoting optimal mental health.
- **Potassium:** Necessary for proper functioning of cells, nerves, and muscle cells. Deficiencies in potassium can cause weakness, fatigue, depression, and anxiety.
- **Chromium:** Helps stabilize blood sugar levels, which in turn helps prevent mood swings and depression.
- **Manganese:** Too little results in low levels of neurotransmitters serotonin and epinephrine, which can result in depression and anxiety.
- **Zinc:** A zinc deficiency may cause depression, anxiety, and lethargy.
- **Calcium:** Deficiencies in calcium affect the nerve fibers, leading to nervousness and irritability.

- **Selenium:** Deficiencies can result in anxiety, confusion, and depression.
- **Omega-3 fatty acids:** Found in flaxseed and fish, they help alleviate stress and depression.

Nature's Medicine Cabinet

A sound diet packed with quality nutrition from vibrant fruits and vegetables will promote your body's and brain's optimal balance, thanks to their powerful vitamins, minerals, and phytonutrients. You can take control of your daily mood, stress level, and overall well-being. Like most people, you'll probably find that feeling a little more healthy because of your new green drinks each day will keep you on a path to better health. With that new lifestyle and on that new path, you'll have the added benefits of increased happiness and mental stability.

Best Produce for Mental Stability

1. Mangoes
2. Cabbage
3. Kale
4. Melons
5. Citrus fruits
6. Berries
7. Romaine
8. Walnuts
9. Almonds
10. Pears

Drinks for Happiness and Mental Stability

Sweet Green Fruitiness

Packed with vitamin C–rich fruits, this green drink will have you sipping yourself to sweetness and pleasure as you kick start your day the healthy way!

INGREDIENTS | SERVES 2

1 cup chopped spinach

2 medium oranges, peeled

1 medium pink grapefruit, peeled and seeded

1 cup pineapple chunks

2 cups water

Combine all ingredients in a blender and blend until desired consistency is reached.

PER SERVING: Calories: 151 | Fat: 1 g | Protein: 3 g | Sodium: 13 mg | Fiber: 6 g | Carbohydrates: 38 g | Sugar: 30 g

Merry Mango Blend

Sweet and bursting with vibrant vitamins from mangoes, pineapples, and romaine, this green drink provides healthy doses of fiber to keep you full and focused throughout the day.

INGREDIENTS | SERVES 2

1 cup chopped romaine lettuce

1 cup mango chunks, peeled and seeded

1 cup pineapple chunks

1 cup vanilla coconut milk

1 cup ice

Combine all ingredients in a blender and blend until desired consistency is reached.

PER SERVING: Calories: 140 | Fat: 3 g | Protein: 1 g | Sodium: 26 mg | Fiber: 3 g | Carbohydrates: 28 g | Sugar: 24 g

Not Your Classic Cabbage Smoothie

Cabbage gets kicked up and sweetened up with the addition of sweet fruits that boast B vitamins, beta-carotene, and tons of minerals that boost brain functioning and focus.

INGREDIENTS | SERVES 2

1 cup cabbage

2 medium peaches, pits removed

1 cup cubed mango, peeled and seeded

½ medium pink grapefruit, peeled and seeded

2 cups organic apple juice, not from concentrate

Combine all ingredients in a blender and blend until desired consistency is reached.

PER SERVING: Calories: 254 | Fat: 1 g | Protein: 3 g | Sodium: 19 mg | Fiber: 6 g | Carbohydrates: 62 g | Sugar: 54 g

A's, B's, and C's of Health

With each ingredient packing tons of vitamins like A, B, and C along with essential minerals and powerful antioxidants, this green drink is a veggie-packed classic that tastes great and makes you feel great, too!

INGREDIENTS | SERVES 2

1 cup chopped broccoli

2 heirloom tomatoes

2 medium carrots, greens removed

½ cup chopped kale leaves

2 cups purified water

1. Juice broccoli, tomatoes, carrots, and kale according to manufacturer's instruction.

2. Stir in the water until all ingredients are well blended.

PER SERVING: Calories: 71 | Fat: 1 g | Protein: 4 g | Sodium: 70 mg | Fiber: 0 g | Carbohydrates: 15 g | Sugar: 7 g

Melon-Kale Morning Smoothie

Sweet melons and oranges combine with kale to kick-start your day (or afternoon!) with vibrant vitamins and omega-packed flax for a better brain, healthier heart, and an overall immunity-boosting blast of all of your daily essentials!

INGREDIENTS | SERVES 2

1 cup chopped kale

1 cup watermelon chunks, rind and seeds removed

1 cup cantaloupe chunks, rind and seeds removed

2 medium oranges, peeled

¼ cup ground flaxseed

Combine all ingredients in a blender and blend until desired consistency is reached.

PER SERVING: Calories: 211 | Fat: 6 g | Protein: 7 g | Sodium: 26 mg | Fiber: 8 g | Carbohydrates: 36 g | Sugar: 24 g

Sweet Green Cabbage Juice

Green apples and sweet pears lend tartness and sweetness to this spiced up green drink that stars vitamin- and mineral-rich cabbage, perfect for any time of the day!

INGREDIENTS | SERVES 2

1 cup cabbage

2 medium green apples, cored

2 medium pears, cored

1 teaspoon cinnamon

1. Juice cabbage, apples, and pears according to manufacturer's instructions.

2. Add cinnamon and stir until all ingredients are well blended.

PER SERVING: Calories: 151 | Fat: 1 g | Protein: 2 g | Sodium: 15 mg | Fiber: 0 g | Carbohydrates: 38 g | Sugar: 20 g

Very Veggie Cabbage Juice

Packed with fiber, beta-carotene, and B vitamins, this green drink combines delicious vegetables that make for a slightly sweetened green drink of vegetable servings you can sip.

INGREDIENTS | SERVES 2

1 cup cabbage

½ cup chopped broccoli

½ cup cauliflower florets

2 medium carrots, peeled

1 medium tomato

1. Juice all ingredients together according to manufacturer's instruction.

2. Stir until all ingredients are well blended.

PER SERVING: Calories: 61 | Fat: 0 g | Protein: 3 g | Sodium: 68 mg | Fiber: 0 g | Carbohydrates: 14 g | Sugar: 7 g

Sweet, Smooth Spinach

With delightfully sweet fruits and a tempting texture, this green drink has it all! Between all of its B vitamins, vitamin C, and plenty of rich minerals, with just one recipe, you can sip your way to sanity . . . sweetly.

INGREDIENTS | SERVES 2

1 cup chopped spinach

1 banana, peeled

1 cup cubed mango, peeled and seeded

1 cup pineapple chunks

2 cups organic apple juice, not from concentrate

1 cup ice

Combine all ingredients in a blender and blend until desired consistency is reached.

PER SERVING: Calories: 261 | Fat: 1 g | Protein: 2 g | Sodium: 24 mg | Fiber: 5 g | Carbohydrates: 65 g | Sugar: 51 g

Vitamin C Strudel

With oats and flax lending a thicker texture to this citrus-stocked cup of spicy goodness, you can savor the pleasure of feeling focused and full of healthy nutrients . . . with the added benefits of brain-boosting, energizing elements, too!

INGREDIENTS | SERVES 2

1 cup chopped kale leaves

1 cup raw oats

⅛ cup ground flaxseed

3 medium oranges, peeled

1 cup pineapple chunks

1" ginger, peeled

2 cups organic apple juice, not from concentrate

Combine all ingredients in a blender and blend until desired consistency is reached.

PER SERVING: Calories: 616 | Fat: 9 g | Protein: 18 g | Sodium: 26 mg | Fiber: 17 g | Carbohydrates: 121 g | Sugar: 51 g

Fruity Fog-Clearer

Sometimes you need a little help clearing the mental fog from your mind, and this green drink is perfect for exactly that. Berries and bright mangoes combine to make this B vitamin–packed green drink of sweetness the healthy way to find focus and mental clarity!

INGREDIENTS | SERVES 2

1 cup chopped spinach

1 cup blueberries

1 cup strawberries, tops removed

2 cups mango chunks, peeled and seeded

2 cups vanilla coconut milk

Combine all ingredients in a blender and blend until desired consistency is reached.

PER SERVING: Calories: 257 | Fat: 6 g | Protein: 3 g | Sodium: 60 mg | Fiber: 6 g | Carbohydrates: 50 g | Sugar: 42 g

Smooth Citrus-Berry Smoothie

Potassium-packed bananas provide smooth sweetness to this vitamin C–rich green drink that has happiness-helping minerals and B vitamins galore!

INGREDIENTS | SERVES 2

1 cup chopped romaine lettuce
2 bananas, peeled
2 cups strawberries, tops removed
1 cup pineapple chunks
2 cups vanilla coconut milk

Combine all ingredients in a blender and blend until desired consistency is reached.

PER SERVING: Calories: 286 | Fat: 6 g | Protein: 3 g | Sodium: 50 mg | Fiber: 8 g | Carbohydrates: 59 g | Sugar: 39 g

Sweet Kale Treat

Sweets aren't always a bad thing. This kale concoction provides a ton of naturally sweet and spicy flavors for a vitamin- and mineral-rich green drink that keeps you satisfied and healthy . . . even through the strongest sweet cravings around!

INGREDIENTS | SERVES 2

1 cup chopped kale
2 medium green apples, cored
2" ginger, peeled
1 teaspoon organic maple syrup
2 cups green tea

Combine all ingredients in a blender and blend until desired consistency is reached.

PER SERVING: Calories: 126 | Fat: 1 g | Protein: 2 g | Sodium: 16 mg | Fiber: 5 g | Carbohydrates: 32 g | Sugar: 21 g

Spicy Pear Dream

Powerful antioxidants and potent vitamins and minerals come from each natural ingredient in this simple, yet delicious, green drink of spicy sweetness.

INGREDIENTS | SERVES 2

1 cup chopped spinach

¼ cup walnuts

¼ cup almonds

1" ginger, peeled

2 pears, peeled and cored

1 teaspoon ground cloves

2 cups purified water

Combine all ingredients in a blender and blend until desired consistency is reached.

PER SERVING: Calories: 296 | Fat: 18 g | Protein: 7 g | Sodium: 18 mg | Fiber: 9 g | Carbohydrates: 34 g | Sugar: 19 g

Sweet Romaine Smoothie

Romaine lettuce gets all jazzed up with plenty of vitamin C, B vitamins, and powerful antioxidants that all boost brain power and help with happiness and mental clarity. Spiced up with the natural zing of ginger, this green drink will make your average morning glass of OJ a thing of the past!

INGREDIENTS | SERVES 2

1 cup chopped romaine lettuce

2 cups blueberries

1 cup pineapple chunks

1" ginger, peeled

2 cups organic apple juice, not from concentrate

Combine all ingredients in a blender and blend until desired consistency is reached.

PER SERVING: Calories: 245 | Fat: 1 g | Protein: 2 g | Sodium: 15 mg | Fiber: 6 g | Carbohydrates: 61 g | Sugar: 47 g

Strawberry Shortcake Smoothie

Whipped up in the blender in a matter of minutes, this drink will have you sipping your way to strawberry shortcake heaven with all-natural ingredients that pack tons of sweetness and essential vitamins and minerals into a delicious, healthy alternative to fattening baked varieties.

INGREDIENTS | SERVES 2

1 cup chopped romaine lettuce

2 cups strawberries, tops removed

2 bananas, peeled

¼ cup ground flaxseed

1 teaspoon ground cinnamon

1 teaspoon ground cardamom

1" ginger, peeled

2 cups organic apple juice, not from concentrate

Combine all ingredients in a blender and blend until desired consistency is reached.

PER SERVING: Calories: 358 | Fat: 6 g | Protein: 6 g | Sodium: 15 mg | Fiber: 12 g | Carbohydrates: 74 g | Sugar: 46 g

Sweet Green Nuttiness

This green drink's ingredients make for a smooth, sweet, and nutty any-time-of-the-day pick-me-up that will boost energy with B vitamins and keep you full and focused . . . just when you need it!

INGREDIENTS | SERVES 2

1 cup chopped spinach

6 prunes, pitted

¼ cup walnuts

¼ cup almonds

1 teaspoon ground cinnamon

2 cups vanilla almond milk

Combine all ingredients in a blender and blend until desired consistency is reached.

PER SERVING: Calories: 350 | Fat: 20 g | Protein: 8 g | Sodium: 164 mg | Fiber: 7 g | Carbohydrates: 41 g | Sugar: 27 g

A Nutty Way to Start the Day

Antioxidant-rich nuts and flaxseed pair with powerful vitamin B–packed romaine and bananas to create a smooth, slightly sweet, and very nutty morning mood-adjusting green drink. It has everything you need to keep you happy, healthy, and vibrant!

INGREDIENTS | SERVES 2

1 cup romaine lettuce
⅛ cup ground flaxseed
¼ cup walnuts
¼ cup almonds
2 bananas, peeled
2 cups purified water

Combine all ingredients in a blender and blend until desired consistency is reached.

PER SERVING: Calories: 334 | Fat: 20 g | Protein: 9 g | Sodium: 3 mg | Fiber: 9 g | Carbohydrates: 36 g | Sugar: 16 g

Sweet and Spicy Kale Smoothie

Juicing up this sweet and spicy kale combination of vibrant veggies and fabulous fruits, you can keep your mental stability and clarity in check . . . with the added benefit of immunity-boosting antioxidants, too!

INGREDIENTS | SERVES 2

1 cup chopped kale
4 carrots, greens removed
1" ginger
1 medium green apple, cored

Combine all ingredients in a blender and blend until desired consistency is reached.

PER SERVING: Calories: 117 | Fat: 1 g | Protein: 3 g | Sodium: 98 mg | Fiber: 0 g | Carbohydrates: 28 g | Sugar: 15 g

Spiced Apple Surprise

Who needs apple pie when you can sip some sweet greens that taste just like the real thing? Antioxidant-rich spices take this green drink featuring vitamin-rich spinach and apples to a delicious new level . . . with fiber-full oats keeping you full, focused, and satisfied!

INGREDIENTS | SERVES 2

1 cup chopped spinach

2 medium red apples, peeled and cored

1 cup raw oats

1 teaspoon ground cinnamon

1 teaspoon ground cloves

2 cups organic apple juice, not from concentrate

Combine all ingredients in a blender and blend until desired consistency is reached.

PER SERVING: Calories: 504 | Fat: 6 g | Protein: 14 g | Sodium: 26 mg | Fiber: 12 g | Carbohydrates: 102 g | Sugar: 40 g

Green Sweetness

Simple and slightly sweet, these four ingredients combine to create a green drink of fiber, fiber, and more fiber for a filling meal or snack that will lift you up instead of weighing you down.

INGREDIENTS | SERVES 2

1 cup chopped kale

1 cup chopped broccoli

2 medium green apples, peeled and cored

2 cups organic apple juice, not from concentrate

Combine all ingredients in a blender and blend until desired consistency is reached.

PER SERVING: Calories: 223 | Fat: 1 g | Protein: 3 g | Sodium: 38 g | Fiber: 4 g | Carbohydrates: 55 g | Sugar: 41 g

CHAPTER 7

Drinks for Stronger Bones

Although dairy products were once considered the most important sources of calcium, research now shows that consuming a diet rich in fresh fruits and vegetables is your best defense against degenerative diseases like osteopenia and osteoporosis. With an increase in dairy allergies among a growing percentage of the population, green drinks deliver quality nutrition with beyond-adequate amounts of the essentials like calcium. Studies also show that the high acid content of traditional calcium sources like milk and cheese actually contribute to the degeneration of bone, so by consuming plenty of low-acid, calcium-rich fruits and vegetables, you can provide your body with exactly what it needs to build strong bones and prevent bone diseases by maintaining the body's healthy acid-alkaline balance . . . without the harsh side effects of traditional dairy products.

Essential Nutrients That Help Retain and Build Bone

In general, most fruits and vegetables are alkalizing, while animal flesh and most processed food products like soda and junk foods are highly acidifying. Based on the acid-alkali theory of bone health, consuming a diet rich in fresh and raw produce coupled with reducing your intake of high-acid foods can help you achieve a healthy degree of alkalinity in the body and thus preserve your bones. The following nutrients are essential for strong bones:

- **Calcium.** The most abundant mineral in bone, calcium builds strong bones and also helps prevent fractures and degeneration.
- **Magnesium.** Another major component in bones, magnesium helps prevent bone loss.
- **Boron.** A trace mineral essential for bone health, boron activates certain hormones that regulate bone growth and health.
- **Vitamin K.** This vitamin helps osteocalcin, the protein found in bone tissue, hang onto calcium.
- **Vitamin D.** This vitamin helps maintain the mineral balance in bone and enhances the absorption of calcium. High levels of vitamin D have been linked to substantial reductions in hip fractures in post-menopausal women.
- **Anthocyanins and proanthocyanidins.** These two compounds found in cells help build collagen and stabilize bone structure while also acting as powerful antioxidants that protect healthy cells from harmful toxins.

Fruits and Vegetables That Boost Bone Health

When fruits and vegetables are added to the diet, it creates an alkaline environment that offsets the acidity of meats and dairy products and helps preserve the structure of the bone. This positive effect on bones is even greater if you eat vegetables that provide calcium, such as broccoli, kale, and turnip greens. Turnip greens, especially, are a calcium powerhouse, supplying 200 milligrams of calcium in a single serving.

Best Sources of Calcium, Magnesium, and Boron

Although milk is high in calcium, there are plenty of reasons why you should be choosing other natural calcium-rich alternatives that are considered healthier options. You will find calcium in abundance in kale, collard greens, broccoli, parsley, and turnip greens, which provide calcium without the acidic fat of dairy products. Collard greens, parsley, and blackberries are packed with magnesium, another essential mineral for bone health. You can find plenty of boron in kale, collard greens, and turnip greens, also.

Best Sources of Vitamins for Bone Health

Excellent sources of vitamin K include kale, collard and turnip greens, broccoli, parsley, lettuce, cabbage, spinach, watercress, asparagus, and string beans. In addition, vitamin D plays a critical role in the preservation of bone health, and most Americans don't get enough. Although the best source of vitamin D is through exposure to direct sunlight for ten to fifteen minutes each day, you may not be able to do this in the dead of winter. To ensure you get enough, consider taking a supplement and eating lots of fatty fish, including salmon, tuna, sardines, catfish, shrimp, and cod. Good produce sources include sunflower seeds, sunflower sprouts, and mushrooms. In addition, some brands of orange juice are fortified with vitamin D. Red grapes and blueberries are high in anthocyanins and proanthocyanidins, which are also essential for bone health.

Fruits and Vegetables That Help Prevent Osteoporosis and Bone Disease

You can find all of the nutrients you need for increased bone health in fresh fruits and vegetables that are suitable for your green drinks, according to the National Institutes for Health.

- Copper is found in nuts, seeds, wheat bran, cereals, whole grain products, and cocoa products.
- Boron is found in avocado, nuts, and prune juice.
- Fluoride is found in fluoridated water and teas.
- Iron is found in parsley, cruciferous veggies, carrots, beets with greens, pineapple, and blackberries.

- Silicon is found in root veggies, cucumbers, and bell peppers.
- Isoflavones are found primarily in soybeans and soy products, chickpeas, and other legumes.
- Magnesium is found in leafy vegetables such as spinach, potatoes, nuts, seeds, whole grains including bran, wheat, and oats, and chocolate. Smaller amounts are found in bananas, broccoli, raisins, and shrimp.
- Manganese is found in cruciferous veggies, spinach, beets, apples, tangerines, pears, and oranges.
- Phosphorous is found in milk, yogurt, ice cream, cheese, peas, meat, and eggs.
- Potassium is found in milk, yogurt, chicken, turkey, fish, bananas, raisins, cantaloupe, celery, carrots, potatoes, and tomatoes.
- Vitamin C is found in citrus fruits, tomatoes and tomato juice, potatoes, Brussels sprouts, cauliflower, broccoli, strawberries, cabbage, and spinach.
- Protein is found in legumes, grains, nuts, seeds, and vegetables.
- Vitamin K is found in collards, spinach, salad greens, broccoli, Brussels sprouts, cabbage, plant oils, and margarine. Patients on anticoagulant medication should work with their physicians to monitor their vitamin K intake to ensure they consume the right amount. Consuming too much or too little vitamin K can interfere with blood clotting.
- Zinc is found in whole grains, dry beans, and nuts. Nutritionists recommend that vegetarians double the RDA, as zinc is harder to absorb on a vegetarian diet. Calcium supplementation may reduce the absorption of zinc.
- Calcium is found in cruciferous veggies, string beans, oranges, celery, carrots, lettuce, watercress, beet greens, kale, parsley, and broccoli.
- Vitamin D is found in sunflower seeds, sunflower sprouts, and mushrooms.

Best Produce for Super Strong Bones

1. Berries
2. Bananas
3. Kale
4. Apples
5. Carrots
6. Pineapples
7. Citrus
8. Ginger
9. Melons
10. Spinach

Drinks for Stronger Bones

Berries and Bananas for Bone Health

The crisp taste of iceberg lettuce is beautifully balanced with the addition of citrus, blackberries, bananas, and yogurt for a flavor combination that will make you enjoy eating better for your health.

INGREDIENTS | SERVES 3

1 cup chopped iceberg lettuce

1 pint blackberries

1 cup pineapple chunks

2 bananas, peeled

1 cup Greek-style yogurt

Magnesium for Bone Health

The magnesium in blackberries can do amazing things for respiratory relief, but it can also help create stronger bones. Playing an important role in the absorption of calcium, a diet rich in this powerful mineral ensures strong bones. Diets deficient in magnesium have also been shown to prevent the body's proper use of estrogen, which can spell disaster for many of the body's cancer-fighting abilities.

1. Place lettuce, blackberries, pineapple, bananas, and ½ cup yogurt in a blender and blend until thoroughly combined.

2. Add remaining ½ cup yogurt, as needed, while blending until desired consistency is achieved.

PER SERVING: Calories: 186 | Fat: 1 g | Protein: 10 g | Sodium: 31 mg | Fiber: 8 g | Carbohydrates: 38 g | Sugar: 23 g

Sweet Green Dreams

Spicy arugula and romaine lettuce pair with pears for a lightly sweet and creamy drink that's as nutritious as it is delicious!

INGREDIENTS | SERVES 2

½ cup arugula

½ cup chopped romaine lettuce

2 medium pears, pitted and peeled

2 cups vanilla almond milk

Combine all ingredients in a blender and blend until desired consistency is reached.

PER SERVING: Calories: 196 | Fat: 3 g | Protein: 2 g | Sodium: 155 mg | Fiber: 7 g | Carbohydrates: 44 g | Sugar: 33 g

Sweetened Kale Chamomile

Kale and sweet fruits get blended into a perfect combination of nutrition that's packed with all you need to keep those bones healthy!

INGREDIENTS | SERVES 2

½ cup chopped kale
1 medium apple, peeled and cored
1 cup seedless green grapes
1 medium pear, peeled and cored
2 cups chamomile tea

Combine all ingredients in a blender and blend until desired consistency is reached.

PER SERVING: Calories: 131 | Fat: 1 g | Protein: 2 g | Sodium: 11 mg | Fiber: 4 g | Carbohydrates: 34 g | Sugar: 24 g

"Green" Apple

While there are no green apples in this drink, it is still packed with powerful vitamins and nutrients.

INGREDIENTS | SERVES 2

1 cup spinach leaves
2 medium red apples, peeled and cored
1 cup coconut milk

Combine all ingredients in a blender and blend until desired consistency is reached.

PER SERVING: Calories: 121 | Fat: 3 g | Protein: 1 g | Sodium: 34 mg | Fiber: 2 g | Carbohydrates: 25 g | Sugar: 19 g

Blackberry Romaine Smoothie

Spiced up with ginger root, this zippy combination of romaine lettuce, blackberries, ginger, and tea creates an antioxidant-packed green drink that's best for boosting bone health.

INGREDIENTS | SERVES 2

1 cup chopped romaine lettuce

2 cups blackberries

1" ginger, peeled

2 cups green tea

1 cup ice

Combine all ingredients in a blender and blend until desired consistency is reached.

PER SERVING: Calories: 69 | Fat: 1 g | Protein: 2 g | Sodium: 4 mg | Fiber: 8 g | Carbohydrates: 15 g | Sugar: 7 g

Grapplenana

Greens get blended with sweet apples and smooth banana in this coconut milk green drink. It's packed with tons of vitamins and minerals that promote your overall health any time of the day.

INGREDIENTS | SERVES 2

½ cup romaine

½ cup spinach

2 medium red apples, peeled and cored

1 banana, peeled

2 cups vanilla coconut milk

Combine all ingredients in a blender and blend until desired consistency is reached.

PER SERVING: Calories: 224 | Fat: 5 g | Protein: 1 g | Sodium: 52 mg | Fiber: 4 g | Carbohydrates: 44 g | Sugar: 33 g

Touch of Tropics with Your Greens

Citrus fruits and coconut milk make this sweet blended green treat a touch of tropical heaven that's perfect for breakfast, dessert, or a simple sweet snack.

INGREDIENTS | SERVES 2

1 cup chopped spinach

1 medium pink grapefruit, peeled and seeded

2 cups frozen strawberries, tops removed

2 cups vanilla coconut milk

Combine all ingredients in a blender and blend until desired consistency is reached.

PER SERVING: Calories: 187 | Fat: 5 g | Protein: 2 g | Sodium: 60 mg | Fiber: 5 g | Carbohydrates: 33 g | Sugar: 25 g

Smooth Green Sweetness

Peaches steal the show in this fruit-packed green drink. Though there is spinach hidden within this smoothie, the berries and bananas add an extra sweetness and smooth texture.

INGREDIENTS | SERVES 2

2 medium peaches, pitted and peeled (peel removal is optional)

1 banana, peeled

1 cup blueberries

1 cup chopped spinach

2 cups vanilla coconut milk

Combine all ingredients in a blender and blend until desired consistency is reached.

PER SERVING: Calories: 246 | Fat: 6 g | Protein: 3 g | Sodium: 58 mg | Fiber: 6 g | Carbohydrates: 48 g | Sugar: 36 g

Blended for Bone Health

Carrots and apples sweeten the spinach leaves in this juice cocktail that is known to build strong bones and improve your overall health.

INGREDIENTS | SERVES 2

1 cup chopped spinach
3 large carrots
1 medium red apple, peeled and cored

1. Juice all ingredients together according to manufacturer's instructions.

2. Stir well.

PER SERVING: Calories: 86 | Fat: 0 g | Protein: 2 g | Sodium: 86 mg | Fiber: 0 g | Carbohydrates: 21 g | Sugar: 13 g

Sweet Veggie Tea

Green tea gets a unique spin in this carrot-filled, ginger-infused drink.

INGREDIENTS | SERVES 2

1 cup chopped romaine lettuce
4 large carrots
1" ginger, peeled
1 cup green tea

Combine all ingredients in a blender and blend until desired consistency is reached.

PER SERVING: Calories: 66 | Fat: 0 g | Protein: 2 g | Sodium: 102 mg | Fiber: 5 g | Carbohydrates: 15 g | Sugar: 7 g

Greens Apple Pie

Traditional apple pie spices combine in this green drink for a spicy, super-delicious combination of fruits and greens.

INGREDIENTS | SERVES 2

1 cup watercress

2 medium red apples, peeled and cored

1" ginger, peeled

1 teaspoon ground cardamom

1 teaspoon cinnamon

Combine all ingredients in a blender and blend until desired consistency is reached.

PER SERVING: Calories: 88 | Fat: 0 g | Protein: 1 g | Sodium: 8 mg | Fiber: 3 g | Carbohydrates: 23 g | Sugar: 16 g

A Carrotful Combination

Loaded with powerful bone-building nutrition, this green drink packs tons of vegetables in one quick and easy serving.

INGREDIENTS | SERVES 2

1 cup spinach

1 cup chopped broccoli

1 cup cauliflower florets

3 large carrots

2 cups water

Combine all ingredients in a blender and blend until desired consistency is reached.

PER SERVING: Calories: 76 | Fat: 1 g | Protein: 4 g | Sodium: 116 mg | Fiber: 6 g | Carbohydrates: 16 g | Sugar: 7 g

Very Berry Bone-Building Green Smoothie

Plain old lettuce gets all jazzed up in this potent, powerful, and simple smoothie that boasts nutritious and delicious ingredients for bone health.

INGREDIENTS | SERVES 2

1 cup chopped iceberg lettuce

1 cup strawberries, tops removed

1 cup blackberries

1 cup pineapple chunks

2 cups water

1 cup ice

Combine all ingredients in a blender and blend until desired consistency is reached.

PER SERVING: Calories: 99 | Fat: 1 g | Protein: 2 g | Sodium: 5 mg | Fiber: 7 g | Carbohydrates: 24 g | Sugar: 16 g

Green Tropical Tonic

A taste of the tropics adds a nutritious spin to this amazing combination of spinach and sweet fruits. This delightful green drink is sure to be one of your favorites!

INGREDIENTS | SERVES 2

1 cup chopped spinach

1 cup pineapple chunks

2 medium oranges, peeled

1 medium red apple, peeled and cored

1 banana, peeled

2 cups vanilla coconut milk

Combine all ingredients in a blender and blend until desired consistency is reached.

PER SERVING: Calories: 291 | Fat: 6 g | Protein: 3 g | Sodium: 58 mg | Fiber: 7 g | Carbohydrates: 60 g | Sugar: 45 g

Kicked-Up Kale

Crisp kale gets a hint of sweetness and zing with the added flavors of peaches, blackberries, and ginger. Combined with antioxidant-rich green tea, this recipe blends into a perfectly paired green drink of delicious nutrition.

INGREDIENTS | SERVES 3

½ cup chopped kale

2 medium peaches, peeled and pitted

2 cups blackberries

1" ginger, peeled

2 cups green tea

Combine all ingredients in a blender and blend until desired consistency is reached.

PER SERVING: Calories: 88 | Fat: 1 g | Protein: 3 g | Sodium: 6 mg | Fiber: 7 g | Carbohydrates: 20 g | Sugar: 13 g

Spiced Blackberries and Greens

Bone-healthy blackberries pair up with splendid spices to take kale to another level. Slightly sweet and super-spicy, this combination of ingredients is packed with nutrition that will promote overall health any time of the day.

INGREDIENTS | SERVES 2

½ cup chopped kale

2 cups blackberries

2" ginger, peeled

1 teaspoon ground cinnamon

¼ teaspoon ground cloves

2 cups green tea

Combine all ingredients in a blender and blend until desired consistency is reached.

PER SERVING: Calories: 80 | Fat: 1 g | Protein: 3 g | Sodium: 10 mg | Fiber: 8 g | Carbohydrates: 18 g | Sugar: 7 g

Smooth Spinach Deliciousness

The addition of apples to this green drink is enough to make any spinach naysayer a devoted green drink lover!

INGREDIENTS | SERVES 2

2 bananas, peeled

1 cup chopped spinach

2 medium green apples, peeled, cored, and chopped

2 cups vanilla almond milk

Combine all ingredients in a blender and blend until desired consistency is reached.

PER SERVING: Calories: 277 | Fat: 3 g | Protein: 3 g | Sodium: 164 mg | Fiber: 6 g | Carbohydrates: 64 g | Sugar: 46 g

Grapefruit Ginger Zest

Forgo the coffee, and reach for this healthy alternative to kick-start your day the right way! With powerful nutritious ingredients, this green drink has everything you want to build your bone health, and everything you need to start your day healthfully.

INGREDIENTS | SERVES 2

1 cup watercress

2 medium grapefruits, peeled and seeded

1 cup blueberries

½" ginger, peeled

2 cups green tea

Combine all ingredients in a blender and blend until desired consistency is reached.

PER SERVING: Calories: 127 | Fat: 1 g | Protein: 3 g | Sodium: 8 mg | Fiber: 5 g | Carbohydrates: 32 g | Sugar: 25 g

A Berry Melon Green Drink

With sweet berries and sweeter melons, this quick and easy drink is packed full of nutrition. And, you can freeze the melons and berries prior to blending to create a sweet green smoothie instead!

INGREDIENTS | SERVES 2

1 cup chopped spinach

1 cup watermelon cubes, rind and seeds removed

1 cup raspberries

1 cup honeydew melon chunks, rind and seeds removed

1 cup water

Combine all ingredients in a blender and blend until desired consistency is reached.

PER SERVING: Calories: 89 | Fat: 1 g | Protein: 2 g | Sodium: 29 mg | Fiber: 5 g | Carbohydrates: 21 g | Sugar: 14 g

Simple Spinach, Carrot, Apple Juice

Sometimes, simplicity is best! Juicing together carotene-rich carrots, quercetin-filled apples, and calcium-packed spinach in one perfect green drink is the simple answer to any question about boosting health and building bones deliciously!

INGREDIENTS | SERVES 2

1 cup chopped spinach

2 medium red apples, cored and chopped

1 medium carrot

1. Juice all ingredients together according to the manufacturer's instructions.

2. Stir until all ingredients are well blended.

PER SERVING: Calories: 111 | Fat: 0 g | Protein: 1 g | Sodium: 35 mg | Fiber: 0 g | Carbohydrates: 29 g | Sugar: 20 g

CHAPTER 8

Drinks for Energy and Stamina

If you find yourself needing a little pick-me-up for your morning perk or afternoon slump, you can whip up a nutritious green drink of fruits and vegetables that will provide the energy and stamina you need. Fruits are packed with simple and complex sugars, carbohydrates, vitamin C, and B vitamins, all of which provide instant and/or sustained energy, as well as iron and copper, power nutrients that promote stamina and endurance. Their vegetable sidekicks make a perfect pairing with their valuable vitamins, minerals, and phytochemicals that support and supplement each and every vibrant sip that will put a pep in your step.

Best Nutrients for Energy and Stamina

If you find that you're chronically tired, and have ruled out more serious deficiencies and illnesses, you could simply be running low on the fuel your body needs to function. Whether you need to power your workout or increase your energy level for work, you'll find all of the necessary nutrients in a glass of a delicious green drink. Packed with all of the essentials and so much more, green drinks combine delicious and nutritious, vibrant, natural foods that will keep your mind alert and focused and your body energized and ready for whatever your day has in store!

Nature's Nutrients for Energy

Here's a look at some of the most important vitamins and nutrients for maintaining high energy and stamina.

- Vitamin B complex refuels cells with energy that can be depleted by a variety of factors, including stress, insomnia, and overworking. Several medical conditions, including iron-deficiency anemia and hypothyroidism, can also cause tiredness and fatigue. Before assuming your fatigue is because of a lack of vitamin B, see your doctor. A simple blood test can rule out medical reasons.
- Vitamin B_{12} is especially crucial for energy and stamina. A lack of vitamin B_{12}, or pernicious anemia, can cause weight loss, lack of muscle control, and yellow-blue color blindness. This deficiency is often triggered by gastrointestinal problems such as bacterial or parasitic infections.
- Folic acid (vitamin B_9) is essential for energy and stamina. A lack of folic acid in the diet may lead to folic acid–deficiency anemia, which can cause insomnia, sleep disorders, and a sore, red tongue.
- Biotin (vitamin B_7) promotes energy production as well as growth and development. Biotin deficiency can result in dermatitis.
- Niacin (vitamin B_3) is required by all cells in the body for energy production and promoting healthy skin, nerves, and proper digestive system functioning.
- Riboflavin (vitamin B_2) is important for growth, nerve function, red blood cell production, healthy skin, and the release of energy from foods.

- Thiamine (Vitamin B$_1$) is necessary for energy production, especially from carbohydrates. It is also important for normal functioning of the heart, nervous system, and muscles.
- Iron deficiencies can cause general anemia, with symptoms that may include tiredness, fatigue, headaches, dizziness, inflammation of the lips, a red tongue, and spoon-like indentations in the fingernails. Overdosing on iron can cause constipation and prevent other minerals from being absorbed. Consume between 18–45 milligrams daily. A quick way to determine if you're iron deficient is to pull down your lower eyelid. If the color of the inner rim is pale pink or whitish, you may be anemic. If it's dark pink, you're not anemic.
- Vitamin C provides energy and boosts the absorption of iron.
- Pantothenic acid helps the body sidestep stress and promotes energy.
- Vitamin E is an antioxidant that can help prevent a chemical reaction called oxidation, which results in free radicals that contribute to aging, cancer, and many other diseases. Vitamin E is also essential for the proper functioning of nerves and muscles.

Special Iron Needs for Women

Most women lose around 35 milliliters of blood (about 2 tablespoons) during a four- to six-day menstrual cycle, which isn't enough to lead to fatigue or anemia. But if you start losing more than 80 milliliters, you could be at an increased risk for anemia, especially if you're a vegetarian who rarely or never eats meat, which is an excellent source of iron. If this sounds like you, talk to your physician. He can administer a blood test to determine if and how much you should supplement. In the meantime, eat more iron-rich foods, including nutrient-dense juice comprised of dark, leafy green vegetables.

Fruits and Vegetables That Provide Energy and Stamina

You can find all the vitamins and minerals to promote energy and stamina in a variety of fresh fruits and vegetables, so mix and match the following produce in your juices for an energy boost.

- Vitamin B complex is found in leafy greens, broccoli, and bananas.
- Vitamin B_{12} is found naturally only in animal products, but you can also find it in small amounts in tofu and tempeh.
- Folic acid (vitamin B_9) is abundant in asparagus, spinach, kale, cabbage, and blackberries.
- Biotin is found in chard, romaine lettuce, carrots, and tomatoes.
- Niacin (vitamin B_3) is abundant in brewer's yeast, rice and wheat bran, and peanuts.
- Riboflavin (vitamin B_2) is found in collard greens, kale, parsley, broccoli, beet greens, and prunes.
- Thiamine (vitamin B_1) is abundant in seeds, nuts, split peas, buckwheat sprouts, sunflower seeds, and garlic.
- Iron is abundant in beets with greens, carrots, apples, blackberries, parsley, broccoli, cauliflower, strawberries, asparagus, chard, cabbage, and pineapple.
- Vitamin C is provided by kale, parsley, broccoli, Brussels sprouts, watercress, cauliflower, citrus fruits, mangoes, papayas, asparagus, and strawberries.
- Pantothenic acid is found in broccoli, cauliflower, and kale.
- Vitamin E is found in tomatoes, carrots, asparagus, watercress, and spinach.

Best Produce for Stamina

1. Zucchini
2. Spinach
3. Kale
4. Collards
5. Carrots
6. Bananas
7. Berries
8. Sweet potatoes
9. Melons
10. Walnuts

Drinks for Energy and Stamina

Carrot Energy Booster

Carrots, spinach, and apples combine for a delightfully sweet and filling smoothie. They provide loads of important vitamins and minerals needed for optimal functioning of all those body systems designed to make you move and help you move faster.

INGREDIENTS | SERVES 3

1 cup chopped spinach

4 medium carrots, peeled

2 medium apples, peeled and cored

2 cups purified water

Carrots for Flushing an Athlete's Fat Stores

Among the many capabilities of carrots, one little-known ability is that they help with the liver's cleansing ability. Carrots aid the liver's cleansing process by keeping it squeaky clean and helping to more efficiently move excess bile and fat stores out of the body.

1. Place spinach, carrots, apples, and 1 cup water in a blender and blend until thoroughly combined.

2. Add remaining 1 cup water, as needed, while blending until desired consistency is achieved.

PER SERVING: Calories: 87 | Fat: 0 g | Protein: 1 g | Sodium: 64 mg | Fiber: 4 g | Carbohydrates: 22 g | Sugar: 15 g

Rapid Recovery Smoothie

Tasty and powerful, this recipe's ingredients provide powerful protein from intense vitamin- and mineral-rich veggies. The addition of the lemon and garlic benefits your body by promoting a healthy metabolic level for more efficient fat burning.

INGREDIENTS | SERVES 3

1 cup watercress

1 cup chopped broccoli

1 celery stalk

½ lemon, peeled

1 clove garlic

2 cups Greek-style yogurt

Yogurt for Rapid Recovery

You know protein delivers recovery aid to your muscles, but what is the best type to deliver maximum benefits and reap the most rewards? Chicken, beef, pork, and fish all come with saturated fats and aren't suitable for vegetarian athletes. If you're not interested in a protein shake of the powdered variety, turn to Greek-style yogurt. It has twice as much protein (20 grams), has lower carbs (9 grams or less), and half the sodium of regular yogurt.

1. Place watercress, broccoli, celery, lemon, garlic, and 1 cup yogurt in a blender and blend until thoroughly combined.

2. Add remaining 1 cup yogurt, as needed, while blending until desired consistency is achieved.

PER SERVING: Calories: 107 | Fat: 1 g | Protein: 17 g | Sodium: 80 mg | Fiber: 1 g | Carbohydrates: 9 g | Sugar: 6 g

Broccoli Blastoff

Broccoli and kale add a great dose of protein in this smoothie. If you're looking for even more protein, there are protein powders in a variety of flavors that would blend nicely with savory smoothies such as this.

INGREDIENTS | SERVES 3

2 kale leaves

1 cup chopped broccoli

½ red bell pepper, seeded and membranes removed

2 celery stalks

1 green onion

1–2 cloves garlic, depending on size

2 cups purified water

1. Place kale, broccoli, pepper, celery, onion, garlic, and 1 cup water in a blender and blend until thoroughly combined.

2. Add remaining 1 cup water, as needed, while blending until desired consistency is achieved.

PER SERVING: Calories: 45 | Fat: 1 g | Protein: 3 g | Sodium: 50 mg | Fiber: 2 g | Carbohydrates: 8 g | Sugar: 2 g

Zucchini Smoothie

The vibrant veggies and cayenne pepper in this recipe make a fat-burning, calorie-zapping smoothie that will fill you up and fire your engines!

INGREDIENTS | SERVES 3

1 cup chopped spinach

1 zucchini

1 medium tomato

2 celery stalks

1 green onion

2 cloves garlic

⅛ teaspoon cayenne pepper

2 cups purified water

1. Place spinach, zucchini, tomato, celery, onion, garlic, cayenne, and 1 cup water in a blender and blend until thoroughly combined.

2. Add remaining 1 cup water, as needed, while blending until desired consistency is achieved.

PER SERVING: Calories: 29 | Fat: 0 g | Protein: 2 g | Sodium: 37 mg | Fiber: 2 g | Carbohydrates: 6 g | Sugar: 3 g

Sweet Spinach Spinner

This sweet spin on vitamin-rich spinach makes a delightful treat you can enjoy before or after an exercise session. The low glycemic index of the ingredients makes a sustainable energy-powering blend of vitamins, minerals, and phytochemicals that will help you perform without the energy crash of caffeinated energy drinks.

INGREDIENTS | SERVES 3

1 cup chopped spinach

4 medium apples, peeled and cored

¼" ginger, peeled

2 cups purified water

1. Place spinach, apples, ginger, and 1 cup water in a blender and blend until thoroughly combined.

2. Add remaining 1 cup water, as needed, while blending until desired consistency is achieved.

PER SERVING: Calories: 106 | Fat: 0 g | Protein: 1 g | Sodium: 8 mg | Fiber: 3 g | Carbohydrates: 28 g | Sugar: 22 g

Powerful Parsnip Smoothie

Packed with vitamin C, parsnips are a tasty ingredient in this surprisingly sweet smoothie. Packed with important minerals for energy and stamina, root veggies are a great way to maximize your smoothie's potency potential.

INGREDIENTS | SERVES 3

1 cup watercress

1 parsnip, peeled

3 medium carrots, peeled

2 cups purified water

1. Place watercress, parsnip, carrots, and 1 cup water in a blender and blend until thoroughly combined.

2. Add remaining 1 cup water, as needed, while blending until desired consistency is achieved.

PER SERVING: Calories: 47 | Fat: 0 g | Protein: 1 g | Sodium: 50 mg | Fiber: 3 g | Carbohydrates: 11 g | Sugar: 4 g

Killer Kale Kickoff

Packed with an abundance of vitamin K, a fat-soluble compound, kale is a healthy way to get your daily recommended amount of vitamin K in a one-stop shop.

INGREDIENTS | SERVES 3

2 kale leaves
4 medium carrots, peeled
1 medium cucumber, peeled
2 green onions
2 cloves garlic
2 cups purified water

1. Place kale, carrots, cucumber, onions, garlic, and 1 cup water in a blender and blend until thoroughly combined.

2. Add remaining 1 cup water, as needed, while blending until desired consistency is achieved.

PER SERVING: Calories: 68 | Fat: 1 g | Protein: 3 g | Sodium: 76 mg | Fiber: 3 g | Carbohydrates: 14 g | Sugar: 5 g

Collide with Collards

Refreshing and nutritious, this blend delivers powerful vitamins and minerals that work as hard as you do. To fuel your body's powerful energy requirements and replenish your muscle's stores, green veggies are your best bet for complete balanced nutrition!

INGREDIENTS | SERVES 3

1 cup collards
1 cup cauliflower florets
1 cup chopped broccoli
1 medium carrot, peeled
2 cups purified water

1. Place collards, cauliflower, broccoli, carrot, and 1 cup water in a blender and blend until thoroughly combined.

2. Add remaining 1 cup water, as needed, while blending until desired consistency is achieved.

PER SERVING: Calories: 31 | Fat: 0 g | Protein: 2 g | Sodium: 36 mg | Fiber: 3 g | Carbohydrates: 6 g | Sugar: 2 g

Protein-Packer Blend

The creamy combination of sweet fruits and almonds blends beautifully with the crisp watercress for a protein-packed delight you're sure to enjoy after a strenuous workout.

INGREDIENTS | SERVES 3

¼ cup almonds

¾ cup purified water

1 cup watercress

1 medium apple, peeled and cored

1 banana, peeled

1 cup Greek-style yogurt

What Is Watercress?

This leafy green veggie is packed with vitamin C, calcium, and potassium, all important vitamins for maintaining a healthy immune system and providing structural support for the bones. But that's not all. Its acid-forming minerals cleanse and normalize the intestines while the chlorophyll stimulates the metabolism and the circulatory system.

1. Combine almonds and water in a blender and emulsify until no almond bits remain.

2. Add watercress, apple, banana, and ½ cup yogurt and blend until thoroughly combined with almond milk.

3. Add remaining ½ cup yogurt, as needed, while blending until desired consistency is achieved.

PER SERVING: Calories: 175 | Fat: 6 g | Protein: 11 g | Sodium: 32 mg | Fiber: 3 g | Carbohydrates: 21 g | Sugar: 13 g

Popeye's Favorite

Popeye had the right idea. This recipe is filled with iron, vitamin K, folate, and fiber and will have you feeling strong and powerful.

INGREDIENTS | SERVES 3

1 cup chopped spinach

1 kale leaf

1 cup chopped broccoli

3 medium apples, peeled and cored

2 cups purified water

Greens for All

When you were a kid, Popeye is one amazing example of what could happen if you ate your spinach! How many times did your parents reference Popeye when trying to get you to eat your spinach? And how often do you reference strength when trying to get your kids to eat greens now? Spinach is packed with vitamins A, B, C, E, and K as well as iron, phosphorous, and fiber. With all of that nutrition delivered in each serving, spinach should be in every athlete's daily diet . . . for strength like Popeye's!

1. Place spinach, kale, broccoli, apples, and 1 cup water in a blender and blend until thoroughly combined.

2. Add remaining 1 cup water, as needed, while blending until desired consistency is achieved.

PER SERVING: Calories: 101 | Fat: 1 g | Protein: 3 g | Sodium: 26 mg | Fiber: 3 g | Carbohydrates: 25 g | Sugar: 17 g

Metabolism Max Out

Vitamin C plays an important part in fighting illness, promoting your body's ability to function properly in every aspect, and optimizing metabolism for a fat-burning effect like no other.

INGREDIENTS | SERVES 3

1 cup watercress

2 cups pineapple chunks

1 medium white grapefruit, peeled and seeded

3 medium tangerines, peeled

1 lemon, peeled

1 cup green tea

1. Place watercress, pineapple, grapefruit, tangerines, lemon, and ½ cup tea in a blender and blend until thoroughly combined.

2. Add remaining ½ cup tea, as needed, while blending until desired consistency is achieved.

PER SERVING: Calories: 136 | Fat: 1 g | Protein: 2 g | Sodium: 8 mg | Fiber: 5 g | Carbohydrates: 35 g | Sugar: 27 g

Banana Berry Boost

You can't beat the taste of smooth bananas and sweet berries blended with creamy yogurt. There's no better follow-up to a satisfying workout than a dose of sweet fruits blended with powerful protein to optimize your muscles' recovery.

INGREDIENTS | SERVES 3

1 cup watercress

2 bananas, peeled

2 cups goji berries

1 cup Greek-style yogurt

1. Place watercress, bananas, goji berries, and ½ cup yogurt in a blender and blend until thoroughly combined.

2. Add remaining ½ cup yogurt, as needed, while blending until desired consistency is achieved.

PER SERVING: Calories: 369 | Fat: 1 g | Protein: 19 g | Sodium: 233 mg | Fiber: 13 g | Carbohydrates: 85 g | Sugar: 44 g

The Goji Berry

Goji berries provide excellent benefits for everything from cancer prevention to eye health. Although research has shown the nutrients and phytochemicals in berries are responsible for preventing serious illnesses and diseases, the goji berry's specific effects are still under review.

Vivacious Vitamin C

Eating a balanced diet of vibrant fruits, vegetables, and leafy greens can ensure you're working toward better health and athletic ability.

INGREDIENTS | SERVES 3

1 cup watercress

½ pineapple, peeled, cored, and cut into chunks

3 medium oranges, peeled

1 lemon, peeled

1 cup strawberries, tops removed

1 cup purified water

Vitamins and Minerals for Proactive Health

How important is vitamin C to an athlete? When was the last time you saw a top-performing athlete take first place hacking and heaving all the way to the finish line? Never! If you're going to keep your body in top shape, sound nutrition isn't the only thing requiring attention. In order to get the biggest bang for your buck out of performance nutrition, load up on vibrant fruits and veggies that do double duty.

1. Place watercress, pineapple, oranges, lemon, strawberries, and ½ cup water in a blender and blend until thoroughly combined.

2. Add remaining ½ cup water, as needed, while blending until desired consistency is achieved.

PER SERVING: Calories: 156 | Fat: 1 g | Protein: 3 g | Sodium: 7 mg | Fiber: 7 g | Carbohydrates: 40 g | Sugar: 29 g

Sweet Potato Smoothie

Even though being an avid athlete means focusing on the healthiest foods that provide ideal nutrition calorie for calorie, cravings for sweet treats creep up every once in a while. Calm those cravings with combinations like this that satisfy with sound nutrition!

INGREDIENTS | SERVES 3

½ cup walnuts

2 cups purified water

1 cup chopped spinach

1 sweet potato, peeled and chopped

1 teaspoon pumpkin pie spice

Walnuts for Athletic Performance

In just ¼ cup of walnuts, you can find almost 100 percent of your daily value of omega 3s with the richness of monounsaturated fats. Not only are walnuts a tasty snack, but they also help athletes perform at their best by improving circulation and heart health, controlling blood pressure, providing essential amino acids, and acting as a powerful antioxidant.

1. Combine walnuts and 1 cup water in a blender and blend until emulsified and no walnut bits remain.

2. Add spinach, sweet potato, pumpkin pie spice, and remaining 1 cup water while blending until desired consistency is achieved.

PER SERVING: Calories: 139 | Fat: 11 g | Protein: 3 g | Sodium: 25 mg | Fiber: 2 g | Carbohydrates: 9 g | Sugar: 2 g

Cacao Craziness

Chocolate cravings can end in guilty consumption of sugar- and fat-laden candy. Satisfy those cravings with pure cacao in a smoothie like this, and candy cravings will be a thing of the past.

INGREDIENTS | SERVES 3

¼ cup almonds

2 cups purified water

1 cup watercress

2 tablespoons powdered natural cacao

2 bananas, peeled

2 medium apples, peeled and cored

Sweet Antioxidant Protection

When you are looking for powerful antioxidants, reach no further than a heaping helping of raw cacao. Protect your body and the hard work you've put into making it an efficient machine by adding raw cacao in sweet or savory smoothies for an extra bit of health.

1. Combine almonds and 1 cup water in a blender and emulsify until no almond bits remain.

2. Add watercress, cacao, bananas, apples, and remaining 1 cup water while blending until desired consistency is achieved.

PER SERVING: Calories: 202 | Fat: 7 g | Protein: 5 g | Sodium: 7 mg | Fiber: 7 g | Carbohydrates: 37 g | Sugar: 21 g

Runner's Delight

Any endurance runner feels amped before and pumped following a run. After all that hard work, you're definitely entitled to enjoy a sweet treat. Instead of undoing all that hard work with empty calories, indulge in the sweet taste of citrus.

INGREDIENTS | SERVES 3

1 cup watercress
3 medium oranges, peeled
1 cup strawberries, tops removed
1 cup raspberries
1 cup Greek-style yogurt

1. Place watercress, oranges, berries, and ½ cup yogurt in a blender and blend until thoroughly combined.

2. Add remaining ½ cup yogurt, as needed, while blending until desired consistency is achieved.

PER SERVING: Calories: 147 | Fat: 1 g | Protein: 10 g | Sodium: 33 mg | Fiber: 7 g | Carbohydrates: 28 g | Sugar: 20 g

A Biker's Best Friend

Nothing keeps sustained energy up like slow-releasing carbohydrates. Root vegetables are the best friend of any distance cyclist on a mission for better times and better health.

INGREDIENTS | SERVES 3

1 cup chopped spinach
2 medium yams, peeled and chopped
2 medium apples, peeled and cored
2 medium carrots, peeled
2 cups purified water

1. Place spinach, yams, apples, carrots, and 1 cup water in a blender and blend until thoroughly combined.

2. Add remaining 1 cup water, as needed, while blending until desired consistency is achieved.

PER SERVING: Calories: 149 | Fat: 0 g | Protein: 2 g | Sodium: 42 mg | Fiber: 5 g | Carbohydrates: 37 g | Sugar: 13 g

Dehydration Fighter

No matter what type of workout you perform, you can come out feeling dehydrated and in need of a boost of energy. A refreshing combination of pineapple, lemon, and cooling cucumbers can deliver exactly what your mind and body need.

INGREDIENTS | SERVES 3

1 cup chopped iceberg lettuce

2 cups pineapple chunks

2 medium cucumbers, peeled

½ lemon, peeled

1 cup Greek-style yogurt

1. Place iceberg, pineapple, cucumbers, lemon, and ½ cup yogurt in a blender and blend until thoroughly combined.

2. Add remaining ½ cup yogurt, as needed, while blending until desired consistency is achieved.

PER SERVING: Calories: 121 | Fat: 1 g | Protein: 9 g | Sodium: 33 mg | Fiber: 3 g | Carbohydrates: 21 g | Sugar: 16 g

A Yogi's Favorite Smoothie

Hot or not, yoga can be a powerful workout. Replenish your body and refresh your senses with this sweet blend of melon, citrus, and veggies. A definite "Yum!" to follow your "Om!"

INGREDIENTS | SERVES 3

1 cup watercress

½ honeydew, rind and seeds removed

2 medium tangerines, peeled

1 medium cucumber, peeled

1 cup Greek-style yogurt

1. Place watercress, honeydew, tangerines, cucumber, and ½ cup yogurt in a blender and blend until thoroughly combined.

2. Add remaining ½ cup yogurt, as needed, while blending until desired consistency is achieved.

PER SERVING: Calories: 145 | Fat: 1 g | Protein: 10 g | Sodium: 64 mg | Fiber: 3 g | Carbohydrates: 27 g | Sugar: 23 g

Oh, My! Omegas

With this tasty recipe, you'll get plenty of omega-3s without the need for salmon or rich meats. If salmon isn't your favorite food, consider smoothies that contain flax for your daily value of omegas.

INGREDIENTS | SERVES 3

1 cup watercress

½ cantaloupe, rind and seeds removed, cut into chunks

1 banana, peeled

1 medium orange, peeled

1 cup raspberries

1 tablespoon flaxseeds

2 cups purified water

1. Place watercress, cantaloupe, banana, orange, raspberries, flaxseeds, and 1 cup water in a blender and blend until thoroughly combined.

2. Add remaining 1 cup water, as needed, while blending until desired consistency is achieved.

PER SERVING: Calories: 129 | Fat: 2 g | Protein: 3 g | Sodium: 21 mg | Fiber: 7 g | Carbohydrates: 28 g | Sugar: 18 g

Flaxseeds for Omega-3s!

Everybody needs omegas. Although many athletes include meats in their diets, some vegetarian and vegan athletes need to turn to alternatives to fulfill their omega needs. Flaxseeds provide amazing amounts of omega-3s that are comparable to rich meats and fish (which are also high in undesirable fat content). Flaxseeds make a mildly nutty addition to your favorite smoothie blends.

Fabulous Fructose

The combination of citrus fruits in this smoothie will give you the nutrients you need after a great workout.

INGREDIENTS | SERVES 3

1 cup chopped romaine lettuce

½ pineapple, peeled and cored

½ medium red grapefruit, peeled and seeded

1 medium tangerine, peeled

½ lemon, peeled

½ lime, peeled

1 cup purified water

1. Place romaine, pineapple, grapefruit, tangerine, lemon, lime, and ½ cup water in a blender and blend until thoroughly combined.

2. Add remaining ½ cup water, as needed, while blending until desired consistency is achieved.

PER SERVING: Calories: 107 | Fat: 0 g | Protein: 2 g | Sodium: 4 mg | Fiber: 4 g | Carbohydrates: 28 g | Sugar: 20 g

Fructose: The Smart Sugar

Fructose, the natural sugar found in fruit, is the healthiest version of sugar because it's an all-natural, nonprocessed version of the table sugars and artificial sweeteners commonly used. As an athlete, fruit is important for its vitamins and minerals and because it can satisfy your cravings for sweets without the unhealthy crash associated with processed sugar or the possible health risks associated with artificial sweeteners.

CHAPTER 9

Drinks for Digestive Health

Your digestive tract is a twenty-five- to thirty-five-foot-long engineering marvel. On the most basic level, it takes the food that your teeth have chopped up, breaks it down, separates the good from the bad, and extracts the essential nutrients to be delivered to the body. But, if just one component of your digestive system malfunctions or is compromised in any way, it can lead to major problems. Fortunately, the fiber in the homemade green drinks detailed in this book adds bulk to your stools and sweeps away harmful toxins. The water helps lubricate the digestive tract, while the many healthful nutrients in each of the ingredients promote digestive health.

Best Nutrients for Tummy Health

To aid digestion, begin by making small changes in your diet. Enzymes are a helpful way to start. You can find formula enzymes at health food stores and in your own freshly made green drinks just by including nutrient-rich foods like papaya, pineapple, pear, apple, carrot, kale, mustard greens, and dandelion greens, all of which help promote the healthy flow of your natural digestive enzymes.

These natural nutrients also cleanse the intestine:

- Aloe vera. You can find aloe vera drops in the health food store. Diluting four ounces of aloe vera drops in juices daily can help eliminate bleeding ulcers and promote healing.
- Beta-carotene. It's found in many fruits and vegetables, including watercress, cruciferous veggies, beet greens, carrots, romaine lettuce, and spinach.
- Acidophilus. This is a general name for a group of probiotics that promote digestion. You can find them in capsule form at your local health food store.
- Rosehips. These are found in rosehip tea and in your health food store or natural supermarket.

In addition, the fiber in produce aids digestion by adding fiber bulk to foods that keep waste moving in the intestine, preventing the toxic buildup that can lead to digestive problems. Don't forget that water is one of the most helpful aids to digestion. Drinking eight to ten glasses of water each day keeps the body hydrated and aids digestion in the intestinal tract. Aerobic exercise and stretching each day also contribute to healthier digestion, keeping your muscles and organs in good shape and keeping things moving.

Benefits of Food Combining

Some nutrition experts believe that following the principles of food combining can also help prevent digestive disorders. According to Paul Pitchford, author of *Healing with Whole Foods*, if you consume combinations of certain foods at the same time, you can avoid putting excess stress on the digestive system. The reason is that different foods require different enzymes to be broken down. Although food combining is not recommended by most mainstream nutritionists or the American Dietetic Society, it is a dietetic movement gaining approval, and you may find the principles extraordinarily helpful.

- Green and nonstarchy vegetables can be combined with protein and healthy starches or fats. These include leafy greens, cauliflower, broccoli, sprouts, celery, cucumber, onion, garlic, green beans, peas, seaweed, and fresh corn.
- Proteins can be combined with green and nonstarchy vegetables easily. These options includes beans, legumes, tofu, tempeh, nuts, seeds, cheese, yogurt, eggs, fish, meat, and fowl.
- Starches can be combined with green and nonstarchy vegetables and fats and oils. Healthy options include whole grains, rice, bread, pasta, potatoes, sweet potatoes, beets, parsnips, carrots, and squash.
- Fats and oils can be combined with green and nonstarchy vegetables, complex starches, and acidic fruits. This group includes avocados, olives, natural butters, natural creams, and minimally processed organic oils.
- Sweet fruit can be combined with sub-acid fruit, including figs, bananas, dates, and dried fruit.
- Acidic fruits can be combined with fats and oils and sub-acid fruits, which include lemon, lime, grapefruit, oranges, tomatoes, strawberries, pineapple, and kiwi.
- Sub-acidic fruits can be combined with acidic fruits or sweet fruits, including apples, berries, pears, apricots, peaches, grapes, plums, cherries, mangoes, and papayas.

Why Green Drinks Aid in Healthy Digestion

Research shows that diets high in fiber and complex carbohydrates, which are found in abundance in fruits' and vegetables' fibrous material (and are low in manufactured and refined foods), have been shown to reduce many digestive disorders, including indigestion, ulcers, low stomach acid, constipation, diarrhea, motion sickness, colitis, diverticulitis, and diverticulosis.

Tips for Increasing Your Fiber

The American College of Gastroenterology recommends consuming at least 20 to 25 grams of fiber daily, which is much higher than the 10 to 15 grams, or lower, that the average American consumes. An easy way to increase your fiber intake is to consume a healthier proportion of high-fiber fruits and vegetables in your green drinks.

The fruits and vegetables highest in fiber include:

- Apples, pears (with skin)
- Beans
- Berries (blackberries, blueberries, raspberries)
- Broccoli
- Chickpeas
- Dates
- Figs
- Lentils
- Parsnips
- Peas
- Prunes
- Pumpkin
- Rutabaga
- Winter squash

Other foods that will add a boost of fiber to your homemade juice include wheat bran, psyllium, sunflower seeds, hemp, oat bran, coconut, almonds, Brazil nuts, peanuts, pecans, walnuts, brown rice, and pumpkin and sunflower seeds.

Best Produce for Digestive Health

1. Spinach
2. Kale
3. Citrus fruits
4. Mangoes
5. Papaya
6. Apples
7. Carrots
8. Ginger
9. Melons
10. Cabbage

Drinks for Digestive Health

Indigestion Inhibitor

Digestion discomfort can be painful, and the resulting gassy symptoms can be downright embarrassing. This delightful blend of sweet fruits and veggies combines with chamomile tea for a wonderful soothing effect on indigestion.

INGREDIENTS | SERVES 3

1 cup watercress
1 medium carrot, peeled
1 medium apple, peeled and cored
1 medium pear, peeled and cored
¼" ginger, peeled
2 cups chamomile tea

1. Place watercress, carrot, apple, pear, ginger, and 1 cup tea in a blender and blend until thoroughly combined.

2. Add remaining 1 cup tea, as needed, while blending until desired consistency is achieved.

PER SERVING: Calories: 71 | Fat: 0 g | Protein: 1 g | Sodium: 21 mg | Fiber: 3 g | Carbohydrates: 18 g | Sugar: 12 g

Why Fruits and Vegetables Aid Digestion

Research shows that diets high in fiber and complex carbohydrates, both found in fruits and vegetables, promote healthy digestive systems and can reduce many digestive disorders. Indigestion, ulcers, low stomach acid, constipation, diarrhea, motion sickness, colitis, and many more can be relieved or reversed with the power of produce.

Perfect Pears and Pineapples

The amazing flavors of pineapples and pears are enhanced by the addition of lemon in this recipe. With vitamins and minerals that aid in digestion and prevent discomfort, this is a perfect blend for any indigestion sufferer.

INGREDIENTS | SERVES 3

1 cup chopped romaine lettuce

2 cups pineapple chunks

2 medium pears, peeled and cored

1 lemon, peeled

2 cups chamomile tea

1. Place romaine, pineapple, pears, lemon, and 1 cup tea in a blender and blend until thoroughly combined.

2. Add remaining 1 cup tea, as needed, while blending until desired consistency is achieved.

PER SERVING: Calories: 132 | Fat: 0 g | Protein: 1 g | Sodium: 6 mg | Fiber: 6 g | Carbohydrates: 35 g | Sugar: 23 g

Amazing Apples for Digestion

Apples star in this delightful recipe because of their high fiber content. With the added benefits from pineapple's vitamin C stores, this combination of deep greens, vibrant fruits, and chamomile tea will make your digestive system perform at its peak.

INGREDIENTS | SERVES 3

1 cup watercress

3 medium apples, peeled and cored

1 cup pineapple chunks

¼" ginger, peeled

2 cups chamomile tea

1. Place watercress, apples, pineapple, ginger, and 1 cup tea in a blender and blend until thoroughly combined.

2. Add remaining 1 cup tea, as needed, while blending until desired consistency is achieved.

PER SERVING: Calories: 108 | Fat: 0 g | Protein: 1 g | Sodium: 7 mg | Fiber: 3 g | Carbohydrates: 28 g | Sugar: 22 g

Dreamy Digestion

On the uncomfortable nights that indigestion creeps up, turn to your blender for quick relief. This sweet fruit and veggie combination provides indigestion relief you can enjoy as dessert or right when the burn hits!

INGREDIENTS | SERVES 3

1 cup chopped romaine lettuce
2 medium apples, cored and peeled
2 medium carrots, peeled
1 medium cucumber, peeled
½ lemon, peeled
2 cups chamomile tea

A Recipe for Sweet Dreams

Indigestion can strike at any time of day, but can be especially uncomfortable at night and can lead to interrupted sleep and moodiness. Taking a two-step approach to relieving your indigestion may help: 1) Use fruit and vegetable combinations shown to regulate stomach acid and promote more alkaline levels of the digestive tract, and 2) drink chamomile tea before bed. Chamomile tea has been shown to aid in indigestion by soothing the esophageal muscles and those of the large and small intestine.

1. Place romaine, apples, carrots, cucumber, lemon, and 1 cup tea in a blender and blend until thoroughly combined.

2. Add remaining 1 cup tea, as needed, while blending until desired consistency is achieved.

PER SERVING: Calories: 83 | Fat: 0 g | Protein: 1 g | Sodium: 32 mg | Fiber: 4 g | Carbohydrates: 21 g | Sugar: 14 g

Pineapple-Papaya Protection

Although romaine lettuce is an important ingredient, its taste is almost completely masked by the flavorful fruit combination in this recipe. This recipe not only protects the stomach lining, but it is also an amazing treat to be enjoyed whenever the craving for fruit strikes!

INGREDIENTS | SERVES 3

1 cup chopped romaine lettuce

2 cups pineapple chunks

2 cups papaya chunks

½ lemon, peeled

¼" ginger, peeled

2 cups chamomile tea

1. Place romaine, pineapple, papaya, lemon, ginger, and 1 cup tea in a blender and blend until thoroughly combined.

2. Add remaining 1 cup tea, as needed, while blending until desired consistency is achieved.

PER SERVING: Calories: 103 | Fat: 0 g | Protein: 1 g | Sodium: 12 mg | Fiber: 4 g | Carbohydrates: 26 g | Sugar: 19 g

Cucumber Cooler

The refreshing combination of sweet citrus, crisp greens, ginger, and cooling cucumbers will perk you up while soothing your tummy. Indigestion stands no chance against the chilling effects of this cool combo.

INGREDIENTS | SERVES 3

1 cup watercress

1 medium pink grapefruit, peeled and seeded

1 medium orange, peeled

2 medium cucumbers, peeled

¼" ginger, peeled

2 cups chamomile tea

1. Place watercress, grapefruit, orange, cucumbers, ginger, and 1 cup tea in a blender and blend until thoroughly combined.

2. Add remaining 1 cup tea, as needed, while blending until desired consistency is achieved.

PER SERVING: Calories: 68 | Fat: 0 g | Protein: 2 g | Sodium: 9 mg | Fiber: 3 g | Carbohydrates: 16 g | Sugar: 12 g

Ginger Ale Smoothie

Ginger ale is the most common remedy for any type of stomach ailment. This natural version of ginger ale provides all of the powerful nutrition without the sometimes uncomfortable and problematic carbonation.

INGREDIENTS | SERVES 3

1 cup watercress
4 medium apples, peeled and cored
¼" ginger, peeled
2 cups chamomile tea

1. Place watercress, apples, ginger, and 1 cup tea in a blender and blend until thoroughly combined.

2. Add remaining 1 cup tea, as needed, while blending until desired consistency is achieved.

PER SERVING: Calories: 106 | Fat: 0 g | Protein: 1 g | Sodium: 6 mg | Fiber: 3 g | Carbohydrates: 28 g | Sugar: 22 g

Smooth Citrus for Smooth Digestion

A delicious remedy for stomach discomfort, this banana blend is a much sweeter and more nutritious alternative to the over-the-counter antacid.

INGREDIENTS | SERVES 3

1 cup watercress
2 cups pineapple chunks
1 medium peach, pitted and peeled
1 medium orange, peeled
2 bananas, peeled
2 cups chamomile tea

1. Place watercress, pineapple, peach, orange, bananas, and 1 cup tea in a blender and blend until thoroughly combined.

2. Add remaining 1 cup tea, as needed, while blending until desired consistency is achieved.

PER SERVING: Calories: 169 | Fat: 1 g | Protein: 2 g | Sodium: 8 mg | Fiber: 6 g | Carbohydrates: 43 g | Sugar: 29 g

Sweet Fiber

Apricots, apples, and banana blend with sweet romaine for a delicious fiber-rich treat that will promote optimal digestion. Deep greens like romaine lettuce can minimize uncomfortable symptoms of indigestion.

INGREDIENTS | SERVES 3

1 cup chopped romaine lettuce

4 apricots, peeled

2 medium apples, peeled and cored

1 banana, peeled

2 cups chamomile tea

Fabulous Fiber

Fiber is absolutely necessary for an efficient digestive system free of toxins, waste, and buildup that may have accrued over the years. Stock up on fiber-rich foods and blend them in delicious smoothies. Not only does blending the fiber-packed fruits and veggies make delicious meal and snack options, but blending them also breaks down the indigestible fiber for the best possible absorption.

1. Place romaine, apricots, apples, banana, and 1 cup tea in a blender and blend until thoroughly combined.

2. Add remaining 1 cup tea, as needed, while blending until desired consistency is achieved.

PER SERVING: Calories: 113 | Fat: 0 g | Protein: 2 g | Sodium: 4 mg | Fiber: 4 g | Carbohydrates: 29 g | Sugar: 20 g

Pears, Apples, and Ginger Drink

There's not much that can compare to the sweet combination of pears, apples, and ginger. This scrumptious blend comforts your stomach with balanced nutrition.

INGREDIENTS | SERVES 3

1 cup watercress
3 medium apples, peeled and cored
3 medium pears, peeled and cored
¼" ginger, peeled
2 cups chamomile tea

1. Place watercress, apples, pears, ginger, and 1 cup tea in a blender and blend until thoroughly combined.

2. Add remaining 1 cup tea, as needed, while blending until desired consistency is achieved.

PER SERVING: Calories: 182 | Fat: 0 g | Protein: 1 g | Sodium: 8 mg | Fiber: 8 g | Carbohydrates: 48 g | Sugar: 34 g

Fiber Effects

Since fiber promotes a more optimal functioning digestive tract, why not enjoy a green smoothie that has a whopping amount of fiber from greens, pears, and apples? This smoothie can get your digestive system working at its full potential in no time.

Move Over, Motion Sickness!

Cabbage is a little-known combatant of motion sickness. Blending the green leafy veggie with bananas, apples, and ginger makes this smoothie both sweet and spicy.

INGREDIENTS | SERVES 3

1 cup chopped cabbage
3 bananas, peeled
2 medium apples, cored and peeled
¼" ginger, peeled
2 cups chamomile tea

1. Place cabbage, bananas, apples, ginger, and 1 cup tea in a blender and blend until thoroughly combined.

2. Add remaining 1 cup tea, as needed, while blending until desired consistency is achieved.

PER SERVING: Calories: 166 | Fat: 1 g | Protein: 2 g | Sodium: 8 mg | Fiber: 5 g | Carbohydrates: 43 g | Sugar: 26 g

Heartburn, Be Gone

This smoothie combines flavorful veggies that will soothe your esophagus and relieve the pain associated with acid indigestion.

INGREDIENTS | SERVES 3

1 cup chopped spinach

2 medium tomatoes

3 celery stalks, leaves intact

1½ cups chamomile tea

Lifestyle Changes for Heartburn Relief

Many people find themselves popping antacids and heartburn relievers numerous times throughout the day just to make the discomfort of acid reflux subside. A great way to combat this debilitating condition is to change your diet to include a wide variety of fruits and vegetables while cutting out caffeine, cigarettes, alcohol, fatty and acidic foods, and carbonation.

1. Place spinach, tomatoes, celery, and ¾ cup tea in a blender and blend until thoroughly combined.

2. Add remaining ¾ cup tea, as needed, while blending until desired consistency is achieved.

PER SERVING: Calories: 25 | Fat: 0 g | Protein: 1 g | Sodium: 45 mg | Fiber: 2 g | Carbohydrates: 5 g | Sugar: 3 g

Spicy Stomach-Soother Smoothie

Spicy arugula and crisp veggies offer a savory taste combination that will soothe your stomach while calming cravings for harsh spicy foods that could aggravate digestion and lead to discomfort.

INGREDIENTS | SERVES 3

1 cup arugula

1 medium green onion

3 celery stalks

1 clove garlic (optional)

2 cups chamomile tea

1. Place arugula, onion, celery, garlic, and 1 cup tea in a blender and blend until thoroughly combined.

2. Add remaining 1 cup tea, as needed, while blending until desired consistency is achieved.

PER SERVING: Calories: 12 | Fat: 0 g | Protein: 1 g | Sodium: 36 mg | Fiber: 1 g | Carbohydrates: 2 g | Sugar: 1 g

Goodbye Gas

Gas is possibly one of the most embarrassing symptoms associated with indigestion and digestive disorders. This smoothie has a combination of gas-fighting foods to get your digestive tract in line.

INGREDIENTS | SERVES 3

1 cup chopped spinach

2 medium carrots, peeled

3 celery stalks, leaves intact

¾ cup petite sweet peas

2 cups chamomile tea

1. Place spinach, carrots, celery, peas, and 1 cup tea in a blender and blend until thoroughly combined.

2. Add remaining 1 cup tea, as needed, while blending until desired consistency is achieved.

PER SERVING: Calories: 46 | Fat: 0 g | Protein: 2 g | Sodium: 122 mg | Fiber: 3 g | Carbohydrates: 10 g | Sugar: 5 g

Tummy Protector

A great way to coat your sensitive stomach against harmful acid is with delicious vegetables like these. Romaine, celery, green onion, tomatoes, and mild chamomile tea deliver protection in every sip.

INGREDIENTS | SERVES 3

1 cup chopped romaine lettuce

3 celery stalks, leaves intact

1 medium green onion

2 tomatoes

2 cups chamomile tea

1. Place romaine, celery, onion, tomatoes, and 1 cup tea in a blender and blend until thoroughly combined.

2. Add remaining 1 cup tea, as needed, while blending until desired consistency is achieved.

PER SERVING: Calories: 26 | Fat: 0 g | Protein: 1 g | Sodium: 40 mg | Fiber: 2 g | Carbohydrates: 5 g | Sugar: 3 g

Red Pepper Relief

Rich in beta-carotene, a powerful antioxidant, red pepper acts to protect your digestive tract from dangerous cancers while also providing your body with rich vitamins and minerals.

INGREDIENTS | SERVES 3

1 cup chopped romaine lettuce

1 red bell pepper, top and seeds removed, ribs intact

2 celery stalks, leaves intact

½ lemon, peeled

1½ cups chamomile tea

1. Place romaine, red pepper, celery, lemon, and ¾ cup tea in a blender and blend until thoroughly combined.

2. Add remaining ¾ cup tea, as needed, while blending until desired consistency is achieved.

PER SERVING: Calories: 23 | Fat: 0 g | Protein: 1 g | Sodium: 26 mg | Fiber: 2 g | Carbohydrates: 5 g | Sugar: 3 g

Keep It Moving

Wonderfully light and delicious, this is a smoothie that will not only taste great, but also relieve constipation and alleviate the uncomfortable symptoms that result!

INGREDIENTS | SERVES 3

1 cup chopped spinach
2 medium zucchini, peeled
3 celery stalks, leaves intact
2 cups chamomile tea

Produce for Constipation Relief

Constipation can really slow you down. The irritating condition can make you feel lethargic, uncomfortable, and irritable. Stay regular by including the recommended 5 servings of fruits and veggies daily. All of this produce contains lots of fiber, which relieves constipation.

1. Place spinach, zucchini, celery, and 1 cup tea in a blender and blend until thoroughly combined.

2. Add remaining 1 cup tea, as needed, while blending until desired consistency is achieved.

PER SERVING: Calories: 32 | Fat: 1 g | Protein: 2 g | Sodium: 52 mg | Fiber: 2 g | Carbohydrates: 6 g | Sugar: 4 g

Cabbage Calms Indigestion

This delightful combination of cabbage and cruciferous veggies provides your body with rich vitamins and minerals. It aids in digestion with vitamin K and carotenes, which act as anti-inflammatory agents.

INGREDIENTS | SERVES 3

1 cup shredded cabbage
1 cup chopped broccoli
1 cup cauliflower florets
1 clove garlic (optional)
2 cups chamomile tea

1. Place cabbage, broccoli, cauliflower, garlic, and 1 cup tea in a blender and blend until thoroughly combined.

2. Add remaining 1 cup tea, as needed, while blending until desired consistency is achieved.

PER SERVING: Calories: 29 | Fat: 0 g | Protein: 2 g | Sodium: 27 mg | Fiber: 2 g | Carbohydrates: 6 g | Sugar: 2 g

Mega Magnesium Blend

With powerful minerals, especially magnesium, the veggies in this recipe promote easier digestion along with overall health for your body and mind.

INGREDIENTS | SERVES 3

1 cup shredded cabbage

1 cup chopped broccoli

1 cup cauliflower florets

2 celery stalks, leaves intact

2 cups chamomile tea

Magnesium Benefits

This powerful mineral is responsible for the proper functioning of our muscles and nerves, so it is very important to men and women of any age and any lifestyle. Magnesium deficiencies can lead to debilitating conditions like diabetes, hypertension, osteoporosis, and irritable bowel syndrome.

1. Place cabbage, broccoli, cauliflower, celery, and 1 cup tea in a blender and blend until thoroughly combined.

2. Add remaining 1 cup tea, as needed, while blending until desired consistency is achieved.

PER SERVING: Calories: 32 | Fat: 0 g | Protein: 2 g | Sodium: 48 mg | Fiber: 3 g | Carbohydrates: 6 g | Sugar: 3 g

The Constipation Cure

Cure the most uncomfortable indigestion symptoms like constipation with delicious smoothies like this one, which features a delicious blend of sweet and crisp vegetables.

INGREDIENTS | SERVES 3

1 cup chopped romaine lettuce

1 cup chopped asparagus

1 cup chopped broccoli

2 medium carrots, peeled

2 cups chamomile tea

1. Place romaine, asparagus, broccoli, carrots, and 1 cup tea in a blender and blend until thoroughly combined.

2. Add remaining 1 cup tea, as needed, while blending until desired consistency is achieved.

PER SERVING: Calories: 40 | Fat: 0 g | Protein: 2 g | Sodium: 42 mg | Fiber: 3 g | Carbohydrates: 8 g | Sugar: 3 g

Cool Off Colitis

Remedy this terrible digestive disorder with vegetables rich in vitamin E. Spinach, asparagus, carrots, tomato, and light chamomile make for a savory, yet slightly sweet, smoothie.

INGREDIENTS | SERVES 3

1 cup chopped spinach

1 cup asparagus

3 medium carrots, peeled

1 medium tomato

2 cups chamomile tea

1. Place spinach, asparagus, carrots, tomato, and 1 cup tea in a blender and blend until thoroughly combined.

2. Add remaining 1 cup tea, as needed, while blending until desired consistency is achieved.

PER SERVING: Calories: 45 | Fat: 0 g | Protein: 2 g | Sodium: 55 mg | Fiber: 3 g | Carbohydrates: 10 g | Sugar: 5 g

CHAPTER 10

Drinks to Boost Immunity

The immune system protects the body from infection and the invasion of harmful toxic and carcinogenic effects on otherwise healthy cells. If you're abnormally tired, catch frequent colds or other infections, or feel sub-par on a regular basis, your immune system may not be working as effectively as it should be. Fruits and vegetables contain many infection-fighting vitamins and antioxidants, including vitamins A, B_6, C, and E, as well as the minerals iron, calcium, zinc, and selenium, which help the body to process and store ingested vitamins and minerals properly. If you're feeling "under the weather," make sure you get a daily nutritional boost by combining your favorite fruits and vegetables in nutrient-rich green drinks.

Nutrients That Fight Germs and Infections

When it comes to fighting infection, more and more studies indicate that diets high in antioxidants reduce colds and flu infections. Antioxidants are powerful phytochemicals found in natural fruits and vegetables, and they help to intercept and destroy free radicals, improving the immune system's functioning and protecting essential cell health.

Free Radicals

Free radicals—which include the superoxide radical, the *hydroxyl radical* and *hydrogen peroxide*—are highly reactive oxygen fragments created by normal chemical processes in the body's cells. Because they lack electrons, they attempt to steal them from other molecules in a process known as *oxidation*. While your body needs some free radicals to fight infection and contract smooth muscles, excess free radicals in the body create toxins that destroy antioxidants and cause harmful damage to otherwise healthy cells (this is the process by which healthy cells become cancerous).

An antioxidant neutralizes oxidants, including free radicals. But when the antioxidant systems of the body are overwhelmed, free radicals stabilize themselves by stealing electrons from antioxidants and causing the generation of more free radicals, which creates further damage. As these chain reactions spread through the body, they attack many vulnerable sites of compromised immunity and cause infection and even chronic disease.

The Most Important Antioxidants for Fighting Infections

The following vitamins help reduce the actions of free radicals and prevent the risk of infection or, more importantly, help heal it:

- Vitamin A is a fat-soluble vitamin that is extremely important in immune defense. Vitamin A has been shown to enhance white blood cell functioning, which helps the body resist and fight off infection.
- Vitamin B_6 helps the immune system function properly by aiding in the production of antibodies that help the body fight infection.

- Vitamin C boosts immunity by increasing the production of white blood cells to help the body fight off infection. It also increases the body's level of interferon, which prevents viruses from even entering the body.
- Vitamin E builds a healthy immune system by triggering the production of cells that kill germs and promote the production of B cells, which create the antibodies that destroy bacteria.
- Beta-carotene enhances the effectiveness of vitamin C, an important vitamin in preventing infections.
- Selenium is a potent antioxidant that helps kill free radicals.
- Bioflavonoids have been shown to reduce the inflammation that accompanies infection. They also boost the action of vitamin C.
- Zinc promotes anti-inflammatory actions in the body.
- Omega-3 fatty acids help decrease inflammation, a reaction to infection that helps rid the body of toxins.
- Copper reduces inflammation.

Best Fruits and Vegetables for Fighting Infections

You can find all of the vitamins and minerals that will help you fight infection in delicious fruits and vegetables that are easy to juice. Enhance their infection-fighting qualities by mixing and matching those with the most potent qualities for your needs.

Where to Find Potent Infection Fighters

Here's a rundown of the best produce sources for fighting infections and germs.

Vitamin or Mineral	Food Source
vitamin A	carrots, sweet potatoes, pumpkin, spinach, kale, red bell peppers
vitamin E	almonds, sunflower seeds, olives, blueberries, tomatoes, spinach, watercress, asparagus, carrots
vitamin C	Brusseis sprouts, broccoli, cauliflower, papayas, oranges, cantaloupe, strawberries
selenium	cruciferous veggies, garlic, oranges, grapes, carrots, radishes

Vitamin or Mineral	Food Source
bioflavonoids	onions, cruciferous veggies, prunes, tomatoes, citrus fruits, cherries, parsley, melons
copper	turnips, garlic, ginger root
zinc	cruciferous veggies, parsley, garlic, carrots, grapes, spinach, tangerines, lettuce, ginger root
omega-3 fatty acids	flaxseed and hemp oils

Best Herbs for Fighting Infections

Echinacea and astragalus are the two most popular herbs used to boost immunity, but they are also supported by the most significant documentation, according to Michael T. Murray, ND, a leading authority on natural medicine and a professor at Bastyr University in Seattle. Murray claims that both echinacea and astragalus exert broad-spectrum effects on the body's natural defense mechanisms, helping to safeguard immunity and boost cell functioning.

Echinacea can be your best friend if you have a bad cold, flu, virus, or other infection caused by a compromised immune system. Studies show echinacea may give sluggish immune systems a much-needed boost for fighting infections by stimulating the thymus gland. Keep in mind, though, that taking echinacea on a daily basis can cause your body to become so adapted and immune to it that it's no longer as effective, so only take the supplement when you're under the weather.

In addition, Murray argues that echinacea also exerts direct antiviral activity and helps prevent the spread of bacteria by blocking a bacterial enzyme called *hyaluronidase*. This enzyme is secreted by bacteria in order to break through the body's first line of defense, the protective membranes such as the skin or mucous membranes.

Murray says that clinical studies have shown astragalus, another herb used for viral infections in traditional Chinese medicine, to be especially effective when used as a preventive measure against the common cold. In addition, it reduces the duration and severity of common cold symptoms and raises white blood cell counts in people with chronic leukopenia (low white blood cell count).

Other herbs that may help fight infection include the following:

- Licorice root is still one of the most used and most important herbs in Chinese medicine and is used extensively for urinary and digestive tract problems. It has a very wide range of uses, including the treatment of tuberculosis, diabetes, and everyday coughs and sore throats.
- Cat's claw may promote a healthier immune system by helping white blood cells fight infection and disease. It's also an ancient remedy for digestive disorders and viruses. Studies show it helps reduce inflammation and fight damaging free radicals that can trigger cancer and heart disease.
- Goldenseal root was used by Native Americans to fight infections and viruses, disorders of the digestive tract, respiratory conditions, urinary tract infections, and infections of the skin and eye. The root is primarily used today to treat bacterial infections

Best Produce for Better Immunity

1. Citrus fruits
2. Melons
3. Greens
4. Pomegranates
5. Apples
6. Celery
7. Ginger
8. Cherries
9. Peas
10. Garlic

Drinks to Boost Immunity

Pomegranate Illness Preventer

Packed with vitamins and minerals that promote health and fight illness, blending these delicious fruits and vegetables is a tasty way to maintain great health.

INGREDIENTS | SERVES 3

1 cup chopped iceberg lettuce

2 cups pomegranate seeds

1 medium orange, peeled

1 banana, peeled

1 cup purified water

Pomegranate Seeds

Pomegranate seeds are also known as pomegranate pips and arils.

1. Place iceberg, pomegranate seeds, orange, banana, and ½ cup water in a blender and blend until thoroughly combined.

2. Add remaining ½ cup water, as needed, while blending until desired consistency is achieved.

PER SERVING: Calories: 155 | Fat: 2 g | Protein: 3 g | Sodium: 6 mg | Fiber: 7 g | Carbohydrates: 37 g | Sugar: 25 g

Cantaloupe for Cancer Prevention

The vibrant color of cantaloupe comes from the high levels of beta-carotene. This smoothie provides a wide variety of vitamins and minerals that work hard in preventing illness and disease.

INGREDIENTS | SERVES 3

1 cup watercress
½ cantaloupe, rind and seeds removed
1 medium apple, peeled and cored
1 banana, peeled
¼" ginger, peeled
1 cup purified water

Beta-Carotene's Fight Against Cancer

Among the many benefits beta-carotene offers, one of the major responsibilities of this strong antioxidant is to combat free radicals from the environment, certain foods, and unhealthy lifestyles. Free radicals can cause abnormal growth in cells, which can lead to dangerous illnesses like cancer. Studies have shown that diets rich in carotenes promote proper cell growth, thereby reducing the chances of cancers and disease.

1. Place watercress, cantaloupe, apple, banana, ginger, and ½ cup water in a blender and blend until thoroughly combined.

2. Add remaining ½ cup water, as needed, while blending until desired consistency is achieved.

PER SERVING: Calories: 94 | Fat: 0 g | Protein: 2 g | Sodium: 20 mg | Fiber: 3 g | Carbohydrates: 24 g | Sugar: 17 g

Breathe Easy with Blackberries

Delicious blackberries are made even more tasty with the addition of lemon and ginger in this recipe. This smoothie packs a healthy dose of much-needed vitamins and minerals, and is rich and satisfying with the addition of protein-packed yogurt.

INGREDIENTS | SERVES 3

1 cup watercress

2 pints blackberries

1 banana, peeled

½ lemon, peeled

½" ginger, peeled

1 cup Greek-style yogurt

Blackberries Promote Respiratory Relief

Rich blackberries are not just tasty—they are also packed with a variety of vitamins and minerals that can aid in overall health. Specifically, the magnesium content in blackberries helps promote respiratory ease. Best known for its ability to relax the muscles and thin mucus most commonly associated with breathing difficulties, blackberries are important help for those in need of breathing assistance.

1. Place watercress, blackberries, banana, lemon, ginger, and ½ cup yogurt in a blender and blend until thoroughly combined.

2. Add remaining ½ cup yogurt, as needed, while blending until desired consistency is achieved.

PER SERVING: Calories: 167 | Fat: 1 g | Protein: 11 g | Sodium: 35 mg | Fiber: 12 g | Carbohydrates: 31 g | Sugar: 17 g

A Grape Way to Bone Health

The sweetness of this smoothie from red grapes and pears just can't be beat! This recipe provides abundant vitamins and minerals with the added benefit of an amazingly refreshing taste.

INGREDIENTS | SERVES 3

1 cup watercress

2 cups red grapes

2 medium pears, cored

1 banana, peeled

1 cup purified water

Grapes' Anthocyanins and Proanthocyanidins

You may never have heard of these two amazing compounds, but they are extremely important in promoting strong bones and optimizing bone health. Anthocyanins and proanthocyanidins are compounds found in cells, and their duty is to ensure the bone structure is stabilized and to promote the collagen-building process that is absolutely imperative for strong bones. The two main foods packed with these strong compounds are deep-red and purple grapes and blueberries.

1. Place watercress, grapes, pears, banana, and ½ cup water in a blender and blend until thoroughly combined.

2. Add remaining ½ cup water, as needed, while blending until desired consistency is achieved.

PER SERVING: Calories: 145 | Fat: 1 g | Protein: 2 g | Sodium: 7 mg | Fiber: 5 g | Carbohydrates: 38 g | Sugar: 26 g

Vitamin C Cancer Prevention

This vitamin C–packed recipe is a delicious blend of grapefruit, pineapple, and orange, intensified by the addition of ginger and vitamin K- and iron-rich spinach.

INGREDIENTS | SERVES 3

1 cup chopped spinach

1 medium grapefruit, peeled and seeded

1 cup pineapple chunks

1 medium orange, peeled

½" ginger, peeled

1 cup purified water

The Amazing Power of C

Not only is this strong vitamin the most well known for illness prevention but it also works absolute wonders in many areas of promoting optimal health. In addition to being a strong supporter of bone health by improving the collagen-building process, building and retaining quality muscle, and improving the efficiency of blood vessels, it actually aids in the body's absorption of iron. Common mineral deficiencies can be reversed by including an abundance of vitamin C with your daily intake of iron-rich foods.

1. Place spinach, grapefruit, pineapple, orange, ginger, and ½ cup water in a blender and blend until thoroughly combined.

2. Add remaining ½ cup water, as needed, while blending until desired consistency is achieved.

PER SERVING: Calories: 80 | Fat: 0 g | Protein: 1 g | Sodium: 9 mg | Fiber: 3 g | Carbohydrates: 20 g | Sugar: 16 g

Sweet Bone Builder

A one-stop shop for many of your fruit and vegetable servings, this delicious recipe satisfies your sweet tooth and dietary needs with vitamins K and C, beta-carotenes, potassium, folate, and protein.

INGREDIENTS | SERVES 3

1 cup chopped romaine lettuce

1 cup pineapple chunks

1 pint strawberries, tops removed

1 banana, peeled

1 cup Greek-style yogurt

1. Place romaine, pineapple, strawberries, banana, and ½ cup yogurt in a blender and blend until thoroughly combined.

2. Add remaining ½ cup yogurt, as needed, while blending until desired consistency is achieved.

PER SERVING: Calories: 140 | Fat: 1 g | Protein: 9 g | Sodium: 30 mg | Fiber: 4 g | Carbohydrates: 27 g | Sugar: 18 g

Low-Sugar Blend

Maintaining a diet that optimizes sugar levels to ensure diabetic health is easy with this drink. The combination of ingredients makes a refreshing treat that will keep you going when you need a boost.

INGREDIENTS | SERVES 3

1 cup watercress

1 celery stalk

1 medium cucumber, peeled

2 medium pears, cored

2 tablespoons mint

1 cup Greek-style yogurt

1. Place watercress, celery, cucumber, pears, mint, and ½ cup yogurt in a blender and blend until thoroughly combined.

2. Add remaining ½ cup yogurt, as needed, while blending until desired consistency is achieved.

PER SERVING: Calories: 125 | Fat: 1 g | Protein: 9 g | Sodium: 46 mg | Fiber: 5 g | Carbohydrates: 23 g | Sugar: 15 g

Cherry Vanilla Respiratory Relief

Move over ice cream! This delicious smoothie will have you wondering, "Where are the greens?" Although the overpowering flavors of cherry and vanilla take center stage, the vitamin and mineral content of all of the ingredients (including the spinach) will do your body a world of good.

INGREDIENTS | SERVES 3

1 cup chopped spinach
2 cups cherries, pitted
1 medium apple, peeled and cored
Pulp of 1 vanilla bean
½" ginger, peeled
2 cups purified water

The Breathing Benefit of Cherries

Cherries have tons of phytochemicals, which ease inflammation in the body. Commonly suggested for patients suffering from inflammation of joints, cherries can also assist in reducing the inflammation of airways and respiratory-related muscles. By including these powerful antioxidant- and vitamin-rich berries in your diet, you'll fight off illnesses that make breathing difficult and promote a more efficient respiratory process.

1. Place spinach, cherries, apple, vanilla, ginger, and 1 cup water in a blender and blend until thoroughly combined.

2. Add remaining 1 cup water, as needed, while blending until desired consistency is achieved.

PER SERVING: Calories: 94 | Fat: 0 g | Protein: 2 g | Sodium: 8 mg | Fiber: 3 g | Carbohydrates: 24 g | Sugar: 19 g

The Sweet Sensation of Health

If your diet and lifestyle leave you feeling like you are in need of refreshment and vitality, this smoothie is for you. Hydrating melon and pineapple combine with rich greens to provide a revitalizing lift.

INGREDIENTS | SERVES 3

1 cup watercress

2 cups cubed watermelon

1 cup pineapple chunks

1 cup kefir

The Body's Need for Water

Cravings, fatigue, lack of focus, and derailed bodily functions can all result from not getting adequate amounts of water. The minimum recommended water intake is eight 8-ounce glasses of water daily, but those who exercise require even more. In addition to the water added while blending, the fruits and vegetable in this smoothie deliver one tasty way to increase your hydration.

1. Place watercress, watermelon, pineapple, and ¾ cup kefir in a blender and blend until thoroughly combined.

2. Add remaining ¼ cup kefir, as needed, while blending until desired consistency is achieved.

PER SERVING: Calories: 106 | Fat: 3 g | Protein: 4 g | Sodium: 38 mg | Fiber: 1 g | Carbohydrates: 18 g | Sugar: 15 g

Apple Celery for Hydration

The fruits and greens in this smoothie provide natural sugars and carbohydrates, and celery regulates water levels.

INGREDIENTS | SERVES 3

1 cup chopped romaine lettuce

3 medium Granny Smith apples, peeled and cored

2 celery stalks

¼" ginger, peeled

2 cups purified water

1. Place romaine, apples, celery, ginger, and 1 cup water in a blender and blend until thoroughly combined.

2. Add remaining 1 cup water, as needed, while blending until desired consistency is achieved.

PER SERVING: Calories: 85 | Fat: 0 g | Protein: 1 g | Sodium: 23 mg | Fiber: 3 g | Carbohydrates: 22 g | Sugar: 17 g

"Pea" Is for Prevention

This tasty blend of watercress, cucumbers, and peas delivers a filling snack with amazing health.

INGREDIENTS | SERVES 3

1 cup watercress

2 medium cucumbers, peeled

1 cup petite sweet green peas

2 cups purified water

1. Place watercress, cucumbers, peas, and 1 cup water in a blender and blend until thoroughly combined.

2. Add remaining 1 cup water, as needed, while blending until desired consistency is achieved.

PER SERVING: Calories: 42 | Fat: 0 g | Protein: 3 g | Sodium: 77 mg | Fiber: 3 g | Carbohydrates: 9 g | Sugar: 4 g

The Power of a Pea

Adding just 1 cup of this sweet veggie to your daily diet will provide over 50 percent of your daily recommended intake of vitamin K, along with vitamins B and C, manganese, folate, fiber, and protein. This results in stronger bones; heightened disease prevention; efficient metabolism of carbohydrates, fats, and proteins; improved cardiac health; and more energy.

Gear Up with Garlic

This savory smoothie makes a delicious meal replacement for an invigorating breakfast, satisfying lunch, or delightful dinner.

INGREDIENTS | SERVES 3

1 cup chopped spinach

1 medium cucumber, peeled

1 celery stalk

1 medium tomato

2–3 cloves garlic, depending on size

2 cups purified water

Garlic Prep for Optimal Benefits

Cooking garlic for as little as 60 seconds has shown to cause it to lose some of its anticancer properties. Packed with vitamins, minerals, and nutrients that work hard to fight cancer and heart disease, prevent bacterial and viral infections, improve iron metabolism, control blood pressure, and act as an anti-inflammatory, garlic's abilities can be optimized by crushing or chopping it and preparing it without heat.

1. Place spinach, cucumber, celery, tomato, garlic, and 1 cup water in a blender and blend until thoroughly combined.

2. Add remaining 1 cup water, as needed, while blending until desired consistency is achieved.

PER SERVING: Calories: 23 | Fat: 0 g | Protein: 1 g | Sodium: 22 mg | Fiber: 1 g | Carbohydrates: 4 g | Sugar: 2 g

Romaine to the Rescue!

Crisp romaine, broccoli, carrots, garlic, and ginger make for one satisfying smoothie that will promote health for your eyes, digestion, muscle repair, and mental clarity.

INGREDIENTS | SERVES 3

2 cups chopped romaine lettuce

½ cup chopped broccoli

2 medium carrots, peeled

1 clove garlic

½" ginger, peeled

2 cups purified water

1. Place romaine, broccoli, carrots, garlic, ginger, and 1 cup water in a blender and blend until thoroughly combined.

2. Add remaining 1 cup water, as needed, while blending until desired consistency is achieved.

PER SERVING: Calories: 30 | Fat: 0 g | Protein: 1 g | Sodium: 36 mg | Fiber: 2 g | Carbohydrates: 7 g | Sugar: 3 g

A Peppery Way to Promote Health

Arugula and red pepper join forces with crisp celery and garlic for a spicy treat in this smoothie.

INGREDIENTS | SERVES 3

1 cup arugula

2 celery stalks

½ red bell pepper, cored with ribs intact

1 clove garlic

1½ cups water

1. Place arugula, celery, red pepper, garlic, and ¾ cup water in a blender and blend until thoroughly combined.

2. Add remaining ¾ cup water, as needed, while blending until desired consistency is achieved.

PER SERVING: Calories: 14 | Fat: 0 g | Protein: 1 g | Sodium: 24 mg | Fiber: 1 g | Carbohydrates: 3 g | Sugar: 1 g

Garlic and Onions Keep the Doctor Away

Although they will probably keep away more people than just the doctor, garlic and onions make for an amazing taste combination that will surprise any green-smoothie skeptic. The watercress, celery, and zucchini downplay the intense flavors of the garlic and onion.

INGREDIENTS | SERVES 3

1 cup watercress
1 celery stalk
1 medium green onion
1 medium zucchini
1 clove garlic
2 cups purified water

1. Place watercress, celery, onion, zucchini, garlic, and 1 cup water in a blender and blend until thoroughly combined.

2. Add remaining 1 cup water, as needed, while blending until desired consistency is achieved.

PER SERVING: Calories: 17 | Fat: 0 g | Protein: 1 g | Sodium: 21 mg | Fiber: 1 g | Carbohydrates: 3 g | Sugar: 2 g

Celery for Diabetic Health

The powerful antioxidant-rich ingredients in this smoothie work together to provide energy, renewed vitality, and overall health.

INGREDIENTS | SERVES 5

1 cup arugula

1 celery stalk

1 medium tomato

½ red bell pepper, cored with ribs intact

1 medium green onion

1 clove garlic

⅛ cup parsley

2 cups purified water

1. Place arugula, celery, tomato, red pepper, onion, garlic, parsley, and 1 cup water in a blender and blend until thoroughly combined.

2. Add remaining 1 cup water, as needed, while blending until desired consistency is achieved.

PER SERVING: Calories: 12 | Fat: 0 g | Protein: 1 g | Sodium: 10 mg | Fiber: 1 g | Carbohydrates: 2 g | Sugar: 2 g

The Importance of Celery for Diabetics

The sodium content in this crisp veggie plays an important role in a diabetic's diet. By consuming this vegetable, the body is more efficient in regulating and maintaining its water balance. Celery is rich in vitamins A, C, K, B_6, and B_1 as well as calcium, potassium, fiber, and folate, and is also a natural diuretic.

Spice It Up Smoothie

If you're worried about too strong of a pepper taste in this smoothe, the mushrooms are a woody ingredient that tones down the peppery flavor of arugula.

INGREDIENTS | SERVES 3

1 cup arugula
1 medium green onion
½ red bell pepper, cored
½ cup mushrooms, stems intact
2 cups purified water

Red Bell Peppers and Vitamins C and A

This beautiful vegetable not only provides a tasty crunch to salads and entrées, but it also provides a whopping dose of both vitamins A and C. Providing almost 300 percent of your recommended daily amount of vitamin C and just over 100 percent of your recommended daily amount of vitamin A, it prevents illnesses like cancer, heart disease, and influenza and protects against free radicals that can cause aged-looking skin, increased fatigue, and zapped energy and mental focus.

1. Place arugula, onion, red pepper, mushrooms, and 1 cup water in a blender and blend until thoroughly combined.

2. Add remaining 1 cup water, as needed, while blending until desired consistency is achieved.

PER SERVING: Calories: 12 | Fat: 0 g | Protein: 1 g | Sodium: 4 mg | Fiber: 1 g | Carbohydrates: 2 g | Sugar: 1 g

Pear Virus Prevention

This refreshing smoothie makes a great snack when your body and mind need a lift. The sweet pears, spicy ginger, and rich cabbage and celery combine with the cooling cucumber for an overall refreshing blend.

INGREDIENTS | SERVES 3

1 cup chopped green cabbage
3 medium pears, cored
1 medium cucumber, peeled
1 celery stalk
½" ginger, peeled
1 cup kefir

1. Place cabbage, pears, cucumber, celery, ginger, and ½ cup kefir in a blender and blend until thoroughly combined.

2. Add remaining ½ cup kefir, as needed, while blending until desired consistency is achieved.

PER SERVING: Calories: 167 | Fat: 3 g | Protein: 4 g | Sodium: 51 mg | Fiber: 7 g | Carbohydrates: 34 g | Sugar: 22 g

Healthy Artichoke Blend

Although artichokes are most commonly used in dips, salads, and entrées, raw artichokes make for a tasty addition to green smoothie recipes such as this one. Artichokes pack a protective punch against disease, inflammation, and bone loss.

INGREDIENT | SERVES 3

1 cup chopped spinach
4 artichoke hearts
1 medium green onion
2 celery stalks
2 cups purified water

1. Place spinach, artichokes, onion, celery, and 1 cup water in a blender and blend until thoroughly combined.

2. Add remaining 1 cup water, as needed, while blending until desired consistency is achieved.

PER SERVING: Calories: 88 | Fat: 0 g | Protein: 6 g | Sodium: 190 mg | Fiber: 10 g | Carbohydrates: 19 g | Sugar: 2 g

Turnip Turnaround

Turnips are most often seen roasted with other root vegetables around the holidays, but most would never think to include them in a green smoothie. The turnips and carrots make for a delicious taste combination.

INGREDIENTS | SERVES 3

1 cup watercress

2 medium turnips, peeled and cut to fit blender

3 medium carrots, peeled

2 celery stalks

2 cups purified water

1. Place watercress, turnips, carrots, celery, and 1 cup water in a blender and blend until thoroughly combined.

2. Add remaining 1 cup water, as needed, while blending until desired consistency is achieved.

PER SERVING: Calories: 53 | Fat: 0 g | Protein: 2 g | Sodium: 123 mg | Fiber: 4 g | Carbohydrates: 12 g | Sugar: 6 g

CHAPTER 11

Drinks for Healthy Breathing

If you suffer from asthma, allergies, and frequent respiratory problems, you may be able to add green drinks to your daily diet as a way to ease and improve breathing processes. A growing number of studies show that you can increase your breathing capacity by consuming a diet rich in vitamins A, C, and D; folic acid; zinc; omega-3 fatty acids; and other valuable natural nutrients. Because these vitamins and minerals are all found in fresh fruits and vegetables, you can create homemade green drinks that contain concentrated "doses" of natural medicine by mixing and matching those that foster better breathing.

Minimizing Respiratory Assailants

While anyone struggling with respiratory challenges should indulge in the healthiest of fruits and vegetables on a regular basis to ensure adequate nutrients for overall health and wellness, there are many measures that can be taken to minimize exposure to unhealthy elements that can complicate breathing issues. Choosing to exercise indoors, minimizing exposure to smoke and smog, and taking measures to ensure indoor air quality of your home can all improve your respiratory health. When it comes to the foods you choose to include in your daily diet, certain foods have shown to protect and improve breathing; berries have specific anthocyanins that act as powerful antioxidants proven to protect the cells specific to the lungs, airways, and smaller components of the respiratory system. Improving your overall health and targeting breathing, specifically, with the foods you choose to include in your green drinks can change your life for the better!

The Best Nutrients for Better Breathing

Although scientists aren't exactly sure why, it appears that a group of allergic problems, including asthma, eczema, and hay fever, often occur together. Fortunately, studies show that basic nutrients play a crucial role in reducing the incidence and severity of these conditions.

The Role of Vitamins D, A, and C

Researchers from around the world, and specifically Costa Rica, found that many people suffering from asthma and other respiratory conditions were deficient in vitamin D, a vitamin supplied by the sun. Low levels of this vitamin were associated with more frequent hospital visits, increased severity of asthma, and higher levels of the allergy marker immunoglobulin E (IgE).

Data analyzed from studies conducted over thirty years in England show that relatively low dietary intakes of vitamins A and C are associated with statistically significant increased odds of asthma and wheezing.

The Role of Folic Acid

According to research published in the Journal of Allergy and Clinical Immunology, two studies of more than 8,000 people showed that those who consumed high levels of folic acid (a B vitamin) had lower levels of the IgE allergy marker, fewer reported allergies, fewer episodes of wheezing, and a reduced incidence of asthma. Those who consumed the lowest levels of folic acid had a 40 percent increase in risk of wheezing, a 30 percent higher risk of elevated IgE, and a 16 percent increase in risk of having asthma.

The Role of Synergy

Many recent studies have supported the importance of nutrient synergy in reducing asthmatic risks. For example, a trial published in the Egyptian nutrition publication *Acta Paediatrica* showed that consuming omega-3 fatty acids, vitamin C, and zinc together was associated with significant improvements in asthma symptoms, lung function, and markers of inflammation in the lungs. While each nutrient alone also yielded benefits, the effects were much greater when the nutrients were consumed together.

The Best Foods to Better Breathing

You can breathe better by creating green drinks from a variety of fresh fruits and vegetables:

- Vitamin D is abundant in sunflower seeds, sprouts, and mushrooms.
- Folic acid can be found in blackberries, cruciferous veggies, spinach, and kale.
- Vitamin A and carotenes are found in romaine lettuce, carrots, parsley, kale, beet greens, spinach, and broccoli.
- Vitamin C is found in citrus fruits, cruciferous veggies, spinach, parsley, asparagus, and watercress.
- Omega-3 fatty acids are found in flaxseed and hemp.
- Zinc is found in cruciferous veggies, garlic, carrots, ginger root, parsley, cucumbers, and lettuce.

Best Produce for Better Breathing

1. Berries	5. Greens	9. Cashews
2. Kiwi	6. Carrots	10. Cucumbers
3. Celery	7. Peaches	
4. Apples	8. Ginger	

Drinks for Healthy Breathing

Breathe Beautifully with Broccoli

This recipe is especially good for older adults afflicted with COPD, allergies, or asthma. It also has the added benefit of aiding eyesight.

INGREDIENTS | SERVES 1

2 cups broccoli florets
1 large cucumber
1 medium zucchini
10 stalks asparagus, trimmed

1. Process the broccoli through an electronic juicer according to the manufacturer's instructions.

2. Add the cucumber.

3. Add the zucchini, followed by the asparagus.

4. Mix the juice thoroughly to combine ingredients and drink immediately.

PER SERVING: Calories: 161 | Fat: 2 g | Protein: 13 g | Sodium: 85 mg | Fiber: 0 g | Carbohydrates: 30 g | Sugar: 15 g

Calming Kiwi

The antioxidants that accompany the naturally occurring vitamin C in this green drink are perfect for protection as well as repair.

INGREDIENTS | SERVES 2

1 cup chopped spinach
1 banana, peeled
2 kiwifruit, peeled
1 cup blackberries
2 cups organic apple juice, not from concentrate

Combine all ingredients in a blender and blend until desired consistency is reached.

PER SERVING: Calories: 253 | Fat: 1 g | Protein: 3 g | Sodium: 26 mg | Fiber: 8 g | Carbohydrates: 61 g | Sugar: 44 g

Blueberry Breathe-Easy Pie

The sweetness of protein-rich kefir and naturally delicious blueberries combines with antioxidant-packed cinnamon for a breathe-easy blend.

INGREDIENTS | SERVES 2

1 cup chopped spinach

2 cups blueberries

1 cup blueberry kefir

1 cup water

1 teaspoon ground cinnamon

Combine all ingredients in a blender and blend until desired consistency is reached.

PER SERVING: Calories: 159 | Fat: 2 g | Protein: 7 g | Sodium: 76 mg | Fiber: 4 g | Carbohydrates: 32 g | Sugar: 25 g

Hempful Helper

Rich in protein, omega-3s, and antioxidants, this green drink's healthy doses of hemp will keep you feeling fit and breathing freely morning, noon, and night.

INGREDIENTS | SERVES 2

1 cup chopped spinach

½ cup hempseed

2 medium carrots, peeled

1 cup sweet peas

2 cups purified water

Combine all ingredients in a blender and blend until desired consistency is reached.

PER SERVING: Calories: 282 | Fat: 18 g | Protein: 17 g | Sodium: 159 mg | Fiber: 6 g | Carbohydrates: 17 g | Sugar: 7 g

Doses of Greens

This cool cucumber blend of greens and fibrous fruit will help you fight breath-constricting bloat.

INGREDIENTS | SERVES 2

1 cup chopped spinach

2 medium green apples, cored

2 cucumbers, peeled

1 celery stalk

2 cups purified water

Combine all ingredients in a blender and blend until desired consistency is reached.

PER SERVING: Calories: 125 | Fat: 1 g | Protein: 2 g | Sodium: 34 mg | Fiber: 6 g | Carbohydrates: 31 g | Sugar: 22 g

Celery Celebration

With calming celery that acts as a natural diuretic and an aromatic antioxidant, this green drink can help relieve pressure on your abdomen and better your breathing by beating bloat and opening airways.

INGREDIENTS | SERVES 2

1 cup chopped romaine lettuce

4 celery stalks

1 English cucumber

2 cups purified water

Combine all ingredients in a blender and blend until desired consistency is reached.

PER SERVING: Calories: 39 | Fat: 0 g | Protein: 2 g | Sodium: 69 mg | Fiber: 3 g | Carbohydrates: 9 g | Sugar: 4 g

Blackberry Blast-Off

With beautiful blackberries and vitamin-rich spinach taking main stage, this green drink's antioxidant power gets pumped up with the delicious addition of zippy ginger root and cloves.

INGREDIENTS | SERVES 2

1 cup spinach

3 cups blackberries

1" ginger, peeled

1 teaspoon ground cloves

2 cups purified water

Combine all ingredients in a blender and blend until desired consistency is reached.

PER SERVING: Calories: 103 | Fat: 1 g | Protein: 4 g | Sodium: 18 mg | Fiber: 12 g | Carbohydrates: 23 g | Sugar: 11 g

Golden Apple Galore

Golden Delicious apples take the spotlight off of sometimes-bitter kale by being brightened with spicy additions that are commonly found in delicious confections like apple pie!

INGREDIENTS | SERVES 2

½ cup chopped kale

4 Golden Delicious apples, cored

1 teaspoon cinnamon

1 teaspoon ground cloves

1" ginger, peeled

2 cups vanilla almond milk

Combine all ingredients in a blender and blend until desired consistency is reached.

PER SERVING: Calories: 301 | Fat: 3 g | Protein: 3 g | Sodium: 168 mg | Fiber: 10 g | Carbohydrates: 66 g | Sugar: 49 g

Tropical Taste Bud Pleaser

No need to tease your taste buds with sugary, artificial concoctions when you have this delicious piña colada–like green drink that provides vitamins C and K, along with essential antioxidants that assist in lung functioning and overall health.

INGREDIENTS | SERVES 2

1 cup chopped romaine lettuce

3 cups pineapple chunks

2 cups coconut milk

Combine all ingredients in a blender and blend until desired consistency is reached.

PER SERVING: Calories: 208 | Fat: 5 g | Protein: 2 g | Sodium: 49 mg | Fiber: 4 g | Carbohydrates: 40 g | Sugar: 31 g

Relaxing Romaine

Sometimes, stress can kill your respiratory relief by tensing up your mind and your body. This relaxing green tea and romaine remedy will surely do the trick to calm your body and mind and better your breathing, too.

INGREDIENTS | SERVES 2

1 cup chopped romaine lettuce

1 English cucumber

1" ginger, peeled

2 cups green tea

Combine all ingredients in a blender and blend until desired consistency is reached.

PER SERVING: Calories: 30 | Fat: 0 g | Protein: 1 g | Sodium: 5 mg | Fiber: 1 g | Carbohydrates: 7 g | Sugar: 3 g

Cool Cucumber Berry Blend

With the light flavors of cucumber and romaine, this berry-packed green drink boasts naturally sweet berries that have tons of anthocyanins that relieve respiratory discomfort.

INGREDIENTS | SERVES 2

1 cup chopped romaine lettuce

1 English cucumber

1 cup blackberries

1 cup blueberries

1 cup raspberries

2 cups organic apple juice, not from concentrate

Combine all ingredients in a blender and blend until desired consistency is reached.

PER SERVING: Calories: 245 | Fat: 2 g | Protein: 4 g | Sodium: 17 mg | Fiber: 11 g | Carbohydrates: 59 g | Sugar: 40 g

Very Berry Creamy Dream

While dairy products can sometimes create phlegm and respiratory discomfort, the probiotic-rich kefir in this recipe has shown to reduce the incidence of reported breathing difficulties in children and adults.

INGREDIENTS | SERVES 2

1 cup chopped spinach

1 cup blackberries

1 cup blueberries

1½ cups blueberry kefir

1 cup water

Combine all ingredients in a blender and blend until desired consistency is reached.

PER SERVING: Calories: 181 | Fat: 2 g | Protein: 10 g | Sodium: 107 mg | Fiber: 6 g | Carbohydrates: 33 g | Sugar: 26 g

Keen on Peaches and Cream

This naturally delicious green drink uses sweet peaches and creamy kefir to boost the vitamin and mineral content of the good-for-you greens that give it its beautiful hue.

INGREDIENTS | SERVES 2

½ cup chopped spinach
4 medium peaches, pitted
1 cup plain kefir
1 cup purified water

Combine all ingredients in a blender and blend until desired consistency is reached.

PER SERVING: Calories: 189 | Fat: 5 g | Protein: 7 g | Sodium: 53 mg | Fiber: 5 g | Carbohydrates: 34 g | Sugar: 30 g

Creamy Cashew Carrot Smoothie

With natural creaminess from antioxidant- and protein-packed cashews, this sweet, creamy treat gets even brighter with vibrant colors and vitamins of sweet carrots and spinach.

INGREDIENTS | SERVES 3

3 cups water
1 cup natural cashews
4 medium carrots, greens removed
1 cup chopped spinach

1. Combine water and cashews in a blender and blend until nuts are emulsified.

2. Add carrots and spinach gradually.

3. Blend until all ingredients are well blended.

PER SERVING: Calories: 298 | Fat: 21 g | Protein: 8 | Sodium: 71 mg | Fiber: 4 g | Carbohydrates: 23 g | Sugar: 6 g

Simple Spinach-Apple Smoothie

In this drink, spinach gets sweetened up with delicious green apples. Packed with fiber and folate, this vitamin-rich drink improves overall health and wellness.

INGREDIENTS | SERVES 2

2 cups chopped spinach

2 medium green apples, cored

2 cups purified water

Combine all ingredients in a blender and blend until desired consistency is reached.

PER SERVING: Calories: 102 | Fat: 0 g | Protein: 1 g | Sodium: 26 mg | Fiber: 5 g | Carbohydrates: 26 g | Sugar: 19 g

Sparkling Spices

This spicy combination of potent antioxidant-rich spices, arugula, and creamy kefir helps keep your body free of toxins and waste while protecting the immune system that safeguards your breathing.

INGREDIENTS | SERVES 2

½ cup arugula

1 medium red apple, cored

2 teaspoons ground cinnamon

2 teaspoons ground cloves

2 teaspoons ground cardamom

1" ginger, peeled

1 cup plain kefir

1 cup purified water

Combine all ingredients in a blender and blend until desired consistency is reached.

PER SERVING: Calories: 140 | Fat: 5 g | Protein: 5 g | Sodium: 57 mg | Fiber: 5 g | Carbohydrates: 23 g | Sugar: 14 g

Cough, Be Gone!

If you're sick of the dizzying number of menthol-scented and -infused products promising relief from respiratory discomfort on the market today, choose to sip this naturally mentholated green drink instead.

INGREDIENTS | SERVES 2

1 cup romaine
1 cup fresh mint leaves
1" ginger, peeled
2 cups hot green tea

Combine all ingredients in a glass or glass blender (not plastic!) and blend until desired consistency is reached. Allow to steep for at least 1 hour.

PER SERVING. Calories: 27 | Fat: 0 g | Protein: 2 g | Sodium: 16 mg | Fiber: 4 g | Carbohydrates: 5 g | Sugar: 0 g

Sweet and Spicy Celery-Kiwi Smoothie

Naturally packed with aromatic ginger and celery, this green drink has a hint of sweetness and a hint of spice to go along with the potent vitamins, minerals, and antioxidants from each of its valuable ingredients.

INGREDIENTS | SERVES 2

1 cup chopped spinach
2 celery stalks, leaves intact
2 kiwifruit, peeled
1" ginger, peeled
2 cups organic apple juice, not from concentrate

Combine all ingredients in a blender and blend until desired consistency is reached.

PER SERVING: Calories: 179 | Fat: 1 g | Protein: 2 g | Sodium: 57 mg | Fiber: 3 g | Carbohydrates: 43 g | Sugar: 34 g

Bing-Bang Blackberry Cream

The greens in this amazing drink aren't even noticeable because of the overpowering flavors of the blackberries, banana, ginger, and coconut milk. Packed with antioxidants and loaded with flavor, this green drink is sure to be a favorite one for breathing easy!

INGREDIENTS | SERVES 2

½ cup spinach

2 cups blackberries

1 banana, peeled

1" ginger, peeled

2 cups vanilla coconut milk

Combine all ingredients in a blender and blend until desired consistency is reached.

PER SERVING: Calories: 209 | Fat: 6 g | Protein: 3 g | Sodium: 53 mg | Fiber: 9 g | Carbohydrates: 37 g | Sugar: 23 g

Breathing Better with Berries

Bursting with berries, this green drink provides a ton of respiratory-rescuing antioxidants intended for better breathing.

INGREDIENTS | SERVES 4

1 kale leaf

1 banana, peeled

1 cup blueberries

1 cup blackberries

1 cup raspberries

2 cups organic apple juice, not from concentrate

Combine all ingredients in a blender and blend until desired consistency is reached.

PER SERVING: Calories: 144 | Fat: 1 g | Protein: 2 g | Sodium: 13 mg | Fiber: 6 g | Carbohydrates: 35 g | Sugar: 22 g

CHAPTER 12

Drinks to Help Diabetes

Until recently, experts thought sugar—including most fruits—was strictly taboo for diabetics. But according to new guidelines by the American Diabetes Association, diabetics can eat pretty much anything they like, provided they pay attention to their diet as a whole and monitor their blood sugar level two hours after meals to see whether any individual food elevates it. Studies show that raw produce is an excellent choice for diabetics because it supplies many needed nutrients for health. Unlike cooked produce, raw fruits, vegetables, and juices help stabilize blood sugar levels.

All about Diabetes

There are two major types of diabetes. Type 1, also known as insulin-dependent diabetes, is caused when your body produces little or no insulin. It is far less common than type 2 diabetes, affecting just 5 percent of people with diabetes. Type 1 diabetes usually develops early in life, and is controlled by daily injections of insulin.

Type 2 (or non-insulin-dependent) diabetes affects 90 to 95 percent of people with diabetes. This type of diabetes usually develops later in life and often goes undiagnosed until symptoms become too troublesome to ignore, according to the American Diabetes Association. In type 2 diabetes, the pancreas may produce insulin, but the body becomes resistant to it.

Other risk factors for diabetes include having a parent or sibling with the disease; being African American, Asian American, Hispanic, or Pacific Islander; having higher than normal blood glucose levels; and having high blood pressure or cholesterol levels. While you can't change your heritage, lifestyle factors can dramatically lower your risk of diabetes. Studies show that borderline diabetics who lost 7 percent of their body weight, consumed a low-calorie, low-fat diet, and exercised moderately reduced their odds of having diabetes by 58 percent. Many type 2 diabetics can control their condition without drugs by following a special diet and getting regular exercise.

Symptoms of Diabetes

According to the ADA, diabetes often goes undiagnosed because many of its symptoms seem so harmless. Some of the more common symptoms include frequent urination, excessive thirst, extreme hunger, unusual weight loss, increased fatigue, irritability, and blurry vision. If you have one or more of these symptoms, see your doctor right away. You can also take an online diabetes risk test to find out if you are at risk for diabetes at *http://diabetes.org*.

Best Nutrients for Diabetes

Sugar was once viewed as the enemy because it was thought to increase blood sugar more than any other food. Scientists now know that carbohydrates, whether they are found in sugar or starchy vegetables like potatoes, have the same effect on blood sugar levels. How many carbs you need depends on your medical condition, weight, and activity levels. Be sure to consult your physician before implementing any new dietary regimen. While these recipes are suggestions for those suffering from diabetes, they in no way take place of a physician's advice or prescription.

Vitamins for Controlling Diabetes

You should consume the following vitamins and minerals daily to keep diabetes in check. Remember that most of these nutrients can be found in fresh fruit and vegetable juices and smoothies:

- Vitamin A: Protects the lining of the digestive system and is also vital for growth and night vision.
- Vitamin B_1 (thiamine): Vital for muscles and heart function.
- Vitamin B_2: Converts B_6 into an active form so the body can more easily use it.
- Vitamin B_6: Helps reduce stress and anxiety.
- Vitamin B_{12}: Helps reduce depression.
- Pantothenic acid: Supports enzyme functions. These enzymes are also needed to break down food and trigger energy release.
- Niacin: Metabolizes carbs and fat and supports your digestive system. Vital for diabetics.
- Biotin (vitamin B_3): Essential for digestion and also triggers enzymes.
- Vitamin E: Diabetics require more vitamin E than other people. Getting enough can also decrease the amount of insulin you need to take to control the disease.

Minerals for Controlling Diabetes

If you have diabetes, be sure to consume adequate amounts of the following minerals.

- Iron: Essential to create energy and transport blood around the body.
- Sodium: Regulates and maintains water balance.
- Potassium: Helps control blood pressure.

- Zinc: Essential for growth and repair. Like the B vitamins, it also supports enzymes.
- Manganese: Low manganese levels may aggravate diabetic conditions. Studies have demonstrated that manganese can help decrease insulin resistance and improve glucose metabolism.
- Calcium: Essential for strong bones and regulating muscles.

Best Produce for Diabetics

If you have diabetes, one of the best ways to control blood sugar levels is to consume a diet high in fruits and vegetables, especially raw produce or produce consumed in homemade juices and smoothies. Here's where to find the vitamins and minerals you need to stay healthy:

- Produce rich in vitamin A includes kale, parsley, carrots, spinach, chard, beet greens, watercress, broccoli, and romaine.
- Fruits and veggies with vitamin B_1 (thiamine) include garlic, sunflower seeds, and buckwheat sprouts.
- Vitamin B_2 is found in broccoli, kale, parsley, beet greens, and prunes.
- Vitamin B_6 is abundant in spinach, turnip greens, bell peppers, prunes, and kale.
- Vitamin B_{12} is found in soy and tempeh.
- Pantothenic acid is abundant in broccoli, kale, and cauliflower.
- Niacin (vitamin B_3) is found in brewer's yeast, wheat bran, and peanuts.
- Vitamin E is abundant in tomatoes, carrots, watercress, asparagus, and spinach.

Foods to Avoid

If you are a diabetic, go easy on the following foods, all of which could cause dangerous spikes in blood sugar:

- Sugar, artificial sweeteners, and honey. However, you may use sweeteners like stevia.

- Candy and chocolate. If you're desperate for chocolate, eat dark chocolate, which contains less sugar and at least 70 percent cocoa solids.
- Avoid foods containing fructose, glucose, and dextrose—all forms of sugar.
- Avoid refined, processed grains found in cakes, biscuits, pies, tarts, breakfast cereals, wheat, rye, barley, corn, rice, bread, pasta, and pastries.
- Don't eat large amounts of vegetables that contain high levels of carbohydrates and starches, including potatoes, carrots, peas, beans, parsnips, and beets. Small amounts are healthy and essential.
- Don't consume large amounts of fruit with a high sugar content, including watermelon, grapes, mangoes, pineapples, oranges, and strawberries.
- Use milk in moderation. It contains sugar.
- Use yogurt and whole-fat cheese in moderation, as both contain sugar.
- Avoid commercially packaged foods like TV dinners, especially lean and light varieties, as well as snack foods and fast foods. All of them contain hidden sugars.
- Fresh fruit juice is high in sugar, so be sure to dilute it, using one part juice to four parts water.

Best Produce for Diabetes

1. Peaches
2. Berries
3. Ginger
4. Greens
5. Pears
6. Broccoli
7. Beets
8. Garlic
9. Bananas
10. Apples

Drinks to Help Diabetes

Ginger-Beet Treat

Beets, while sweet, can help to regulate blood sugar. Helping maintain a stable blood sugar level is the ideal green drink goal!

INGREDIENTS | SERVES 2

½ head romaine lettuce, chopped

4 beets, greens removed

½" ginger, peeled

2 cups water

Combine all ingredients in a blender and blend until desired consistency is reached.

PER SERVING: Calories: 99 | Fat: 1 g | Protein: 5 g | Sodium: 141 mg | Fiber: 8 g | Carbohydrates: 21 g | Sugar: 13 g

Blueberry Strudel

Many diabetics struggle with adhering to meal plans that, while helping them achieve health goals, seem too restrictive and result in "cheating." Green drinks like this recipe are full of filling fiber and craving-calming naturally sweet excitement.

INGREDIENTS | SERVES 3

1 cup chopped spinach

2 bananas, frozen

1 cup blueberries

½ cup oats

1 teaspoon cinnamon

2 cups unsweetened vanilla almond milk

Combine all ingredients in a blender and blend until desired consistency is reached.

PER SERVING: Calories: 274 | Fat: 4 g | Protein: 7 g | Sodium: 111 mg | Fiber: 8 g | Carbohydrates: 57 g | Sugar: 26 g

Chai-Choco Diabetic Dream

While dates blend into a chocolatey-like sweet treat, their natural state boasts vitamins and minerals without all the bad stuff the processed chocolates provide. Enjoy this sweet chocolatey goodness any time you get a chocolate craving.

INGREDIENTS | SERVES 2

1 cup chopped romaine lettuce

4 pitted dates

Pulp of 1 vanilla bean

1 teaspoon cardamom

2 cups unsweetened vanilla almond milk

Combine all ingredients in a blender and blend until desired consistency is reached.

PER SERVING: Calories: 138 | Fat: 3 g | Protein: 2 g | Sodium: 153 mg | Fiber: 3 g | Carbohydrates: 28 g | Sugar: 24 g

Sweet Green Goodness

By using frozen bananas, you can enjoy sweeter green drinks and a more "icy" consistency. This green drink combines a variety of low-glycemic fruits for optimal taste and minimal blood-sugar spike.

INGREDIENTS | SERVES 2

½ cup chopped spinach

2 red apples, cored

1 banana, peeled and frozen

1 teaspoon cinnamon

2 cups unsweetened coconut milk

Combine all ingredients in a blender and blend until desired consistency is reached.

PER SERVING: Calories: 232 | Fat: 6 g | Protein: 1 g | Sodium: 53 mg | Fiber: 7 g | Carbohydrates: 47 g | Sugar: 32 g

Sweet Peach-Berry

With all of the healthy elements of greens, fruits, and natural additions, this sweet green drink will satisfy a sweet tooth at any time of day.

INGREDIENTS | SERVES 2

½ cup chopped iceberg lettuce

1 cup blueberries

½ cup blackberries

1 medium peach, pitted

1 cup unsweetened coconut milk

Combine all ingredients in a blender and blend until desired consistency is reached.

PER SERVING: Calories: 128 | Fat: 3 g | Protein: 2 g | Sodium: 25 mg | Fiber: 5 g | Carbohydrates: 25 g | Sugar: 19 g

Colorful Combo

This sweet green drink is as easy on the stomach as it is on the eyes.

INGREDIENTS | SERVES 2

1 cup chopped spinach

1 medium Granny Smith apple, peeled and cored

1 medium carrot, peeled

2 cups purified water

Combine all ingredients in a blender and blend until desired consistency is reached.

PER SERVING: Calories: 55 | Fat: 0 g | Protein: 1 g | Sodium: 33 mg | Fiber: 2 g | Carbohydrates: 14 g | Sugar: 10 g

Kale-Carrot Combo Smoothie

For those who choose to naysay kale because of the deep-green veggie's strong taste, this sweet green treat is perfect! Combining sweet vegetables and creamy fruits with potent and powerful phytonutrient-rich kale, this green drink packs a punch of nutrition without a bunch of bitterness!

INGREDIENTS | SERVES 2

1 cup chopped kale

2 large carrots, peeled

1 medium red apple, peeled and cored

1 banana, peeled

2 cups purified water

Combine all ingredients in a blender and blend until desired consistency is reached.

PER SERVING: Calories: 137 | Fat: 1 g | Protein: 3 g | Sodium: 63 mg | Fiber: 0 g | Carbohydrates: 34 g | Sugar: 19 g

Apple Pie in a Cup

Diabetes diagnoses don't mean sweet treats are out of the question; you just have to use natural ingredients more creatively. This green drink combines naturally delicious fruits, vegetables, spices, and almond milk that blend perfectly in one cup.

INGREDIENTS | SERVES 2

½ cup chopped romaine lettuce

2 medium red apples, peeled and cored

1 teaspoon cinnamon

½ teaspoon cloves

2 cups unsweetened vanilla almond milk

Combine all ingredients in a blender and blend until desired consistency is reached.

PER SERVING: Calories: 175 | Fat: 3 g | Protein: 2 g | Sodium: 154 mg | Fiber: 4 g | Carbohydrates: 38 g | Sugar: 31 g

Sweet and Spicy Green Pears

The romaine in this green drink, while potent in its vitamins and minerals, gets deliciously overpowered by the delightful flavors of sweet pears and spicy cinnamon.

INGREDIENTS | SERVES 2

½ head romaine lettuce, chopped

2 medium pears, peeled and cored

1 teaspoon cinnamon

2 cups water

Combine all ingredients in a blender and blend until desired consistency is reached.

PER SERVING: Calories: 131 | Fat: 1 g | Protein: 3 g | Sodium: 14 mg | Fiber: 9 g | Carbohydrates: 33 g | Sugar: 19 g

The Power of Parsley

Making a powerful green drink doesn't always mean combining fruits and vegetables. Packing a bunch of parsley into this savory treat pumps up the nutritional content as well as the flavor!

INGREDIENTS | SERVES 2

1 cup chopped spinach

1 bunch parsley

1 medium tomato

1 medium carrot, greens removed

2 cups purified water

Combine all ingredients in a blender and blend until desired consistency is reached.

PER SERVING: Calories: 38 | Fat: 0 g | Protein: 2 g | Sodium: 53 mg | Fiber: 3 g | Carbohydrates: 8 g | Sugar: 3 g

Sweet Beet Greens

Using every inch of those deliciously sweet beets in this green drink means using the greens, too! Packing tons of flavorful fruits into this nutrient-rich smoothie, you can sip your way to health happily.

INGREDIENTS | SERVES 2

½ cup beet greens

1 cup chopped beets, greens removed

1 medium Granny Smith apple, peeled and cored

1 medium pear, peeled and cored

2 cups purified water

1 cup ice

Combine all ingredients in a blender and blend until desired consistency is reached.

PER SERVING: Calories: 121 | Fat: 0 g | Protein: 2 g | Sodium: 75 mg | Fiber: 6 g | Carbohydrates: 31 g | Sugar: 21 g

Green Garlic Smoothie

The garlic in this savory green drink ensures that your allicin intake for the day is covered.

INGREDIENTS | SERVES 2

1 cup chopped romaine lettuce

1 cup chopped broccoli

2 medium carrots, peeled

2 cloves garlic

2 cups water

Combine all ingredients in a blender and blend until desired consistency is reached.

PER SERVING: Calories: 49 | Fat: 0 g | Protein: 2 g | Sodium: 59 mg | Fiber: 3 g | Carbohydrates: 11 g | Sugar: 4 g

Better Peanut Butter Dream

This green drink will taste so similar to your favorite chocolate–peanut butter treat, you'll forget it's healthy!

INGREDIENTS | SERVES 2

1 cup chopped spinach

8 dates, pitted

½ cup almonds

2 cups unsweetened vanilla almond milk

Combine all ingredients in a blender and blend until desired consistency is reached.

PER SERVING: Calories: 380 | Fat: 20 g | Protein: 10 g | Sodium: 164 mg | Fiber: 8 g | Carbohydrates: 46 mg | Sugar: 34 g

Smooth Blue Banana

Combining the protein-packed, probiotic-rich kefir with naturally smooth bananas and sweet blueberries, this delightful combination of healthy ingredients will keep you feeling full, focused, and blood sugar–balanced throughout the day.

INGREDIENTS | SERVES 2

1 cup chopped spinach

2 bananas, peeled

2 cups blueberries

1 cup blueberry kefir

1 cup water

Combine all ingredients in a blender and blend until desired consistency is reached.

PER SERVING: Calories: 261 | Fat: 2 g | Protein: 8 g | Sodium: 77 mg | Fiber: 7 g | Carbohydrates: 59 g | Sugar: 39 g

Cinnamon Sweetness

With each ingredient in this antioxidant-rich green drink providing an overall health and wellness boost (along with craving-calming fiber), this sweet treat is perfect anytime you're in the mood for something sweet and spicy.

INGREDIENTS | SERVES 2

1 cup chopped romaine lettuce

½ cup natural cashews

2 cups unsweetened vanilla almond milk

4 teaspoons ground cinnamon

Combine all ingredients in a blender and blend until desired consistency is reached.

PER SERVING: Calories: 303 | Fat: 19 g | Protein: 7 g | Sodium: 159 mg | Fiber: 5 g | Carbohydrates: 32 g | Sugar: 17 g

Not Your Everyday Oatmeal

This green drink has natural ingredients like creamy bananas, sweet apples, spicy cloves and cardamom, and wonderful walnuts for a morning meal that satisfies your taste buds, leaves you feeling full and focused, and naturally nurtures your needs for vitamins, minerals, and antioxidants.

INGREDIENTS | SERVES 4

1 cup chopped spinach

2 bananas, peeled

1 medium red apple, cored

¼ cup walnuts, shelled

1 teaspoon ground cloves

1 teaspoon ground cardamom

1 teaspoon cinnamon

3 cups unsweetened vanilla almond milk

1 cup raw oats

Combine all ingredients in a blender and blend until desired consistency is reached.

PER SERVING: Calories: 343 | Fat: 9 g | Protein: 9 g | Sodium: 123 mg | Fiber: 9 g | Carbohydrates: 60 g | Sugar: 23 g

Vivacious Green Vitamins

From folate and other B vitamins to vitamins C and K, this green drink combines leafy greens, cruciferous vegetables, and vibrant bell peppers with potent additions that keep your blood sugar stable and your savory cravings satisfied.

INGREDIENTS | SERVES 2

1 cup chopped spinach

½ cup chopped broccoli

2 medium tomatoes

1 red bell pepper, ribs and seeds removed

1 clove garlic

1 medium carrot, peeled

Combine all ingredients in a blender and blend until desired consistency is reached.

PER SERVING: Calories: 67 | Fat: 1 g | Protein: 3 g | Sodium: 49 mg | Fiber: 0 g | Carbohydrates: 14 g | Sugar: 8 g

Broccoli for Blood Health

Cruciferous vegetables are great for controlling blood pressure, cholesterol, and blood sugar levels. Opt for this broccoli blend when your savory cravings come calling, and be splendidly satisfied.

INGREDIENTS | SERVES 1

1 cup chopped broccoli

1 cup chopped kale

2 green apples, cored

Combine all ingredients in a blender and blend until desired consistency is reached.

PER SERVING: Calories: 253 | Fat: 2 g | Protein: 6 g | Sodium: 59 mg | Fiber: 0 g | Carbohydrates: 62 g | Sugar: 39 g

CHAPTER 13

Drinks for Fasting

A juice fast is considered an extreme form of detoxification because no solid food is consumed. While considered the most popular "go-to" for a quick cleanse, relying on juices without fiber can be counterproductive and actually keep you from achieving your detox goals. Proponents of juice fasting claim the process gives the body a much-needed "spring cleaning," allowing it to take a break from the laborious process of digestion. Claiming juice fasting assists the immune system in clearing out dead, diseased, and damaged cells, promoters of juice fasts neglect to share that the many natural nutrients found in the fiber of fresh juice revitalizes the immune system. Critics of juice fasting insist the practice is unnecessary and potentially dangerous. They claim it can lead to malnutrition, dehydration, diarrhea, and a serious electrolyte imbalance.

The Case Against Juice Fasts

The American Dietitian Association and most medical doctors are not enthused by the latest juice fast diets, especially those that are ultra restrictive and have you drinking sweet and spicy lemonade for weeks at a time. As juice fasts have become increasingly popular among celebrities, medical professionals have sounded the alarm over possible risks from lengthy or repeated fasts, claiming that juice fasts may result in vitamin deficiencies, muscle breakdown, blood-sugar problems, and frequent liquid bowel movements. Because juice fasts are skimpy on solid foods and fiber, those using them are urged to "move things along" by using daily enemas and laxatives and staying close to the bathroom. Not a pleasurable experience in the least, juice fasts may yield a faster weight loss on the scale, but that water weight is quickly regained.

Crash diets also take a toll on your body chemistry, lowering your blood sugar levels and depleting your body's supply of important minerals necessary for maintaining normal electrolyte balances. If you're suffering from a chronic disease such as diabetes, cancer, or a heart condition, you're particularly vulnerable to changes in body chemistry, so don't embark on a fast without your doctor's approval. Because of their low nutrient value and potential dangers, fasts and detox diets are not recommended for children, pregnant women, seniors, and those with digestive conditions.

Types of Juice and Smoothie Fasts

There are many detox diet guides, each with its own magic formula for helping you cleanse your body of unwanted toxins and excess weight. Some have you drinking nothing but lemonade, fruit juice, or purées, claiming this will help flush out environmental or dietary toxins. Others instruct you to eliminate entire food groups, such as dairy and meat products or even all solid foods, in an effort to purify your system. Despite their claims, most are so dangerously low in calories and nutrients that they can lead to serious imbalances in the body.

Juice Fasts Aren't Necessary

According to experts at the Mayo Clinic, your body is already well-equipped to flush out toxins via your kidneys, liver, and skin. Cleansing diets that claim to remove "bad" toxins from your system may remove or even deplete your intestines of healthy bacteria required for healthy functioning.

You're Not Cleansed, You're Starving

Proponents claim they feel lighter and more energetic after fasting; in fact, studies of starvation show the longer you fast, the more lethargic and less focused you become. And because most of these diets contain very little protein, it can be difficult for the body to rebuild lost muscle tissue. Also, medical experts attribute the "high" you feel not to cleansing, but to the body kicking into starvation mode.

Best Fasting Foods

For those who want to give it a try, what follows is a list of the best fruits for green drink fasting. Although there is no medical research proving these fruits are effective in cleansing your body, they certainly supply a lot of healthy nutrients.

Best Internal Cleansers

Beets, cabbage, wheatgrass, sprouts, lemons, carrots, celery, green peppers, oranges, parsley, apples, and grapefruit will all help your body to detox naturally. The best diuretics include watermelon, parsley, cucumber, lemon, kiwifruit, asparagus, and cantaloupe with the seeds.

Bulking agents, including psyllium husks and flaxseed, will curb your appetite and keep you near the bathroom. Herbs that juicing proponents tout as cleansers include herbal teas like dandelion and nettle, which purportedly help cleanse the liver and kidneys.

Getting Started on a Green Drink Fast

Fasting proponents claim you'll get the most from your fast—which typically last three to five days—by preparing yourself physically and mentally for the challenge. Before you start a fast, it is *strongly* recommended that you consult your doctor to discuss the effects the fast may have on your body. To make the transition from solid to liquid foods, about five days before your fast, begin weaning off of foods such as grains, breads, dairy, fish, and meat, and consume a pre-fat diet rich in cooked vegetables, salads, fruits, and green drinks. The next day, limit your foods to raw salads, fruits, and green drinks, becoming progressively stricter as your fast approaches but being careful not to eliminate water from your diet. Try replacing breakfast with green drinks and gradually work up to ingesting only green drinks before dinner.

What to Expect

During a short fast lasting a few days, the pH balance of your stomach changes, becoming more alkaline. As your stomach contracts and the digestive tract is cleansed, you will experience the most dramatic weight loss as water, minerals, and water soluble vitamins are heavily excreted and you lose up to 75 grams of protein per day. You're also likely to experience hunger, headaches, light-headedness, and copious urination.

During longer fasts lasting anywhere from four days to a week, the liver begins to eliminate chemicals and toxins in your body, which may make you feel nauseous, exhausted, nervous, and short of breath. You may develop bad breath, diarrhea, body odor, and skin eruptions. During extended fasts lasting two weeks or longer, blood toxins are eliminated from the body as deep tissue cleansing and organ detox begins. You may experience anything from stress and irritability to a sense of euphoria and well-being, which medical science attributes not to cleansing and regeneration, but to starvation.

Best Produce for Fasting

1. Citrus fruits
2. Melons
3. Apricots
4. Celery
5. Berries
6. Cauliflower
7. Ginger
8. Fennel
9. Cinnamon
10. Garlic

Drinks for Fasting

Fast Feast

Substitute mustard greens for the turnip greens in this recipe for a peppery flavor.

INGREDIENTS | SERVES 2

6 medium carrots, peeled
1 cup turnip greens
1 red bell pepper, seeded
½ cup chopped kale

Storing Juice

If you make more juice than you can drink at once, use a vacuum seal device and store the juice in the refrigerator. Most juices will retain their nutrients for at least twenty-four hours when sealed and refrigerated, the exception being the more volatile, citrus-based juices, which should be consumed as soon as possible.

1. Process the carrots through an electronic juicer according to the manufacturer's instructions.

2. Add the turnip greens, followed by the pepper.

3. Add the kale.

4. Stir or shake the juice to combine the ingredients and enjoy.

PER SERVING: Calories: 110 | Fat: 1 g | Protein: 3 g | Sodium: 146 mg | Fiber: 0 g | Carbohydrates: 25 g | Sugar: 11 g

Luscious Liquid Lunch

Gorgeous color and lively flavor! If cilantro is not to your liking, substitute fresh parsley or a combination of parsley and mint.

INGREDIENTS | SERVES 1

2 kale leaves
½ cup chopped spinach
½ cup cilantro
2 medium apples, cored
1 medium pear, cored
½ lemon, peeled
1" ginger, peeled

1. Process the kale, spinach, and cilantro through an electronic juicer according to the manufacturer's instructions.

2. Add the apples, followed by the pear.

3. Add the lemon and the ginger.

4. Stir or shake the juice to combine the ingredients and enjoy.

PER SERVING: Calories: 394 | Fat: 2 g | Protein: 11 g | Sodium: 105 mg | Fiber: 0 g | Carbohydrates: 97 g | Sugar: 56 g

Powerhouse Green Juice

The powerful combination of spinach and beets will fill you up and keep you energized throughout the day.

INGREDIENTS | SERVES 1

4 celery stalks, leaves intact

1 bunch parsley

2 cups chopped spinach

⅓ medium cucumber

2 carrots, peeled

1 beet, trimmed

2 leaves Swiss chard

Give It a Squeeze

Some people find the flavor of greens-based juices less than appetizing, but adding a healthy squeeze of lemon juice or a dash of hot sauce can do a lot to perk up the flavor and tickle your taste buds.

1. Process the celery and parsley through an electronic juicer according to the manufacturer's instructions.

2. Add the spinach, followed by the cucumber and the carrots.

3. Add the beet and the Swiss chard.

4. Mix the juice thoroughly to combine the ingredients and serve alone or over ice.

PER SERVING: Calories: 168 | Fat: 2 g | Protein: 8 g | Sodium: 436 | Fiber: 0 g | Carbohydrates: 35 g | Sugar: 17 g

Watermelon Fast

Some juicers swear by the effectiveness of single-ingredient, one-day fasts for cleansing the system, losing weight, and restoring the body's alkaline balance.

INGREDIENTS | SERVES 3

5–6-pound watermelon, divided into thirds

1 cup chopped spinach, divided into thirds

Juice only one third of the watermelon and spinach for breakfast, lunch, and dinner. Consume each portion immediately after juicing.

PER SERVING: Calories: 229 | Fat: 1 g | Protein: 5 g | Sodium: 15 mg | Fiber: 0 g | Carbohydrates: 57 g | Sugar: 47 g

Blues Buster

Fasting can bring on some mood swings, so if you feel your good humor slipping away, try this.

INGREDIENTS | SERVES 1

1 cup broccoli florets
½ cup chopped spinach leaves
4 leaves Swiss chard
½ red bell pepper, seeded

1. Process the broccoli through an electronic juicer according to the manufacturer's instructions.

2. Add the spinach, followed by the chard.

3. Add the bell pepper.

4. Mix the juice thoroughly to combine the ingredients and serve alone or over ice.

PER SERVING: Calories: 67 | Fat: 1 g | Protein: 5 g | Sodium: 198 mg | Fiber: 0 g | Carbohydrates: 13 g | Sugar: 5 g

Green Carrot Mango Juice

The sweetness of mango and carrot complement the earthy flavor of the spinach in this smoothie.

INGREDIENTS | SERVES 1

3 large carrots, peeled
1 mango, peeled and seeded
1 cup chopped spinach

1. Process the carrots, mango, and spinach through an electronic juicer according to the manufacturer's instructions.

2. Serve the juice alone or over ice.

PER SERVING: Calories: 220 | Fat: 1 g | Protein: 5 g | Sodium: 175 mg | Fiber: 0 g | Carbohydrates: 53 g | Sugar: 39 g

Apricot Cooler

This makes a perfect choice when you're craving something sweet.

INGREDIENTS | SERVES 1

1 cup chopped kale

4 fresh apricots, pitted

¼ honeydew melon, peeled and seeds removed

1 medium pear, cored

½ cup raspberries

1. Process the kale, apricots, and melon through an electronic juicer according to the manufacturer's instructions.

2. Add the pear, followed by the raspberries.

3. Mix the juice to combine the ingredients and serve over ice.

PER SERVING: Calories: 323 | Fat: 2 g | Protein: 8 g | Sodium: 74 mg | Fiber: 0 g | Carbohydrates: 79 g | Sugar: 53 g

Sunset Supper

This juice has great color and a fantastic flavor. For easier juicing, cut the greens from the beets and add them separately.

INGREDIENTS | SERVES 1

1 cup spinach

5 medium carrots, peeled

2 medium cucumbers

2 medium beets, complete with greens

1. Process the spinach and carrots through an electronic juicer according to the manufacturer's instructions.

2. Add the cucumbers one at a time.

3. Add the beets, followed by the greens.

4. Mix the juice to combine the ingredients and serve over ice.

PER SERVING: Calories: 301 | Fat: 2 g | Protein: 11 g | Sodium: 460 mg | Fiber: 0 g | Carbohydrates: 69 g | Sugar: 36 g

Collard Classic

Red pepper and tomato provide a nice flavor balance for the greens in this recipe.

INGREDIENTS | SERVES 1

1 kale leaf
1 collard leaf
1 celery stalk, with leaves intact
1 medium carrot, peeled
½ red bell pepper, seeded
1 large tomato
½ cup arugula
¼ cup parsley

Collard Greens

A staple of traditional Southern cooking, collards are rich in nutrients. They contain protein, thiamine, niacin, and potassium, as well as vitamin A, vitamin C, vitamin E, vitamin K, riboflavin, vitamin B$_6$, folate, calcium, and manganese. It doesn't get much healthier than that!

1. Process the kale and collard leaves through an electronic juicer according to the manufacturer's instructions.

2. Add the celery, followed by the carrot and the red pepper.

3. Add the tomato, the arugula, and the parsley.

4. Mix the juice to combine the ingredients and serve over ice.

PER SERVING: Calories: 118 | Fat: 2 g | Protein: 7 g | Sodium: 122 mg | Fiber: 0 g | Carbohydrates: 24 g | Sugar: 10 g

Orange Spinach Delight

The greens take a back seat to the lively fresh taste of the orange in this recipe.

INGREDIENTS | SERVES 1

4 medium oranges, peeled
2 cups chopped spinach
1 cup parsley

Ask an Athlete

Many professional athletes praise the power of parsley to boost performance. So if your juice fast has left you feeling a little low on energy, be sure to throw in a handful to your fasting favorites.

1. Process the oranges through an electronic juicer according to the manufacturer's instructions.

2. Add the spinach and parsley.

3. Mix the juice to combine the ingredients and serve over ice.

PER SERVING: Calories: 100 | Fat: 1 g | Protein: 4 g | Sodium: 81 mg | Fiber: 0 g | Carbohydrates: 22 g | Sugar: 14 g

Cantaloupe Cinnamon Cooler

On a juice fast, you can treat yourself to a whole melon without guilt! It will help fill you up and satisfies those hunger pangs.

INGREDIENTS | SERVES 2

½ cup chopped romaine lettuce
1 whole cantaloupe, peeled, seeded, and cut into chunks
½ teaspoon cinnamon

1. Process lettuce through the electronic juicer according to the manufacturer's directions. Do the same with the melon chunks.

2. Add the cinnamon and mix. Serve the juice alone or over ice.

PER SERVING: Calories: 97 | Fat: 1 g | Protein: 2 g | Sodium: 45 mg | Fiber: 0 g | Carbohydrates: 23 g | Sugar: 22 g

Ginger Celery Cooler

Distinctly Asian flavor makes this perfect for a summer snack! Add a dash of soy sauce for some zip.

INGREDIENTS | SERVES 1

½ cup chopped spinach
3 celery stalks, with leaves intact
1 small clove garlic, peeled
1" ginger, peeled
1 medium cucumber
2 scallions, trimmed

1. Process the spinach and celery through an electronic juicer according to the manufacturer's instructions.

2. Add the garlic and the ginger, followed by the cucumber and the scallions.

3. Mix the juice to combine the ingredients and serve.

PER SERVING: Calories: 85 | Fat: 1 g | Protein: 4 g | Sodium: 119 mg | Fiber: 0 g | Carbohydrates: 19 g | Sugar: 9 g

Satsuma Fennel Treat

Satsuma, or honey citrus, are small mandarin oranges that become widely available from October through Christmas.

INGREDIENTS | SERVES 1

½ cup chopped iceberg lettuce
3 satsuma, peeled
½ fennel bulb
¼ lemon or lime, peeled

How to Choose the Best Satsuma

Choose fruit that is small but heavy for its size for the greatest juice yield. Satsuma is prone to mold, so store in the refrigerator.

1. Process the lettuce and satsuma segments through an electronic juicer according to the manufacturer's instructions.

2. Add the fennel bulb, followed by the lemon or lime.

3. Mix the juice thoroughly to combine the ingredients and serve alone or over ice.

PER SERVING: Calories: 104 | Fat: 0 g | Protein: 2 g | Sodium: 64 mg | Fiber: 0 g | Carbohydrates: 26 g | Sugar: 16 g

Red Velvet Juice

This vibrantly colored juice is not exactly a piece of cake, but sweet and satisfying all the same!

INGREDIENTS | SERVES 1

½ cup chopped spinach

3 medium carrots, peeled

2 large Granny Smith apples, cored

1 medium orange, peeled and in segments

¼ beet, trimmed

Sugar in the Morning

When fasting, it's best to consume sweet fruit juices in the morning, go to green juices at lunch, and confine yourself to simple, one or two fruit combinations in the late afternoon for a quick pick-me-up.

1. Process the spinach, carrots, and apples through an electronic juicer according to the manufacturer's instructions.

2. Add the orange segments, followed by the beet.

3. Mix the juice thoroughly to combine the ingredients and serve alone or over ice.

PER SERVING: Calories: 384 | Fat: 2 g | Protein: 5 g | Sodium: 159 mg | Fiber: 0 g | Carbohydrates: 98 g | Sugar: 69 g

Vitamin Mixer

Alfalfa sprouts are low in calories but high in protein, with a fabulous mix of vitamins to boot.

INGREDIENTS | SERVES 1

1 lemon, peeled

2 cups alfalfa sprouts

1" ginger, peeled

2 medium carrots, trimmed

3 medium cucumbers

½ cup parsley

1. Process the lemon through an electronic juicer according to the manufacturer's instructions.

2. Add the sprouts, followed by the ginger and the carrots.

3. Add the cucumbers one at a time, followed by the parsley.

4. Mix the juice thoroughly to combine the ingredients and serve alone or over ice.

PER SERVING: Calories: 235 | Fat: 2 g | Protein: 11 g | Sodium: 125 mg | Fiber: 0 g | Carbohydrates: 55 g | Sugar: 23 g

Gadzooks

As this recipe proves, sometimes the simplest combinations provide maximum benefits.

INGREDIENTS | SERVES 1

½ cup chopped romaine lettuce

3 medium zucchini

2 stalks celery, with leaves

Zucchini Benefits

If you grow a garden, juicing is a wonderful way to rid yourself of too many zucchini. Very low in calories, zucchini is rich in vitamin A and potassium, a heart-friendly electrolyte that helps reduce blood pressure and heart rate by countering the effects of sodium.

1. Process the lettuce, zucchini, and the celery through an electronic juicer according to the manufacturer's instructions.

2. Mix or shake the juice to combine the ingredients and serve alone or over ice.

PER SERVING: Calories: 133 | Fat: 2 g | Protein: 9 g | Sodium: 121 mg | Fiber: 0 g | Carbohydrates: 24 g | Sugar: 19 g

Nutrition Star

The starfruit, also known as carambola, is cultivated throughout the tropics. It provides vitamins C and A.

INGREDIENTS | SERVES 1

3 starfruit

1 medium slice honeydew melon, peeled

½ cup chopped iceberg lettuce

1. Process the starfruit and melon through an electronic juicer according to the manufacturer's directions. Add the lettuce.

2. Mix or shake the juice to combine the ingredients and serve alone or over ice.

PER SERVING: Calories: 114 | Fat: 1 g | Protein: 3 g | Sodium: 29 mg | Fiber: 0 g | Carbohydrates: 26 g | Sugar: 19 g

Cauliflower Combo

Another feast for your fast, this is the juicing equivalent of a big chef's salad!

INGREDIENTS | SERVES 1

1 cup cauliflower florets

1 cup red cabbage

1 orange bell pepper, seeded

4 scallions

½ head romaine lettuce, chopped

1 cup cherry tomatoes

Cauliflower Caution

Like other members of the cruciferous family, excessive consumption of cauliflower may cause swelling of the thyroid gland and thyroid hormone deficiency. This is due to the presence of certain plant compounds known as goitrogens. So if you have a history of thyroid dysfunction, limit your cruciferous intake.

1. Process the cauliflower through an electronic juicer according to the manufacturer's instructions.

2. Add the cabbage, followed by the pepper and the scallions.

3. Add the lettuce and the tomatoes.

4. Whisk or shake the juice thoroughly to combine the ingredients and serve alone or over ice.

PER SERVING: Calories: 174 | Fat: 2 g | Protein: 10 g | Sodium: 88 mg | Fiber: 0 g | Carbohydrates: 35 g | Sugar: 19 g

Eden Elixir

Some say Eve ate an apple, others say a pomegranate. Either way, this will put you in paradise.

INGREDIENTS | SERVES 1

6 medium carrots, peeled

2 kale leaves

4 Brussels sprouts

1 medium apple, cored, or ¼ cup
  pomegranate seeds

Brussels Sprouts and Cancer Prevention

Three major systems in the body that figure into cancer risk are the body's detox system, its antioxidant system, and its anti-inflammatory system. Chronic imbalances in any of these three systems can increase the risk of cancer, and when imbalances in all three systems occur simultaneously, the risk of cancer increases. The good news is that Brussels sprouts have been seen to have a significant impact on the health of each of these systems without the negative impact on the thyroids sometimes associated with the cruciferous group.

1. Process the carrots through an electronic juicer according to the manufacturer's instructions.

2. Add the kale, followed by the Brussels sprouts and the apple or pomegranate seeds.

3. Whisk the juice to combine the ingredients and serve alone or over ice.

PER SERVING: Calories: 343 | Fat: 3 g | Protein: 12 g | Sodium: 324 mg | Fiber: 0 g | Carbohydrates: 79 g | Sugar: 38 g

CHAPTER 14

Heart-Healthy Drinks

Just as exercise can help reduce blood pressure and prevent risks of heart disease, green drinks can have a wonderful impact on the health of your heart. Bulking up on vitamins and minerals can strengthen your heart and help it to work more efficiently. Over the past few decades, researchers have made strong correlations between a healthy diet and a healthy heart. By choosing natural, fresh fruits, vegetables, and heart-healthy additions, you can improve your overall health while also improving your cardiovascular system. Green drinks packed with delicious and nutritious ingredients can supply all of the necessary nutrients your body needs to keep your heart pumping as it should.

How Your Heart Works

In a healthy person, the heart beats at a normal rate, retrieving blood in need of oxygen and delivering it to the lungs. Once the lungs have removed the impurities and infused the blood with oxygen, the heart continues to pump the newly oxygenated blood to the rest of the body . . . and the cycle repeats again and again and again. Conversely, in an unhealthy person, the rate of the heart's beating, efficiency of the blood's retrieval and delivery, and the stress of the entire process can be overwhelming and eventually lead to complications that result in heart disease and heart attacks. In addition, the quality of a person's diet can directly affect the health of the heart by minimizing or maximizing the amount of plaque generated and deposited on the walls of the main arteries that allow blood to flow freely through the valves of the heart. There are no debates about the importance of a nutritious diet when it comes to the health of your heart, so you can safeguard and optimize your cardiovascular health by choosing fresh fruits and vegetables to include in your green drinks daily.

Vitamins and Minerals That Promote Heart Health

While improving your overall quality of health through a diet rich in all of the essential vitamins and minerals your body needs, there are a few select micronutrients that specifically target heart health:

- **Vitamin E:** The American Heart Association has pinpointed vitamin E as a heart-healthy diet necessity after conducting a study in which participants who supplemented their diet with vitamin E showed a 40 percent reduction in the incidence of heart attack and stroke. Vitamin E can be found in natural food options like nuts, seeds, and heart-healthy oils.
- **Vitamin D:** Commonly known as the "sunshine vitamin," vitamin D has been shown to help fight cancer, treat diabetes, build strong bones, and prevent heart disease. While the older recommendations for vitamin D were around 200 IUs per day, many physicians are now recommending a heart-healthy dose of 2000 IUs per day.

- **Potassium:** One of the heart-healthy minerals that can be easily consumed through your nutrient-rich diet is potassium, the essential mineral responsible for regulating muscle contractions and assisting in the electrical impulses between cells. According to a report in the March 2011 issue of *Current Hypertension Reports*, 4,700 mg of potassium daily can lower blood pressure and reduce the risk of heart attack and stroke by 8–15 percent.
- **Magnesium:** The other essential mineral for heart health is magnesium, which has shown to assist in maintaining a healthy blood pressure, preventing calcium buildup in arteries, and improving fat metabolism; with a diet rich in foods that provide magnesium, these three benefits can drastically improve the quality of your cardiovascular system's functioning.

Best Foods for a Healthy Heart

By including heart-healthy foods that provide a wide array of heart-healthy vitamins and minerals in your daily green drinks, you can ensure your body is absorbing the nutrients it needs to fend off detrimental heart-health illnesses and diseases.

Best Produce for Heart Health

1. Nuts
2. Seeds
3. Healthy oils
4. Spinach
5. Avocados
6. Beans
7. Citrus fruits
8. Tomatoes
9. Cantaloupe

Heart-Healthy Drinks

Cabbage Carrot Blend

There are at least a hundred different types of cabbage grown throughout the world. This recipe blends this tasty green with carrots and ginger, the perfect combination of sweet and spicy.

INGREDIENTS | SERVES 3

1 cup shredded green cabbage

3 medium carrots, peeled

2 celery stalks

1" ginger, peeled and sliced

2 cups purified water

1. Place cabbage, carrots, celery, ginger, and 1 cup water in a blender and blend until thoroughly combined.

2. Add remaining 1 cup water, as needed, while blending until desired texture is achieved.

PER SERVING: Calories: 39 | Fat: 0 g | Protein: 1 g | Sodium: 69 mg | Fiber: 3 g | Carbohydrates: 9 g | Sugar: 4 g

Powerful Pepper Trio

This smoothie's mix of spicy arugula, peppers, and garlic combines for a savory treat you can enjoy anytime.

INGREDIENTS | SERVES 3

1 cup arugula

1 red bell pepper, cored

1 green bell pepper, cored

1 yellow bell pepper, cored

1 clove garlic

2 cups purified water

1. Place arugula, peppers, garlic, and 1 cup water in a blender and blend until thoroughly combined.

2. Add remaining 1 cup water, as needed, while blending until desired texture is achieved.

PER SERVING: Calories: 40 | Fat: 0 g | Protein: 2 g | Sodium: 6 mg | Fiber: 2 g | Carbohydrates: 9 g | Sugar: 3 g

Zesty Arugula Smoothie

Cilantro pairs perfectly with spicy arugula, sweet red pepper, and garlic in this flavor-packed smoothie.

INGREDIENTS | SERVES 3

1 cup arugula

1 red bell pepper, cored

2 tablespoons cilantro

1 clove garlic

2 cups purified water

1. Place arugula, pepper, cilantro, garlic, and 1 cup water in a blender and blend until thoroughly combined.

2. Add remaining 1 cup water, as needed, while blending until desired texture is achieved.

PER SERVING: Calories: 17 | Fat: 0 g | Protein: 1 g | Sodium: 6 mg | Fiber: 1 g | Carbohydrates: 3 g | Sugar: 2 g

Great Garlic

Just one small clove of garlic helps promote a strong heart—it takes center stage in this recipe, mixing nicely with spinach and celery.

INGREDIENTS | SERVES 3

1 cup chopped spinach

1 celery stalk

1 medium tomato

3 cloves garlic, peeled

2 cups purified water

1. Place spinach, celery, tomato, garlic, and 1 cup water in a blender and blend until thoroughly combined.

2. Add remaining 1 cup water, as needed, while blending until desired texture is achieved.

PER SERVING: Calories: 16 | Fat: 0 g | Protein: 1 g | Sodium: 21 mg | Fiber: 1 g | Carbohydrates: 3 g | Sugar: 1 g

A Savory Celery Celebration

Celery is a powerful ingredient for anyone needing a diet that is low in sodium. It also helps with water retention.

INGREDIENTS | SERVES 3

1 cup watercress
3 celery stalks
1 medium cucumber, peeled
1 clove garlic
1 cup purified water

1. Place watercress, celery, cucumber, garlic, and ½ cup water in a blender and blend until thoroughly combined.

2. Add remaining ½ cup water, as needed, while blending until desired texture is achieved.

PER SERVING: Calories: 17 | Fat: 0 g | Protein: 1 g | Sodium: 38 mg | Fiber: 1 g | Carbohydrates: 3 g | Sugar: 2 g

Squash Surprise

When you take a look at the color of this smoothie, you'll see the vibrant colors of the veggies, and thus their valuable nutrition. The bright-green spinach, yellow squash, and orange carrot combine for an aesthetically and palate-pleasing smoothie.

INGREDIENTS | SERVES 3

1 cup chopped spinach
½ butternut squash, peeled, seeded, and cubed
1 medium carrot, peeled
2 cloves garlic
2 cups purified water

1. Place spinach, squash, carrot, garlic, and 1 cup water in a blender and blend until thoroughly combined.

2. Add remaining 1 cup water, as needed, while blending until desired texture is achieved.

PER SERVING: Calories: 44 | Fat: 0 g | Protein: 1 g | Sodium: 25 mg | Fiber: 2 g | Carbohydrates: 11 g | Sugar: 3 g

Turnip Temptation

When was the last time you ate a turnip?
This rarely enjoyed root vegetable is a great addition to any diet.

INGREDIENTS | SERVES 3

1 cup chopped romaine lettuce

2 turnips, peeled and cut to fit blender

2 medium carrots, peeled

2 celery stalks

2 cups purified water

Turnip Lanterns

Pumpkins aren't the only vegetable that have been carved for Halloween. The Irish started the tradition of carving lanterns on Halloween, but originally turnips were used. Turnip lanterns were left on doorsteps in order to ward off evil spirits. At Samhain, candle lanterns carved from turnips—*Samhnag*—were part of the traditional Celtic festival. Large turnips were hollowed out, carved with faces, and placed in windows to ward off harmful spirits.

1. Place romaine, turnips, carrots, celery, and 1 cup water in a blender and blend until thoroughly combined.

2. Add remaining 1 cup water, as needed, while blending until desired texture is achieved.

PER SERVING: Calories: 46 | Fat: 0 g | Protein: 1 g | Sodium: 105 mg | Fiber: 3 g | Carbohydrates: 10 g | Sugar: 6 g

Health Harvest Juice

In late summer and early autumn, it's hard to come home from the farmers' market without feeling that you've just bought more than you could ever eat! Juicing is a great way to manage this bounty and take advantage of all the goodness the season provides.

INGREDIENTS | SERVES 1

1 small beet, greens optional

6 medium carrots, peeled

1 cup chopped spinach

2 celery stalks, with leaves intact

1 medium cucumber

1 medium grapefruit, peeled, seeded, and sectioned

1 kiwifruit

1 red or black plum, pitted

2 medium Bosc or Anjou pears, cored

2 medium apples, cored

1. Process the beet and carrots through an electronic juicer according to the manufacturer's instructions.

2. Add the spinach, celery, and cucumber.

3. Add the grapefruit sections, followed by the kiwi.

4. Add the plum and the pears, followed by the apples.

5. Whisk or shake the juice to combine and serve over ice, if desired.

PER SERVING: Calories: 681 | Fat: 3 g | Protein: 11 g | Sodium: 210 mg | Fiber: 0 g | Carbohydrates: 173 g | Sugar: 121 g

Cucumber Pear Plus

The "plus" in this recipe comes from sugar snap peas, a rich source of folate. Snap peas have 150 percent more vitamin C than regular garden peas and also contain phytosterols, which help lower cholesterol.

INGREDIENTS | SERVES 1

3 medium pears, cored

1 medium cucumber, peeled

2 cups chopped spinach

6 kale leaves

½ leaf Swiss chard

½ lemon, peeled

1 cup sugar snap peas

Snap!

Sugar snap peas also are a good source of riboflavin, vitamin B_6, pantothenic acid, magnesium, phosphorus, and potassium in addition to fiber, vitamin A, vitamin K, thiamine, iron, and manganese.

1. Process the pears through an electronic juicer according to the manufacturer's instructions.

2. Add the cucumber, followed by the spinach.

3. Roll the kale and chard leaves together to compress and add to the juicer.

4. Add the lemon and the snap peas.

5. Whisk the juice to combine the ingredients and serve immediately.

PER SERVING: Calories: 596 | Fat: 5 g | Protein: 25 g | Sodium: 416 mg | Fiber: 0 g | Carbohydrates: 134 g | Sugar: 60 g

Grapeberry Cocktail

Grapes are rich in the phytochemical resveratrol, a powerful antioxidant that has been found to play a protective role against cancers of the colon and prostate, heart disease, degenerative nerve disease, Alzheimer's, and viral/fungal infections. It also has marvelous benefits for aging skin.

INGREDIENTS | SERVES 1

½ cup chopped romaine lettuce

3 cups Concord grapes

1 medium apple, cored

½ cup blackberries

All about Blackberries

Blackberries help to lower your risk of heart disease and stroke, and they may lower your risk of certain cancers. Blackberries may also help to prevent diabetes and age-related cognitive decline. When choosing blackberries, be sure they don't have the hulls or green leaves attached. If they do, it means they were picked too early and they will not ripen after they have been picked.

1. Process the romaine and grapes through an electronic juicer according to the manufacturer's instructions.

2. Add the apple, followed by the blackberries.

3. Mix the juice thoroughly and enjoy.

PER SERVING: Calories: 315 | Fat: 2 g | Protein: 4 g | Sodium: 10 mg | Fiber: 0 g | Carbohydrates: 80 g | Sugar: 68 g

Red Bells Make Hearts Ring

Red peppers star in this simple, savory smoothie that tastes great and makes for a strong heart.

INGREDIENTS | SERVES 3

1 cup arugula

1 red bell pepper, top and seeds removed and ribs intact

2 medium cucumbers, peeled

2 celery stalks

2 cups chamomile tea

1. Place arugula, red pepper, cucumbers, celery, and 1 cup tea in a blender and blend until thoroughly combined.

2. Add remaining 1 cup tea, as needed, while blending until desired consistency is achieved.

PER SERVING: Calories: 36 | Fat: 0 g | Protein: 2 g | Sodium: 29 mg | Fiber: 2 g | Carbohydrates: 7 g | Sugar: 4 g

Sweet Flax and Fiber

Flaxseed's nutritional qualities include plentiful protein, complex carbs, and outstanding omega-3s. This recipe is sweetened with antioxidant-rich berries.

INGREDIENTS | SERVES 2

1 cup chopped spinach

2 medium red apples, peeled and cored

⅛ cup ground flaxseed

1 teaspoon cinnamon

2 cups vanilla almond milk

Combine all ingredients in a blender and blend until desired consistency is reached.

PER SERVING: Calories: 215 | Fat: 5 g | Protein: 3 g | Sodium: 163 mg | Fiber: 6 g | Carbohydrates: 41 g | Sugar: 31 g

Omegas and Beyond

Great for the brain, blood, and heart, omega-3s and omega-6s are nature's powerhouses. With fiber-rich spinach, omega-packed flax and walnuts, and sweet pears, this green drink is the perfect combination of heart-healthy ingredients in one single cup.

INGREDIENTS | SERVES 2

½ cup chopped spinach
⅛ cup ground flaxseed
2 medium pears, peeled and cored
¼ cup walnuts, shelled
2 cups vanilla coconut milk

Combine all ingredients in a blender and blend until desired consistency is reached.

PER SERVING: Calories: 315 | Fat: 16 g | Protein: 4 g | Sodium: 53 mg | Fiber: 9 g | Carbohydrates: 41 g | Sugar: 27 g

Apple-Flax Smoothie

Between the fiber content and the healing antioxidant powers of flax and cinnamon, this sweet apple treat will keep your heart healthy and your mouth happy!

INGREDIENTS | SERVES 2

1 cup chopped spinach
1 cup raw oats
⅛ cup ground flaxseed
2 medium green apples, cored
1 teaspoon ground cinnamon
2 cups vanilla almond milk

Combine all ingredients in a blender and blend until desired consistency is reached.

PER SERVING: Calories: 535 | Fat: 11 g | Protein: 17 g | Sodium: 166 mg | Fiber: 17 g | Carbohydrates: 97 g | Sugar: 34 g

Carrot Commando

This sweet drink makes for a healthy breakfast, lunch, dinner, or simple snack.

INGREDIENTS | SERVES 2

1 cup chopped kale
6 medium carrots, peeled
1" ginger, peeled
1 teaspoon ground cloves

1. Juice kale, carrots, and ginger together according to the manufacturer's instructions.

2. Transfer to a blender and blend in ground cloves.

3. Stir until all ingredients are well blended.

PER SERVING: Calories: 98 | Fat: 1 g | Protein: 3 g | Sodium: 143 mg | Fiber: 0 g | Carbohydrates: 22 g | Sugar: 9 g

Gracious Grapes

Red grapes provide a ton of potassium, and blend perfectly with the subtle flavor of romaine lettuce and the sweetness of a green apple and pear.

INGREDIENTS | SERVES 2

1 cup chopped romaine lettuce
2 cups red grapes
1 medium pear, cored
1 green apple, cored

1. Juice all ingredients together according to the manufacturer's instructions.

2. Stir until all ingredients are well blended.

PER SERVING: Calories: 164 | Fat: 1 g | Protein: 1 g | Sodium: 6 mg | Fiber: 0 g | Carbohydrates: 43 g | Sugar: 33 g

Pineapple Perfection

The vitamin C found in this sweet drink does wonders for protecting your heart and boosting your immunity.

INGREDIENTS | SERVES 2

1 cup chopped spinach
3 cups pineapple chunks
1 cup red grapes
2 cups unsweetened coconut milk

Combine all ingredients in a blender and blend until desired consistency is reached.

PER SERVING: Calories: 238 | Fat: 6 g | Protein: 2 g | Sodium: 60 mg | Fiber: 4 g | Carbohydrates: 48 g | Sugar: 38 g

Wonderful Waldorf

With the sweetness of grapes and the nutty flavors of walnuts and flax, you'll feel like you're drinking a Waldorf salad as you sip this delicious and nutritious green drink.

INGREDIENTS | SERVES 2

1 cup chopped romaine lettuce
1 medium green apple, cored
2 cups red grapes
1 English cucumber
¼ cup walnuts, shelled
⅛ cup ground flaxseed
2 cups purified water

Combine all ingredients in a blender and blend until desired consistency is reached.

PER SERVING: Calories: 257 | Fat: 11 g | Protein: 5 g | Sodium: 8 mg | Fiber: 7 g | Carbohydrates: 39 mg | Sugar: 28 g

A Healthy, Happy Heart

Keep yourself happy and healthy by boosting your vitamin and mineral intake with veggies and fruits and cholesterol-lowering oats.

INGREDIENTS | SERVES 2

1 cup chopped spinach

1 medium carrot, peeled

1 medium red apple, cored

1 medium pear, cored

1 cup raw oats

2 cups unsweetened vanilla almond milk

Combine all ingredients in a blender and blend until desired consistency is reached.

PER SERVING: Calories: 508 | Fat: 8 g | Protein: 15 g | Sodium: 187 mg | Fiber: 15 g | Carbohydrates: 97 g | Sugar: 35 g

Sweet Heart

Sweetness isn't only found in the fabulous fruits you have available. You can maximize your vitamins and minerals by combining fruits and vegetables in every meal and snack possible . . . just as in this sweet green drink for your sweet heart.

INGREDIENTS | SERVES 2

1 cup chopped spinach

2 medium carrots, peeled

2 kiwifruit, peeled

1 cup pineapple chunks

2 cups unsweetened vanilla almond milk

Combine all ingredients in a blender and blend until desired consistency is reached.

PER SERVING: Calories: 212 | Fat: 3 g | Protein: 3 g | Sodium: 208 mg | Fiber: 6 g | Carbohydrates: 45 g | Sugar: 36 g

Drinks for Kids' Health

No doubt about it: kids love juice! Even the pickiest eaters can get greedy when it comes to a wholesome, healthful glass of fresh juice or a delicious smoothie. You can creatively include a variety of nutrient-rich foods in kids' green drinks that can provide them with all of the benefits they need to stay healthy and build strong bodies. While experts recommend that babies and toddlers should avoid unpasteurized juices in favor of mother's milk, toddlers and young children who are eating solid foods, as well as older children, can enjoy a myriad of benefits in nutritious, delicious green drinks.

Kid-Friendly Drinks

Here are some rules to keep in mind when creating green drinks for and with your kids. First of all, keep it simple. Don't overwhelm them with too many complex flavors and don't think you can sneak in potent ingredients like kale or turnips without them suspecting something. Those fruits and vegetables that have strong flavors for adults are even more powerful to the younger palates.

Second, try to begin introducing green drinks by keeping the ingredients' flavors subtle and on the mild side. Bean sprouts, for example, have very little flavor, but plenty of the nutrition your child needs. Even if they won't touch greens on their dinner plate, you can easily create green drinks that include nutrient-rich essentials and simply mask their flavors with strongly flavored additions like apples, pineapple, grapes, carrots, and juices. By paying attention to your child's likes and dislikes, you can introduce a variety of flavors, include overpowering ingredients that will minimize the "not-so-tempting" flavors, and gradually change the amounts of the ingredients to include more and more of the less-liked varieties and fewer and fewer of the overpowering elements. Children eat and drink things that taste good (healthy or not), so if you choose your recipes and ingredients wisely, you're more likely to be successful in your quest to get your non-veggie-eater some necessary nutrients.

Third, dilute your green drinks with filtered water. Children's digestive systems are more delicate, and some may be prone to allergies or have sensitivities to certain foods. Just as some adults need time for their systems to adjust to certain produce, so do kids, so take it easy in the beginning.

Fourth, never put any child under the age of twelve on any type of fast . . . especially a juice fast! Still developing systems and child-size metabolisms are more easily thrown out of whack when too much of an emphasis is placed on one food group or another.

Last, but certainly not least, keep it fun! Ask them to help dream up their own imaginative combinations, write their own recipes, and give your green drinks silly or kid-friendly names. Most children are far more likely to sample something called Green Goblin Juice than they are to try a Chlorophyll Cocktail.

Green Drinks Provide What Kids Need

Whether you're weaning your toddler off of milk or helping your high schooler study for exams, you can improve your child's chances to thrive by ensuring he or she receives all of the needed nutrients and consumes a diet rich in natural foods that optimize nutritional values. Children of all ages are in need of adequate amounts of vitamin A, all of the B vitamins, vitamin C, and vitamin E, as well as the minerals calcium, potassium, magnesium, zinc, copper, and iron; the recommended daily amount of these vitamins and minerals varies depending upon a number of factors, such as age, weight, activity level, pre-existing conditions, etc. Without enough of any of the vital vitamins and minerals, your child could suffer from symptoms that can range from lightheadedness to frequent illness, anemia to impeded protein synthesis. The bottom line is that children require nourishment for all of their body's systems as well as proper brain development and optimal cognitive functioning; by preparing green drinks packed with nutrient-rich fruits and vegetables, you can ensure your child will be consuming clean sources of plentiful vitamins, minerals, and phytochemicals each and every day!

Best Produce for Kids' Health

1. Melons
2. Berries
3. Pumpkin
4. Citrus
5. Grapes
6. Peaches
7. Greens
8. Pears
9. Peas
10. Nuts

Drinks for Kids' Health

Cantaloupe Quencher

Kids love fresh cantaloupe! Juice running down their little chins, they can't get enough of this powerful vitamin-rich fruit, which makes it the perfect star of a green smoothie recipe like this one.

INGREDIENTS | SERVES 3

1 cup chopped iceberg lettuce

2 cups cantaloupe cubes, rind and seeds removed

2 bananas, peeled

1 cup almond milk

1 cup ice

Protect Your Family with Vitamins and Antioxidants

Although many people get the flu shot, exercise regularly, and try to eat a diet that will promote illness protection, when was the last time your child was guzzling vitamin C for the health benefits or finishing off his spinach because of the rich iron content? Children eat what tastes great, and when you make nutritious food delicious, they arm their own bodies with immunity-building protection.

1. Place iceberg, cantaloupe, bananas, and ½ cup almond milk in a blender and blend until thoroughly combined.

2. Add remaining ½ cup almond milk and ice, as needed, while blending until desired consistency is achieved.

PER SERVING: Calories: 93 | Fat: 1 g | Protein: 2 g | Sodium: 72 mg | Fiber: 2 g | Carbohydrates: 21 g | Sugar: 16 g

Wonderful Watermelon

Watermelon's super powers don't end with its amazing hydrating effects, which make it one of the top go-to summer fruits. This delicious smoothie with the hidden taste of romaine will make even your pickiest eater love veggies.

INGREDIENTS | SERVES 3

1 cup chopped romaine lettuce

2 cups watermelon chunks, rind and seeds removed

2 bananas, peeled

½ cup Greek-style yogurt

1 cup ice

A Great Gatorade Alternative

Packed with delicious flavor and hydrating power, watermelon offers up the added benefit of much-needed electrolytes for active kids. Most commercial drinks that promise a boost of balancing electrolytes are packed with sugars. Sweet homemade green smoothies are a smarter choice for your youngster following any high-endurance activity.

1. Place romaine, watermelon, bananas, and yogurt in a blender and blend until thoroughly combined.

2. Add ice, as needed, while blending until desired consistency is achieved.

PER SERVING: Calories: 125 | Fat: 1 g | Protein: 6 g | Sodium: 17 mg | Fiber: 3 g | Carbohydrates: 27 g | Sugar: 17 g

Honeydew for Your Honeys

This smooth, slightly sweet treat is delicious without being overpowering. With a very cool color and a taste your kids will love, this recipe makes a fruity green milkshake that delivers loads of vitamins and minerals.

INGREDIENTS | SERVES 3

1 cup chopped romaine lettuce

2 cups honeydew cubes, rind and seeds removed

2 bananas, peeled

½ cup Greek-style yogurt

1 cup ice

1. Place romaine, honeydew, bananas, and yogurt in a blender and blend until thoroughly combined.

2. Add ice, as needed, while blending until desired consistency is achieved.

PER SERVING: Calories: 136 | Fat: 1 g | Protein: 6 g | Sodium: 36 mg | Fiber: 3 g | Carbohydrates: 30 g | Sugar: 20 g

Strawberry Breakfast Smoothie

A deliciously rich strawberry banana smoothie will be your kids' favorite breakfast after just one taste.

INGREDIENTS | SERVES 3

1 cup chopped romaine lettuce

2 pints strawberries, tops removed

2 bananas, peeled

1 cup strawberry kefir

1 cup ice

1. Place romaine, strawberries, bananas, and kefir in a blender and blend until thoroughly combined.

2. Add ice, as needed, while blending until desired consistency is achieved.

PER SERVING: Calories: 181 | Fat: 2 g | Protein: 6 g | Sodium: 46 mg | Fiber: 6 g | Carbohydrates: 40 g | Sugar: 26 g

Blueberry Burst

*Even kids who say they hate blueberries love this smoothie,
since it tastes more like ice cream than a green smoothie.*

INGREDIENTS | SERVES 3

1 cup watercress

2 pints blueberries

2 bananas, peeled

1 cup blueberry kefir

1 cup ice

Blueberries and Bananas for Overall Health

Not only does the delicious blend of blueberries and bananas taste great, but this combination also makes an amazingly nutritional treat for youngsters. The rich potassium, magnesium, B_6, and electrolyte stores of the bananas add to the vitamin C, sapronins, and powerful antioxidants of the blueberries. It's a delicious way to promote heart health, mental clarity and focus, energy, and immune-fighting power.

1. Place watercress, blueberries, bananas, and kefir in a blender and blend until thoroughly combined.

2. Add ice, as needed, while blending until desired consistency is achieved.

PER SERVING: Calories: 228 | Fat: 2 g | Protein: 6 g | Sodium: 49 mg | Fiber: 7 g | Carbohydrates: 53 g | Sugar: 36 g

Green Machine

This smoothie appeals to youngsters because the overall taste is sweet and the color is very different from ordinary juices. This flavorful combination is a nutrition-packed drink for any child or adult.

INGREDIENTS | SERVES 3

1 cup chopped spinach

4 medium Granny Smith apples, peeled and cored

2 bananas, peeled

2 cups purified water

1 cup ice

1. Place spinach, apples, bananas, and 1 cup water in a blender and blend until thoroughly combined.

2. Add remaining 1 cup water and ice, as needed, while blending until desired consistency is achieved.

PER SERVING: Calories: 175 | Fat: 1 g | Protein: 2 g | Sodium: 9 mg | Fiber: 5 g | Carbohydrates: 46 g | Sugar: 31 g

Lead by Example

Monkey see, monkey do. Kids look to their parents for cues on what is desirable in regard to speech, behavior, and even food likes and dislikes. Show your child that you indulge in green smoothies and enjoy them; you'll be nurturing yourself with powerful nutrition while being a positive role model. You'll discourage your child from being a picky eater, and she'll reap the benefits of a healthy, balanced diet.

Sweet Pumpkin Pie

Masking an entire cup of spinach in the delicious flavors of sweet pumpkin pie is an excellent idea. Sweet potatoes and almond milk, along with intense aromatic spices, will never give away the star ingredient: spinach!

INGREDIENTS | SERVES 3

1 cup chopped spinach
2 sweet potatoes, peeled and cubed
1 teaspoon cinnamon
1 teaspoon pumpkin pie spice
2 cups almond milk
1 cup ice

1. Place spinach, sweet potatoes, cinnamon, pumpkin pie spice, and 1 cup almond milk in a blender and blend until thoroughly combined.

2. Add remaining 1 cup almond milk and ice, as needed, while blending until desired consistency is achieved.

PER SERVING: Calories: 97 | Fat: 2 g | Protein: 2 g | Sodium: 147 mg | Fiber: 2 g | Carbohydrates: 19 g | Sugar: 7 g

Green Lemonade

Most kids won't pass up lemonade! Revamp the old nutrition-lacking version of lemonade by blending this mix of real lemons, sweet apples, raw honey or agave nectar, vitamin-rich spinach, and green tea.

INGREDIENTS | SERVES 3

1 cup chopped spinach
2 medium apples, peeled and cored
4 lemons, peeled
1 tablespoon raw honey or agave nectar
2 cups green tea
1 cup ice

1. Place spinach, apples, lemons, honey or agave, and 1 cup tea in a blender and blend until thoroughly combined.

2. Add remaining 1 cup tea and ice, as needed, while blending until desired consistency is achieved.

PER SERVING: Calories: 98 | Fat: 0 g | Protein: 1 g | Sodium: 10 mg | Fiber: 4 g | Carbohydrates: 27 g | Sugar: 19 g

Grapefruit Tangerine

Grapefruit can be tart, but combining it with tangerines, pineapple, and soothing green tea makes a delicious balance of flavors for one remarkably sweet and refreshing smoothie your kids will enjoy.

INGREDIENTS | SERVES 3

1 cup watercress

2 medium grapefruits, peeled and seeded

2 medium tangerines, peeled

1 cup pineapple chunks

1 cup green tea

1 cup ice

1. Place watercress, grapefruits, tangerines, pineapple, and ½ cup tea in a blender and blend until thoroughly combined.

2. Add remaining ½ cup tea and ice, as needed, while blending until desired consistency is achieved.

PER SERVING: Calories: 114 | Fat: 0 g | Protein: 2 g | Sodium: 6 mg | Fiber: 4 g | Carbohydrates: 29 g | Sugar: 24 g

Great Grape

With balanced nutrition and a great taste your kids will love, this is one sweet treat you'll never feel guilty about giving them!

INGREDIENTS | SERVES 3

1 cup watercress

3 cups red grapes

2 medium pears, cored and peeled

1 cup almond milk

1 cup ice

1. Place watercress, grapes, pears, and almond milk in a blender and blend until thoroughly combined.

2. Add ice, as needed, while blending until desired consistency is achieved.

PER SERVING: Calories: 151 | Fat: 1 g | Protein: 2 g | Sodium: 61 mg | Fiber: 5 g | Carbohydrates: 37 g | Sugar: 29 g

Chocolate Banana Blitz

Kids love chocolate! A brilliant way to transform a plain old green vegetable into pure deliciousness is to add chocolatey carob.

INGREDIENTS | SERVES 3

1 cup chopped romaine lettuce

2 tablespoons carob powder

3 bananas, peeled

Pulp of 1 vanilla bean or 1 teaspoon vanilla extract

1 cup vanilla kefir

1 cup ice

1. Place romaine, carob powder, bananas, vanilla, and kefir in a blender and blend until thoroughly combined.

2. Add ice, as needed, while blending until desired consistency is achieved.

PER SERVING: Calories: 162 | Fat: 2 g | Protein: 6 g | Sodium: 45 mg | Fiber: 4 g | Carbohydrates: 36 g | Sugar: 21 g

The Chocolate Alternatives

Powdered raw cacao and carob are two alternatives to the not-so-healthy chocolate enhanced with sugars that can bring out undesirable overstimulation in your little one. By including the flavors of the chocolate alternatives, you can provide a chocolate-flavored delight packed with rich antioxidants and amazing vitamins and minerals. Healthy, no sugar, no additives, no guilt!

Peas, Please!

This veggie-packed smoothie actually tastes sweet. If your kids like peas and love carrots, this smoothie's a sure thing; if your kiddo is anti-veggie, this smoothie's probably going to get him to admit they're not half bad.

INGREDIENTS | SERVES 3

1 cup chopped spinach

1 cup sweet peas

2 medium carrots, peeled

1 medium apple, peeled and cored

1 cup green tea

1 cup ice

1. Place spinach, peas, carrots, apple, and tea in a blender and blend until thoroughly combined.

2. Add ice, as needed, while blending until desired consistency is achieved.

PER SERVING: Calories: 70 | Fat: 0 g | Protein: 3 g | Sodium: 106 mg | Fiber: 4 g | Carbohydrates: 17 g | Sugar: 10 g

The Lonely Sweet Pea

Very rarely do kids get heaping helpings of peas on a regular basis. Peas provide more than 50 percent of the recommended daily amount of vitamin K and are packed with vitamin Bs and C, folate, iron, zinc, manganese, and protein. They also promote brain health, bone strength, heart health, and disease-fighting protection.

Watercress Citrus Burst

For kids who love citrus fruits, this recipe is absolutely amazing. Blending an entire cup of greens into a deliciously sweet, tangy, and refreshing treat is one great-tasting way to get fiber.

INGREDIENTS | SERVES 3

1 cup watercress
3 cups pineapple chunks
1 medium tangerine, peeled
½ lemon, peeled
1 cup Greek-style yogurt
1 cup ice

1. Place watercress, pineapple, tangerine, lemon, and yogurt in a blender and blend until thoroughly combined.

2. Add ice, as needed, while blending until desired consistency is achieved.

PER SERVING: Calories: 147 | Fat: 1 g | Protein: 9 g | Sodium: 34 mg | Fiber: 3 g | Carbohydrates: 29 g | Sugar: 22 g

Green Peaches 'n Cream

Fresh or frozen ingredients, fireside or poolside, this smoothie is a mouthwatering way to deliver fresh ingredients, no added sugars, an entire cup of greens, and plentiful fruit servings to kids who need and deserve great-tasting nutrition.

INGREDIENTS | SERVES 3

1 cup chopped romaine lettuce
3 medium peaches, pitted
2 bananas, peeled
1 cup vanilla kefir
1 cup ice

1. Place romaine, peaches, bananas, and kefir in a blender and blend until thoroughly combined.

2. Add ice, as needed, while blending until desired consistency is achieved.

PER SERVING: Calories: 178 | Fat: 1 g | Protein: 6 g | Sodium: 44 mg | Fiber: 5 g | Carbohydrates: 39 g | Sugar: 29 g

Sweet Pears

Pears have a unique flavor that blends deliciously with the crisp watercress, sweet bananas, and kefir to make this drink. It provides intense vitamins and minerals in every scrumptious sip.

INGREDIENTS | SERVES 3

1 cup watercress
4 medium pears, peeled and cored
2 bananas, peeled
2 cups vanilla kefir
1 cup ice

1. Place watercress, pears, bananas, and 1 cup kefir in a blender and blend until thoroughly combined.

2. Add remaining 1 cup kefir and ice, as needed, while blending until desired consistency is achieved.

PER SERVING: Calories: 300 | Fat: 2 g | Protein: 9 g | Sodium: 91 mg | Fiber: 9 g | Carbohydrates: 68 g | Sugar: 46 g

Vanilla Banana Blend

You'll love the rich vitamin, mineral, antioxidant, and probiotic power of these amazing ingredients.

INGREDIENTS | SERVES 3

1 cup chopped romaine lettuce
4 bananas, peeled
Pulp of 1½ vanilla beans or 1½ teaspoons vanilla extract
2 cups vanilla kefir
1 cup ice

1. Place romaine, bananas, vanilla, and 1 cup kefir in a blender and blend until thoroughly combined.

2. Add remaining 1 cup kefir and ice, as needed, while blending until desired consistency is achieved.

PER SERVING: Calories: 236 | Fat: 2 g | Protein: 9 g | Sodium: 86 mg | Fiber: 4 g | Carbohydrates: 50 g | Sugar: 33 g

Green Cherry Vanilla Milkshake

This recipe is specifically for the serious doubters who don't believe a child will consume greens blended in a smoothie. Give a try and be pleasantly surprised!

INGREDIENTS | SERVES 3

1 cup chopped spinach

2 cups cherries, pitted

1 banana, peeled

Pulp of 1½ vanilla beans or 1½ teaspoons vanilla extract

2 cups vanilla kefir

1 cup ice

1. Place spinach, cherries, banana, vanilla, and 1 cup kefir in a blender and blend until thoroughly combined.

2. Add remaining 1 cup kefir and ice, as needed, while blending until desired consistency is achieved.

PER SERVING: Calories: 195 | Fat: 2 g | Protein: 9 g | Sodium: 92 mg | Fiber: 3 g | Carbohydrates: 39 g | Sugar: 31 g

Green Chocolate Dream

Your little ones will fall for the deliciously rich flavors of this recipe, with the only question being, "Are there seconds?"

INGREDIENTS | SERVES 3

1 cup chopped spinach

2 tablespoons carob powder

3 bananas, peeled

2 cups almond milk

1 cup ice

1. Place spinach, carob, bananas, and 1 cup almond milk in a blender and blend until thoroughly combined.

2. Add remaining 1 cup almond milk and ice, as needed, while blending until desired consistency is achieved.

PER SERVING: Calories: 155 | Fat: 3 g | Protein: 3 g | Sodium: 116 mg | Fiber: 4 g | Carbohydrates: 35 g | Sugar: 19 g

Nuts 'n Honey

Trail mixes, cereals, granola, and even candy bars make this delicious and healthy blend of ingredients a sugar-packed, preservative-enhanced trap. By combining these fresh ingredients at home, you'll know exactly where the finished product came from.

INGREDIENTS | SERVES 3

⅛ cup almonds

⅛ cup walnuts

1 tablespoon ground flaxseed

2 cups almond milk

1 cup chopped romaine lettuce

2 bananas, peeled

1½ tablespoons raw honey or agave nectar

1 cup ice

1. Combine nuts, flax, and 1 cup almond milk in a blender and emulsify until no nut bits remain.

2. Add romaine, bananas, and agave or honey and blend until thoroughly combined.

3. Add remaining 1 cup almond milk and ice, as needed, while blending until desired consistency is achieved.

PER SERVING: Calories: 220 | Fat: 9 g | Protein: 4 g | Sodium: 109 mg | Fiber: 4 g | Carbohydrates: 35 g | Sugar: 24 g

Flaxseeds for Kids

If your child isn't wild about salmon, or any fish for that matter, you can add omega-3s to his diet in an undetectable form. Ground flaxseeds provide a mild nutty flavor without an extreme taste. Sold at grocery stores and mega marts around the country, organic ground flaxseeds are an inexpensive way to boost your child's omega intake.

Pineapple Melon Smoothie

Sweet pineapple and the naturally syrupy cantaloupe make for a wonderful duo in this recipe.

INGREDIENTS | SERVES 3

1 cup chopped romaine lettuce

2 cups pineapple chunks

2 cups cantaloupe chunks, rind and seeds removed

1 cup green tea

1 cup ice

1. Place romaine, pineapple, cantaloupe, and ½ cup tea in a blender and blend until thoroughly combined.

2. Add remaining ½ cup tea and ice, as needed, while blending until desired consistency is achieved.

PER SERVING: Calories: 93 | Fat: 0 g | Protein: 2 g | Sodium: 19 mg | Fiber: 3 g | Carbohydrates: 23 g | Sugar: 19 g

Very Vitamin C!

This recipe has big helpings of vitamin C–rich fruits, mineral-boasting greens, and delicious chamomile for a refreshing and sweet breakfast, lunch, snack, or dessert.

INGREDIENTS | SERVES 3

1 cup watercress

2 medium tangerines, peeled

2 cups pineapple chunks

1 cup grapefruit chunks, peeled and seeded

1 cup green tea

1 cup ice

1. Place watercress, tangerines, pineapple, grapefruit, and ½ cup tea in a blender and blend until thoroughly combined.

2. Add remaining ½ cup tea and ice, as needed, while blending until desired consistency is achieved.

PER SERVING: Calories: 112 | Fat: 0 g | Protein: 2 g | Sodium: 7 mg | Fiber: 3 g | Carbohydrates: 29 g | Sugar: 22 g

CHAPTER 16

Drinks for Pregnancy

Pregnancy is one of the most beautiful experiences a woman can have in her lifetime, and it is a time where quality nutrition becomes a priority. To ensure that the expectant body has everything available to safeguard her health and minimize common discomforts like nausea, morning sickness, fatigue, and joint and back pain, and to prevent more serious complications like preeclampsia and gestational diabetes, consuming a diet rich in whole, natural, clean foods that optimize nutrition bite-for-bite is absolutely imperative. Green drinks can help guarantee that the prenatal diet is packed with the best nutrients available, and that the building blocks needed to create a healthy, happy baby are available around the clock.

Healthy Moms Make Healthy Babies

There is no doubt about it: The diet you consume during your pregnancy will directly affect the health of your baby. Through your diet, your baby will receive all of the vitamins, minerals, protein, carbohydrates, fats, and antioxidants it needs. By consuming a diet rich in healthy foods that maximize nutrition, you can ensure the proper growth of your baby, promote a healthier and happier pregnancy, and even increase your chances of having an easier delivery.

The healthy lifestyle and diet you choose during your pregnancy can also improve your chances of having a baby that has the taste for that same lifestyle and diet as she grows. New research is showing a strong correlation between moms who choose to exercise and diet healthfully during pregnancy and their children choosing healthier food options, living more active lifestyles, and showing lower incidences of eating disorders as they grow.

Vitamins and Minerals for Pregnancy

Pregnancy can take a toll on your body, so it is important to get the right vitamins and minerals, such as:

- **Vitamin A:** Promotes the growth and health of cells and tissues for mom and baby. The well-known vitamin A antioxidant, beta-carotene, also acts as a powerful antioxidant to ward off illnesses, prevent unhealthy cell damage, and promote proper cell growth.
- **Vitamin D:** Aids in promoting healthy calcium balance by helping the body to absorb sufficient amounts to be used by mom and baby.
- **Folic acid:** A B vitamin whose job is mainly to promote the healthy cell development required in DNA and genetic processes, folic acid, consumed in sufficient amounts is imperative in maintaining healthy blood cells and reducing the risks of certain folic acid deficiencies like anemia, impaired fetal growth, abnormal digestive functioning, and even spina bifida.
- **Vitamins B_6 and B_{12}:** Two essential vitamins required by the body in order to create nonessential amino acids (the building blocks of protein) used to create necessary body cells. The requirements of both increase in pregnancy due to the formation of the baby's red blood cells.

- **Vitamin C:** From protecting mom and baby from harmful illnesses and diseases to ensuring the proper formation and growth of red blood cells, bones, and other tissues, vitamin C is a powerful antioxidant that multitasks in a number of important processes. It also helps the expectant mom to absorb sufficient amounts of iron. Vitamin C is absolutely imperative in the prenatal diet.

- **Calcium:** A little-known fact about calcium during pregnancy is that the fetus will get what she needs for calcium whether it is available in the diet or not; if the expectant mom is not consuming enough calcium through her diet, the body will rob the calcium stores of the mom in order to ensure the fetus has enough. By consuming enough calcium through a nutrient-rich diet, you can ensure you and your baby have sufficient amounts of this valuable mineral while also preventing serious situations like high blood pressure and toxemia.

- **Iron:** Because iron is essential in the formation of hemoglobin in the blood, a prenatal diet rich in this mineral is important for both mom and baby. The risk of becoming anemic (iron deficient) during pregnancy is much higher than in the nonpregnant population, and consuming iron-rich foods like leafy greens and iron-rich additions will help ensure that the body's iron stores remain at a healthy level.

- **Zinc:** Zinc is needed for cell growth and brain development and becomes especially important for pregnancy. While the daily requirement rises only slightly (from 8 mg to 11 mg daily), it is important to focus on including zinc-rich foods in the diet to ensure that adequate amounts necessary to optimize the development and growth of the fetus are available.

- **Sodium:** This mineral can be one that is healthy to an extent, and hazardous past a certain intake level. During pregnancy, fluids are fluctuating and sodium is necessary to maintain a healthy balance of those fluids, *but* a high sodium intake via processed foods can result in dangerous and debilitating situations. Focusing on foods that provide natural forms of sodium, and limiting the unnatural provisions of the mineral, will keep you in the "safe zone." The goal of 2,400 daily mg will ensure that your body maintains proper fluid balance, regular blood pressure, and relaxed muscles without excessive bloating and discomfort.

Best Fruits for Pregnancy

The following is a list of the best fruits to eat during your pregnancy.

- Apples
- Avocados
- Bananas
- Blackberries
- Blueberries
- Cantaloupe
- Grapefruit
- Grapes
- Honeydew melons
- Kiwi
- Lemons
- Limes
- Mangoes
- Oranges
- Papayas
- Peaches
- Pears
- Pineapples
- Pomegranates
- Raspberries
- Strawberries
- Tomatoes

Best Vegetables for Pregnancy

- Beets
- Broccoli
- Cabbage
- Carrots
- Cauliflower
- Celery
- Corn
- Green beans
- Kale
- Onions
- Peas
- Peppers
- Potatoes
- Romaine lettuce
- Spinach
- Squash
- Sweet potatoes
- Zucchini

Drinks for Pregnancy

Maternity Medley

This delicious smoothie recipe combines sweet fruits and luscious watercress with the zing of ginger to provide important vitamins and minerals for your pregnancy.

INGREDIENTS | SERVES 3

1 cup watercress
½ mango, peeled and seeded
½ pineapple, peeled and cored
2 medium tangerines, peeled
¼" ginger, peeled
1 cup red raspberry tea

Make Calories Count in Pregnancy

Although many women strive for complete nutrition while also appreciating the increase in caloric requirements suggested in pregnancy, some fear excess troublesome weight gain. In order to ensure that your nutrition and your weight gain are ideal for your pregnancy, make every calorie count. Empty-calorie foods like fried foods and sugary treats deliver empty nutrition for your body and your baby and lead to excessive sodium, sugar, and fat intake, which will result in stubborn post-baby pounds.

1. Place watercress, mango, pineapple, tangerines, ginger, and ½ cup tea in a blender and blend until thoroughly combined.

2. Add remaining ½ cup tea, as needed, while blending until desired consistency is achieved.

PER SERVING: Calories: 123 | Fat: 0 g | Protein: 2 g | Sodium: 8 mg | Fiber: 4 g | Carbohydrates: 31 g | Sugar: 24 g

Fertility Found

A blend of berries, melon, and vanilla downplay the subtle taste of spinach for a deliciously sweet and tart smoothie that provides vitamins, minerals, and phytochemicals for better health for mom and baby.

INGREDIENTS | SERVES 3

1 cup chopped spinach

2 cups cranberries

1 cup cantaloupe chunks, rind and seeds removed

Pulp of ½ vanilla bean

1 cup kefir

Copper for Fertility

Alternative and holistic medicine promotes the use of herbs, vitamins, minerals, and herbal teas to remedy infertility in both men and women. Copper enhances iron absorption and reproductive health in the body. Copper is abundant in deep leafy greens, so add more to your diet to increase copper consumption.

1. Place spinach, cranberries, cantaloupe, vanilla pulp, and ½ cup kefir in a blender and blend until thoroughly combined.

2. Add remaining ½ cup kefir, as needed, while blending until desired consistency is achieved.

PER SERVING: Calories: 97 | Fat: 3 g | Protein: 4 g | Sodium: 49 mg | Fiber: 4 g | Carbohydrates: 16 g | Sugar: 10 g

Baby, Be Happy

This simple recipe makes a sweet veggie smoothie you're sure to enjoy. Combining iron-rich spinach, peas, and vitamin-rich carrots will satisfy your increasing iron needs.

INGREDIENTS | SERVES 3

1 cup chopped spinach
1 cup sweet peas
3 medium carrots, peeled
2 cups red raspberry tea

1. Place spinach, peas, carrots, and 1 cup tea in a blender and blend until thoroughly combined.

2. Add remaining 1 cup tea, as needed, while blending until desired consistency is achieved.

PER SERVING: Calories: 53 | Fat: 0 g | Protein: 3 g | Sodium: 121 mg | Fiber: 4 g | Carbohydrates: 12 g | Sugar: 5 g

Veggies for Vitamins

This delicious savory blend of spicy arugula, tomato, onion, cucumber, celery, and garlic combines with natural tea to give your body an amazing amount of vitamins and minerals.

INGREDIENTS | SERVES 3

1 cup arugula
1 medium tomato
1 medium cucumber, peeled
1 celery stalk
1 medium green onion
1 clove garlic
2 cups red raspberry tea

1. Place arugula, tomato, cucumber, celery, onion, garlic, and 1 cup tea in a blender and blend until thoroughly combined.

2. Add remaining 1 cup tea, as needed, while blending until desired consistency is achieved.

PER SERVING: Calories: 23 | Fat: 0 g | Protein: 1 g | Sodium: 18 mg | Fiber: 1 g | Carbohydrates: 4 g | Sugar: 3 g

Folate for Fine Spines

This eclectic mix of veggies and fruits meets a variety of vitamin and mineral requirements.

INGREDIENTS | SERVES 3

1 cup chopped spinach

2 medium carrots, peeled

2 medium red Gala apples, peeled and cored

1 banana, peeled

2 cups red raspberry tea

Importance of Folate in Pregnancy

Among the important vitamins and minerals found to prevent birth defects, one of the most well known is folate. Studies have shown that ideal levels of folate in pregnancy reduce or remedy the chance of neural and spinal-tube defects. You can take a prenatal vitamin that includes folate, but what about natural sources? Eating a diet rich in deep leafy greens and vibrant-green vegetables can provide a great amount of folate naturally.

1. Place spinach, carrots, apples, banana, and 1 cup tea in a blender and blend until thoroughly combined.

2. Add remaining 1 cup tea, as needed, while blending until desired consistency is achieved.

PER SERVING: Calories: 107 | Fat: 0 g | Protein: 1 g | Sodium: 37 mg | Fiber: 4 g | Carbohydrates: 27 g | Sugar: 18 g

Luscious Legs in Pregnancy

Two amazing benefits of this blend are better circulation and reduced swelling in the legs.

INGREDIENTS | SERVES 3

1 cup watercress

1 medium grapefruit, peeled and seeded

½ cantaloupe, rind and seeds removed

½ pineapple, peeled and cored

1 cup strawberries, tops removed

1 cup red raspberry tea

1. Place watercress, grapefruit, cantaloupe, pineapple, strawberries, and ½ cup tea in a blender and blend until thoroughly combined.

2. Add remaining ½ cup tea, as needed, while blending until desired consistency is achieved.

PER SERVING: Calories: 144 | Fat: 1 g | Protein: 3 g | Sodium: 22 mg | Fiber: 5 g | Carbohydrates: 36 g | Sugar: 29 g

Stomach Soother

Digestive problems can be easily remedied with smoothies like this one. The comforting ginger will soothe your stomach while satisfying your taste buds.

INGREDIENTS | SERVES 3

1 cup watercress

3 medium apples, peeled and cored

1 banana, peeled

½" ginger, peeled

2 cups red raspberry tea

1. Place watercress, apples, banana, ginger, and 1 cup tea in a blender and blend until thoroughly combined.

2. Add remaining 1 cup tea, as needed, while blending until desired consistency is achieved.

PER SERVING: Calories: 116 | Fat: 0 g | Protein: 1 g | Sodium: 6 mg | Fiber: 3 g | Carbohydrates: 30 g | Sugar: 21 g

Morning Sickness Savior

One of the major discomforts of pregnancy can be the queasiness, nausea, and vomiting brought on by almost anything. This smoothie recipe is perfect for occasional or constant sufferers.

INGREDIENTS | SERVES 3

1 cup watercress

1 medium grapefruit, peeled and seeded

½ lemon, peeled

½" ginger, peeled

1 cup red raspberry tea

1. Place watercress, grapefruit, lemon, ginger, and ½ cup tea in a blender and blend until thoroughly combined.

2. Add remaining ½ cup tea, as needed, while blending until desired consistency is achieved.

PER SERVING: Calories: 33 | Fat: 0 g | Protein: 1 g | Sodium: 6 mg | Fiber: 1 g | Carbohydrates: 8 g | Sugar: 6 g

Berries for Baby

Blending berries is a great way to ward off cravings for sweet, processed foods during pregnancy.

INGREDIENTS | SERVES 3

1 cup watercress

2 bananas, peeled

1 cup blueberries

1 cup strawberries, tops removed

2 cups kefir

1. Place watercress, bananas, berries, and 1 cup kefir in a blender and blend until thoroughly combined.

2. Add remaining 1 cup kefir, as needed, while blending until desired consistency is achieved.

PER SERVING: Calories: 208 | Fat: 6 g | Protein: 7 g | Sodium: 69 mg | Fiber: 4 g | Carbohydrates: 35 g | Sugar: 23 g

Refreshing Raspberry Blend

The tanginess of raspberries is heightened by the sweet pineapple and sour lemon in this recipe. Simple, quick, and delicious, this smoothie will be a favorite go-to when you're in need of a delicious snack on the run.

INGREDIENTS | SERVES 3

1 cup watercress
1 cup raspberries
½ pineapple, peeled and cored
½ lemon, peeled
1½ cups kefir

1. Place watercress, raspberries, pineapple, lemon, and ¾ cup kefir in a blender and blend until thoroughly combined.

2. Add remaining ¾ cup kefir, as needed, while blending until desired consistency is achieved.

PER SERVING: Calories: 164 | Fat: 4 g | Protein: 5 g | Sodium: 54 mg | Fiber: 5 g | Carbohydrates: 29 g | Sugar: 20 g

Incredible Edible Iron

With loads of essential iron that will improve the blood health of both mom and baby, this savory smoothie is a delicious way to get more of what you need in your daily diet.

INGREDIENTS | SERVES 2

2 cups spinach leaves
½ medium sweet potato, baked and skin removed
2 cups red raspberry tea
1 cup ice (optional)

1. Combine spinach, sweet potato, and tea in a blender and blend until thoroughly combined.

2. Add ice and blend until desired consistency is achieved.

PER SERVING: Calories: 37 | Fat: 0 g | Protein: 2 g | Sodium: 35 mg | Fiber: 2 g | Carbohydrates: 8 g | Sugar: 2 g

Combat Candida

Candida causes uncomfortable digestive problems, so ward off the yeast with a quality diet and green drinks like this one to maintain a comfortable pregnancy.

INGREDIENTS | SERVES 2

1 cup cabbage
½ cup broccoli spears
2 cups red raspberry tea

1. Process the cabbage and broccoli through an electronic juicer according to the manufacturer's instructions.

2. Add to a blender and blend with the red raspberry tea, and stir to combine completely.

PER SERVING: Calories: 18 | Fat: 0 g | Protein: 1 g | Sodium: 15 mg | Fiber: 0 g | Carbohydrates: 4 g | Sugar: 2 g

Stress Reliever

Pregnancy can cause hormonal fluctuations that lead to moodiness and excess stress. Melt that stress away with a cool combination of melon and ginger for a total-body transforming treat that will soothe the body and the soul.

INGREDIENTS | SERVES 2

1 cup romaine
½ cup cantaloupe chunks, rind and seeds removed
½ cup honeydew chunks, rind and seeds removed
½ cup watermelon chunks, rind and seeds removed
1" ginger, peeled
1 cup ice

1. Combine romaine, melons, and ginger in a blender and blend until thoroughly combined.

2. Add ice and blend until desired consistency is achieved.

PER SERVING: Calories: 47 | Fat: 0 g | Protein: 1 g | Sodium: 17 mg | Fiber: 1 g | Carbohydrates: 11 g | Sugar: 9 g

Essential Cs

This sweet drink will keep your immunity on high alert to help ward off any potential viruses during your pregnancy.

INGREDIENTS | SERVES 2

1 cup plain kefir
½ cup red raspberry tea
1 medium orange, peeled
1 cup pineapple chunks

Combine all ingredients in a blender and blend until desired consistency is reached.

PER SERVING: Calories: 144 | Fat: 4 g | Protein: 5 g | Sodium: 49 mg | Fiber: 3 g | Carbohydrates: 24 g | Sugar: 19 g

Oh, Baby!

Plain kefir and sweet tangerines fill this drink with healthy bacteria and immunity-boosting vitamins and antioxidants.

INGREDIENTS | SERVES 2

2 cups plain kefir
4 medium tangerines, peeled
1 cup ice

1. Combine kefir and tangerines in blender and blend until thoroughly combined.

2. Add ice and blend until desired consistency is achieved.

PER SERVING: Calories: 234 | Fat: 9 g | Protein: 9 g | Sodium: 98 mg | Fiber: 3 g | Carbohydrates: 33 g | Sugar: 27 g

Perfect Protein

With all of the added caloric expenditure flowing to support the growing baby inside of you, this protein-packed smoothie is perfect for an on-the-go breakfast, lunch, dinner, or snack!

INGREDIENTS | SERVES 2

1 cup spinach
2 cups blueberry kefir
1 cup blueberries
½ cup almonds
½ cup walnuts
½ cup water (optional)

1. Combine the spinach, blueberry kefir, blueberries, almonds, and walnuts in a blender and blend until nuts are emulsified.

2. Add water gradually until desired consistency is achieved.

PER SERVING: Calories: 554 | Fat: 36 g | Protein: 23 g | Sodium: 138 mg | Fiber: 8 g | Carbohydrates: 42 g | Sugar: 29 g

Strawberry Savior

Fruits packed with antioxidants and tons of naturally occurring sugars (fructose) can be the perfect savior for a low-blood-sugar slump in the morning or the middle of the day. Forgo the coffee and reach for this quick blended natural pick-me-up instead.

INGREDIENTS | SERVES 2

1 cup spinach
2 cups strawberries, tops removed
1 cup strawberry kefir
1 cup red raspberry tea
½" ginger, peeled and grated
1 cup ice

1. Combine spinach, strawberries, kefir, tea, and ginger in a blender until completely emulsified and well blended.

2. Add ice, as needed, until desired consistency is achieved.

PER SERVING: Calories: 122 | Fat: 2 g | Protein: 7 g | Sodium: 77 mg | Fiber: 3 g | Carbohydrates: 22 g | Sugar: 17 g

Go-Go-Ginger Juice

The simplicity of ginger root can be deceiving. Once you boil your favorite tea and steep this natural antioxidant-rich root with mind-boggling benefits, you'll never be satisfied with normal tea again.

INGREDIENTS | SERVES 2

1 cup spinach

3 cups purified water

5 tea bags of natural, organic green, white, or chamomile tea

1" ginger, peeled and diced into ⅛" slices

1. Boil water in stainless steel pot; remove from heat.

2. Add tea bags and ginger slices and cover, and allow to steep for 4 hours.

3. In a blender, combine steeped tea, ginger, and spinach and blend (adding ice if desired) until desired consistency is achieved.

PER SERVING: Calories: 7 | Fat: 0 g | Protein: 1 g | Sodium: 12 mg | Fiber: 0 g | Carbohydrates: 1 g | Sugar: 0 g

The Better Choco-Peanut-Butter

If you're craving chocolate and peanut butter, skip the candy alternative and opt for the healthy option that will provide a ton of natural antioxidants and protein.

INGREDIENTS | SERVES 2

1 cup spinach

2 cups almond milk, unsweetened

10 dates, pitted

½ cup natural almonds

1 teaspoon vanilla extract

Combine all ingredients in a blender and blend until desired consistency is reached.

PER SERVING: Calories: 375 | Fat: 20 g | Protein: 10 g | Sodium: 173 mg | Fiber: 8 g | Carbohydrates: 43 g | Sugar: 31 g

Breathe Easy with Blue and Blackberries

Blueberries and blackberries contain powerful anthocyanins that help the respiratory system function at its best. When you feel the need to reach for a sweet treat, do yourself a favor and blend up this naturally delicious and nutritious treat that brings breathe-easy benefits in every delightful sip.

INGREDIENTS | SERVES 2

1 cup spinach
2 cups blueberry kefir
1 cup blueberries
1 cup blackberries
1 cup unsweetened vanilla almond milk

1. Combine spinach, kefir, blueberries, and blackberries in a blender and blend until completely emulsified.

2. Add almond milk gradually until desired consistency is achieved.

PER SERVING: Calories: 261 | Fat: 4 g | Protein: 13 g | Sodium: 214 mg | Fiber: 6 g | Carbohydrates: 46 g | Sugar: 38 g

Glossary

Amino acids A simple organic compound that contains both a carboxyl (-COOH) and an amino (-NH$_2$) group.

Antioxidants Substances found in many foods, including fruits, vegetables, seeds, and nuts. The most common antioxidants are beta-carotene, vitamins A, C, and E, lutein, lycopene, and selenium. Antioxidants gobble up and neutralize free radicals in the body that can lead to serious diseases like cancer, heart disease, and other diseases.

Calorie deficit When you burn more calories than you consume. For example, if you only consume 1,200 or 1,500 calories when your body needs 2,000 calories to function normally, your body will force your system to get the energy it needs from your stored fat cells. Your body requires a 3,500 caloric deficit in order to burn one pound.

Carbohydrates The body's major source of energy. They are found in simple and complex sugars, starches, fibers, and starchy vegetables. Simple carbohydrates including glucose and fructose are abundant in fruits and vegetables; the simple sugar sucrose is found in beets and cane sugar; and lactose, another simple sugar, is found in milk. Complex carbohydrates, including starches and fiber, are primarily found in whole grains and legumes. Complex carbohydrates provide more nutrients than simple carbohydrates, and are more filling because they take longer to digest.

Centrifugal Juicing The juicing process that chops and grinds the fruit and vegetables into tiny particles and dispenses a mixture of juice and microscopic particles, producing a very high yield of drinkable juice. However, this is not technically true juice extraction and produces a lower quality of "living juice."

Chlorophyll A molecule in plants that plays a crucial role in photosynthesis, a process in which plants absorb energy from sunlight and use it to create carbohydrates from CO_2 and water.

Complete protein A food that contains all the essential amino acids essential for the growth of cells.

Dash A few drops.

Detoxification The process of removing toxic substances or qualities from your body.

Dice To cut into small cubes, about ¼-inch squares.

Dietary minerals Inorganic elements necessary for body function in humans and animals.

Drizzle To lightly sprinkle drops of liquid over a food.

Enzyme A substance that acts as a catalyst to bring about a specific biochemical reaction in your body.

Floret The flower or bud end of broccoli or cauliflower.

Folic acid A form of the water-soluble vitamin B$_9$. It helps keep your blood healthy.

Free radicals Substances produced in the body by exposure to environmental toxins such as cigarette smoke and radiation. They trigger cellular changes that can lead to cancer, heart disease, and many other conditions.

Fructose The natural sugar found in fruit, slightly sweeter than table sugar and okay for consumption by diabetics.

Glucose   The simplest natural sugar.

Grate   To shave into tiny pieces using a grater.

Grind   To reduce a large chunk of something to the consistency of sand.

Hypertension   Unusually high blood pressure, especially arterial blood pressure.

Indoles   Found in cabbages, they stimulate enzymes that make estrogen less effective and could reduce the risk for breast cancer.

Insoluble fiber   Insoluble fiber does not absorb or dissolve in water. Insoluble fiber will pass through your digestive system and remain close to its original form. It is a great tool to combat constipation and help clean out your digestive tract.

Isoflavones   Found in soy, they imitate human estrogen and help to reduce menopausal symptoms and osteoporosis.

Keratin   The insoluble protein substance that forms the basis of your hair and nails.

Living juice   A concept created by Dr. Norman Walker. According to Walker, when juice heats to 122°F, the enzymes from the fruits and vegetables die. Therefore, "living juice" is juice that comes from raw fruits or vegetables that have never been heated up to 122°F. This juice lasts longer and contains more vitamins and nutrients than "dead juice."

Mastication   A juicing process that mimics the natural process we use to chew food. An auger (or sometimes two augers) rotates and gently chews up the food to extract high-quality "living juice." This difference in juice quality is actually visible—juices are much darker and more flavorful.

Nutrient   An element required by the body for growth and function.

Osteoporosis   A medical condition where bones become weak and break easily.

Oxidation   A process that occurs when juice is heated during the juicing process or exposed to open air for long periods of time. Essential vitamins and nutrients can escape during oxidation. The more a juice oxidizes, the shorter shelf life it has.

Phytochemicals   Non-nutritive plant chemicals that have protective or disease-preventive properties. There are more than a thousand known phytochemicals. It is well-known that plants produce these chemicals to protect themselves, but recent research demonstrates that they can also protect humans against diseases. Some of the well-known phytochemicals are lycopene in tomatoes, isoflavones in soy, and flavonoids in fruits. They are not essential nutrients and are not required by the human body for sustaining life.

Proanthocyanidins   Responsible for the anti-adhesion properties of cranberry. Consumption of cranberries will reduce the risk of urinary tract infections and improve dental health.

Purée   To reduce a food to a thick, creamy texture.

Savory   A popular herb with a fresh, woodsy taste.

Soluble fiber   Soluble fiber attracts water and forms a gel, which slows down digestion. This is what makes you feel full longer.

Slice   To cut into thin pieces.

Standard American Diet (SAD)   A term used to describe a diet that includes a high intake of red meats, sugary desserts, high-fat foods, and refined grains.

Steep   To let dry ingredients sit in hot water until the flavor seeps into the liquid.

Whisk   To rapidly mix and introduce air into the mixture.

Zest   Small slivers of peel, usually from a lemon, lime, or orange.

Standard U.S./Metric Measurement Conversions

VOLUME CONVERSIONS

U.S. Volume Measure	Metric Equivalent
⅛ teaspoon	0.5 milliliter
¼ teaspoon	1 milliliter
½ teaspoon	2 milliliters
1 teaspoon	5 milliliters
½ tablespoon	7 milliliters
1 tablespoon (3 teaspoons)	15 milliliters
2 tablespoons (1 fluid ounce)	30 milliliters
¼ cup (4 tablespoons)	60 milliliters
⅓ cup	90 milliliters
½ cup (4 fluid ounces)	125 milliliters
⅔ cup	160 milliliters
¾ cup (6 fluid ounces)	180 milliliters
1 cup (16 tablespoons)	250 milliliters
1 pint (2 cups)	500 milliliters
1 quart (4 cups)	1 liter (about)

WEIGHT CONVERSIONS

U.S. Weight Measure	Metric Equivalent
½ ounce	15 grams
1 ounce	30 grams
2 ounces	60 grams
3 ounces	85 grams
¼ pound (4 ounces)	115 grams
½ pound (8 ounces)	225 grams
¾ pound (12 ounces)	340 grams
1 pound (16 ounces)	454 grams

OVEN TEMPERATURE CONVERSIONS

Degrees Fahrenheit	Degrees Celsius
200 degrees F	95 degrees C
250 degrees F	120 degrees C
275 degrees F	135 degrees C
300 degrees F	150 degrees C
325 degrees F	160 degrees C
350 degrees F	180 degrees C
375 degrees F	190 degrees C
400 degrees F	205 degrees C
425 degrees F	220 degrees C
450 degrees F	230 degrees C

BAKING PAN SIZES

U.S.	Metric
8 × 1½ inch round baking pan	20 × 4 cm cake tin
9 × 1½ inch round baking pan	23 × 3.5 cm cake tin
11 × 7 × 1½ inch baking pan	28 × 18 × 4 cm baking tin
13 × 9 × 2 inch baking pan	30 × 20 × 5 cm baking tin
2 quart rectangular baking dish	30 × 20 × 3 cm baking tin
15 × 10 × 2 inch baking pan	30 × 25 × 2 cm baking tin (Swiss roll tin)
9 inch pie plate	22 × 4 or 23 × 4 cm pie plate
7 or 8 inch springform pan	18 or 20 cm springform or loose-bottom cake tin
9 × 5 × 3 inch loaf pan	23 × 13 × 7 cm or 2 lb narrow loaf or pâté tin
1½ quart casserole	1.5 liter casserole
2 quart casserole	2 liter casserole

Index